IN STARRY REALMS

IN STARRY REALMS

SIR ROBERT S. BALL, D. SC., LL.D., F.R.S.

WITH NUMEROUS ILLUSTRATIONS

CHEAP EDITION

GYAN

Published by

GYAN

Gyan Publishing House
5, Ansari Road
Daryaganj, New Delhi-110002
Phone: 011-47034999, 9811692060
E-mail: books@gyanbooks.com

Distribution Network
gyanbooks.com
India, USA, Canada, UK, Australia, France

ISBN : 978-81-212-9604-5(PB)
First Published, 1892

2nd Impression 2023

Printed at: Gyan Press, Delhi.

IN STARRY REALMS
Author: SIR ROBERT S. BALL

IN STARRY REALMS

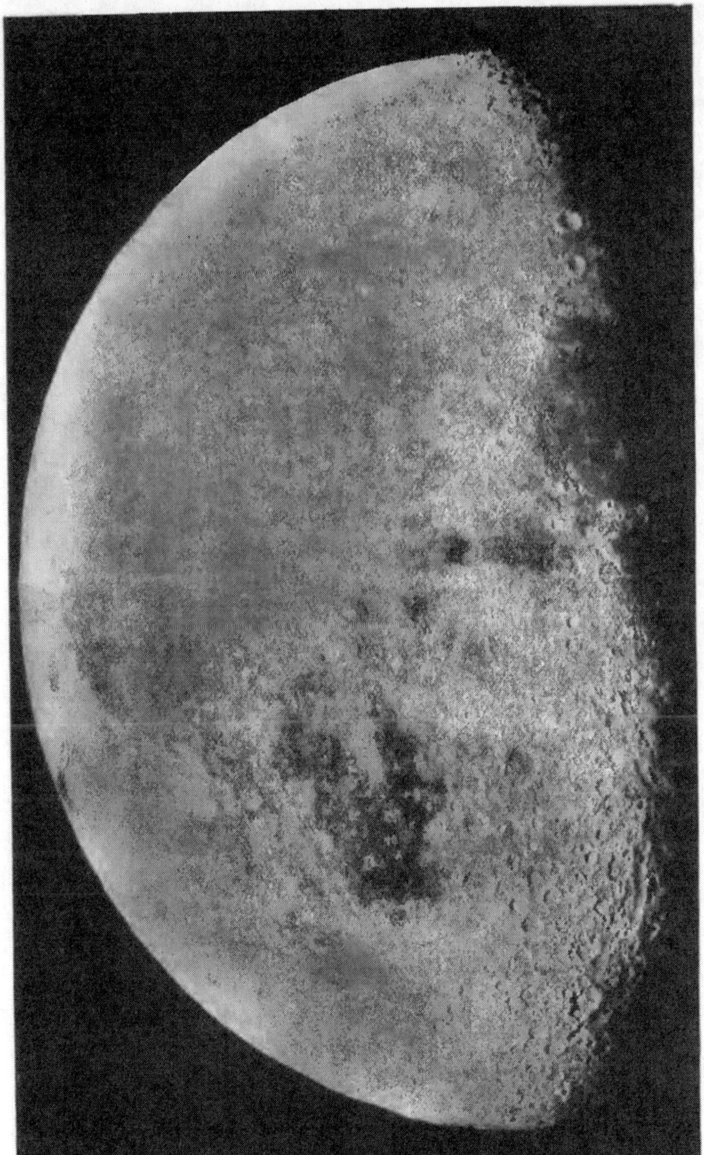

IN STARRY REALMS

BY

SIR ROBERT S. BALL, D.Sc., LL.D., F.R.S.

LOWNDEAN PROFESSOR OF ASTRONOMY AND GEOMETRY IN THE UNIVERSITY OF CAMBRIDGE

AUTHOR OF "GREAT ASTRONOMERS," "IN THE HIGH HEAVENS," ETC.

WITH NUMEROUS ILLUSTRATIONS

CHEAP EDITION

1912

PREFACE TO THE NEW EDITION.

Leaving the general features of "In Starry Realms" unaltered, I have endeavoured to correct the present edition and bring it, as far as possible, up to date. This has been particularly necessary in the chapters on "Showers of Shooting Stars" and on "Photographing the Stars," but the latter subject would now need volumes to itself. Probably the recent discoveries in Radio-Activity will, at no distant date, cause some modification to be required in our present views as to the sustentation of the sun's heat. At present, however, there is no adequate reason for making any alteration of moment in the chapters here given on this subject.

ROBERT S. BALL.

Cambridge,
21*st August*, 1906.

PREFACE TO THE ORIGINAL EDITION.

THE contents of this little volume have within the last few years seen the light in various periodicals. Chapters I—VII and XV—XVII appeared in *Good Words;* VIII—X in the *Girl's Own Paper;* XI, XIV, XVIII, XIX in various newspapers; XII, XIII in *A* 1; XXI in *Macmillan's Magazine;* XXII in the *Contemporary Review;* XXIII in *Longman's Magazine;* while XX was a presidential address delivered at the Midland Institute, Birmingham.

A few alterations have been found necessary in gathering them into a consecutive whole, and each chapter has been carefully revised.

With respect to the illustrations, several of which did not accompany the papers in their original form, I am indebted to the kindness of Mr. A. Cowper Ranyard, the editor of *Knowledge,* for permission to reproduce the photograph of the Moon, taken with the Great Refractor of the Lick Observatory (Frontispiece), Mr. Lassell's picture of the Great Nebula in Orion, and drawings of the Rev. F. Howlett's photographs of sun-spots of 1882–3. To the Council of the Royal Society I owe thanks for a similar favour in regard to the Krakatoa diagrams.

The object of the book is to give the general reader some sketches of specially interesting matters relating to the different heavenly bodies. They may be regarded as supplementary to a treatise on elementary astronomy such as my little volume, "Starland."

I am indebted to my friends, Rev. Maxwell Close, Dr. A. Rambaut, and Mr. L. Steele, for their aid in revising the work.

ROBERT S. BALL.

OBSERVATORY, CO. DUBLIN.
April, 1892.

CONTENTS.

CHAPTER | PAGE

I.—The Heat of the Sun 1

II.—Expenditure and Supply 15

III.—How the Heat is Kept Up 26

IV.—What We Owe to the Sun 40

V.—The Constant Face of the Moon . . . 49

VI.—The Moon's History 63

VII.—The Lunar World 77

VIII.—A Visit to an Observatory 97

IX.—An Evening with the Telescope . . . 113

X.—Notes on Nebulæ 124

XI.—Venus and Mercury 141

XII.—Mars as a World 149

XIII.—The Greatest Planet 180

XIV.—The Names of the Planets 195

XV.—A Falling Star 202

CHAPTER PAGE

XVI.—FIRE-BALLS 216

XVII.—SHOWERS OF SHOOTING STARS 228

XVIII.—THE NUMBER OF THE STARS 248

XIX.—THE EXTENT OF THE SIDEREAL HEAVENS . . 255

XX.—THE MOVEMENTS OF THE STARS 261

XXI.—PHOTOGRAPHING THE STARS 292

XXII.—AN ASTRONOMER'S THOUGHTS ABOUT KRAKATOA 319

XXIII.—DARWINISM AND ITS RELATION TO OTHER BRANCHES OF SCIENCE 343

LIST OF ILLUSTRATIONS.

PAGE

Photograph of the Moon . . . *Frontispiece*

Sunspots 10

The Solar Prominences 12

The Solar Corona 13

The Lunar Disc shown against the Map of Europe 51

Lunar Orbit compared with Circumference of the Sun 52

View from the Surface of the Moon . . . 81

Lunar Craters compared with the Area of England 89

The Meridian Circle 107

The Sun and its Attendant Worlds . . . 114

Saturn and his Rings 119

The Great Nebula in Orion 120

The Great Spiral Nebula 139

Orbits of the Earth and Mars 152

PAGE

VIEW OF MARS 155

WEIGHING THE PLANETS 174

ORBITS OF JUPITER AND THE EARTH 181

COMPARATIVE SIZES OF THE SUN AND THE PLANETS . 183

VIEWS OF JUPITER 185

KRAKATOA : ERUPTION OF, AUGUST 26-27 . . . 333

KRAKATOA : PROGRESS OF SKY PHENOMENA . . . 336

KRAKATOA : NORTHERN LIMIT OF SKY PHENOMENA . 339

CHAPTER I.

THE HEAT OF THE SUN.

THERE is not in the whole range of modern science a more fruitful subject for discussion than the sun and his connection with the earth. In the first place it is the function of the sun's attracting power to constrain the earth to follow that orbit in which she performs her annual revolution. The same office is also filled by the sun in the guidance of the several planets which, like our earth, are controlled by the one great central power. There are other functions in which the sun appears to be more obviously our benefactor by contributing several of the necessaries for our welfare. Chief among these is his provision of the *heat* by which life is sustained. The study of the benefits conferred on us by the sun in this particular opens up most interesting questions. As the great dispenser of *light* to the surrounding worlds, the functions of the sun illustrate other branches of science. Indications of the sun's interference in terrestrial affairs of somewhat minor moment are not wanting. The swing of the magnetic needle is connected in some occult manner with sunbeams, and phenomena of this class seem destined, at a time now perhaps not far distant, to become of great scientific interest. I propose to devote this and the few following chapters to the more important relations of the sun to the earth. I shall strive to illustrate the different functions which the sun has to perform, and I shall point out how it is that he is enabled to send down his benefits upon the dwellers on this earth with a profuseness that shows no signs of exhaustion.

Let us begin by considering the extent to which we are indebted to the sun for maintaining the earth in the same orbit year after year. It would almost seem as if our globe were always trying to escape from the thraldom of the sun. If the sun were to withhold that attractive power by which the earth is maintained in the course that it at present follows, dire calamity must immediately result. This globe of ours is hurrying along at a pace of eighteen miles a second, and if the sun's attraction no longer restrained it the globe would not continue to revolve in a circle, but would at once start off in a straight line on a voyage through space. Every minute would take us more than a thousand miles, and by the time a hundred days had elapsed we should be twice as far from the sun as we are at present. His light and his heat would be reduced to one-fourth part of what we now enjoy. With every successive minute the sun's influence would still further abate, and it is almost needless to add that all known forms of life would have to vanish from the globe. It is, therefore, satisfactory to know that we possess sufficient grounds for our belief that the sun's attraction will never decline from what it is at this moment, and therefore that there is no cause for apprehension that life may be chased from this globe by a dissolution of the bond of attraction between the earth and sun.

There is, however, another aspect of the earth's relation to the sun which requires such close attention that it must necessarily form the chief subject with which we have to deal. For the preservation of life on this earth it is not only necessary that the distance of our globe from the sun shall never greatly alter from what it is at present, but also that the present amount of the radiation from the source of heat shall continue without perceptible variation. These considerations introduce questions which do not admit of being summarily disposed of. They involve some problems that are not at all simple. Indeed, it is only in modern times that the subject has become properly understood. We have here to consider not alone some matters of primary significance as regards the continuance of life on this earth, but also various scientific problems of the highest interest and importance. I therefore propose to discuss how it comes to pass that the sun's power to radiate heat to the earth is maintained at a rate which appears to be constant.

There seems to be sufficient reason for the belief that the heat at present emitted from the sun is neither greater nor less to any sensible extent than that which our luminary used to dispense ages ago. Where the vine and the olive now grow, the vine and the olive were growing twenty centuries back. We must not, however, place too strong a reliance on what seems an obvious deduction from such a fact. Darwin has taught us how by natural selection an organism can continue to preserve its adaptation to the environment notwithstanding the gradual change of the surrounding conditions. The facts, so far as they are known to us, fail to show any grounds for supposing that there have been any important changes in the climates of the earth within historic times. We have geological evidence far earlier than any historical testimony as to the character of the climates which prevailed at various epochs of remote antiquity. The records of the rocks demonstrate unquestionably that our globe has passed through many striking vicissitudes so far as heat and cold are concerned. Those records prove that there have been periods during which some of the fairest regions of this globe were desolated by a frost so intense that they became thickly cased with solid ice. There have also been periods when conditions of an opposite character have prevailed. The polar regions which now seem the perennial abode of impenetrable ice once enjoyed a succession of long and delightful summers, diversified by winters remarkable alike for their brevity and their mildness. The Arctic solitudes, now so dismal and so barren, then nourished plants and animals that can only thrive under genial conditions of climate.

No doubt the question as to the origin of these great climatic changes, which have so frequently occurred in the course of geological time, presents many difficulties. Opinion is divided as to what the cause of these changes may have been. I do not now enter into this subject, because for our present purpose it suffices to note one very important conclusion. Those who are competent to pronounce on the question of the cause of the geological variations of climate are in substantial accordance with the view that several changes have not been due to any actual variations in the amount of heat radiated from the sun. In other words, there is not the slightest reason for the belief that the sun has been during geological times either appreciably hotter or appreciably colder than at the present moment.

One of the indications of the existence of sunbeams throughout geological times is afforded by the eyes of certain fossil animals. It may, for instance, be specially noted that the great fish-like reptile, the Ichthyosaurus, which lived during a remote period of this earth's history, possessed an eye apparently unequalled in size and complexity by the eye of any other animal living or extinct.

There is no reason for being surprised that the sun should have attracted the earth by the force of gravitation a million years ago with just the same intensity as it does at present. The gravitation between two masses does not necessarily involve anything in the nature of *expenditure.* Two cannon balls, for instance, placed at a certain distance apart attract each other with a certain force, and that force remains the same after any lapse of time, provided the masses of the cannon balls and the distance between them continue unchanged. The case is, however, totally different, if it be radiation of heat and not attraction of gravitation that is the phenomenon in question. For example, let us regard one of the cannon balls as a red-hot body dispensing heat around so as to warm the objects in its vicinity. Here, evidently, the question of *time* enters as an important element. The hot body will, in general, be able to impart heat to a cold one, so long as the one retains an excess of temperature over the other. It is, however, in the nature of a heated object to pour forth its heat by radiation, and ultimately to cool down to the temperature of the bodies which surround it. It thus appears that the dispensing of heat from a body at a high temperature, being essentially of the nature of expenditure, cannot be maintained without the source being in some manner replenished. Even the greatest body, if also the hottest body, only contains a limited and perfectly definite quantity of heat. In the process of cooling a heated object gradually pays out from its stores of heat, until, at last, its temperature approximates to that of the surrounding objects. From that time the radiation ceases to have appreciable amount, or, to speak more accurately, the heat which the body loses is restored by the heat which it receives by the radiation of other objects. No matter how magnificent be the dimensions of the radiating mass, or how exalted be its temperature, it cannot escape from the application of these principles. It must ultimately cool down and cease to operate as a source of heat to the other objects around.

It is unavoidable that the sun himself must run his course in accordance with the doctrines we have been here considering. The great source of light and heat cannot escape from the legitimate consequences of continuous expenditure. Unless there is some process of restoration by which the results of solar extravagance are neutralised, impoverishment and ultimate exhaustion are inevitable. If, therefore, the sun receives no supply of heat, or of what is equivalent to heat, the time must ultimately arrive when his stores of radiant energy shall have been all expended, and the great globe can then no longer remain as a source of life and light to the worlds which circulate around him. We know that the fire which gladdens our hearth requires occasional renewal by fuel else it will go out; so too that glowing globe in the heavens which gladdens and beautifies the earth must also go out unless its energies be recuperated from some source or other.

The amount of heat squandered by the sun is truly prodigious. The earth intercepts only an extremely small proportion of the total radiation of sunbeams. It would be easy to show that the sun distributes sufficient light and heat to maintain two thousand million planets in the same comfortable circumstances as those in which our earth is placed. The greater part of that radiation is entirely lost, or, at least, lost in so far as any of the planets are concerned. Our fellow-worlds—Jupiter, Saturn, Venus, Mercury, and Mars—do, no doubt, intercept a little of the heat that would otherwise depart altogether from our system, but the total amount of radiant solar energy that all the planets together can utilise is utterly inappreciable when compared with that which streams away into space, and has gone from us for ever. The quantity of heat radiated from the sun is one of the most astounding facts in nature. Let us consider with the help of a few illustrations the wealth of radiation which our great central hearth pours forth. We shall make use of some of the facts collected in Professor Young's well-known treatise on the sun.

When an engineer is designing the furnaces to supply a steam engine he has to arrange that the heating surfaces of the boilers shall have an extent duly proportioned to the work which the engine has to do. Each square foot of boiler exposed to the flame is capable of generating so much steam per hour, and may thus be regarded as the equivalent of so much horse-power. Let us consider an area of a single square foot on the sun's surface, and suppose that all the heat which passes through it on its way to outer space could be collected and applied to the generation of steam in a boiler. The generation of steam in that boiler would be so copious that a mighty engine of ten thousand horse-power might be maintained in continuous action. Indeed a great Atlantic liner could be driven at full speed at a heat expenditure not larger than that which flows out through each square foot of the sun. It would be easy to show that if the heat from an area on the sun of an acre or two in extent could all be utilised by a system of boilers, they would generate as much steam as would suffice to sustain in full work every steam engine in the world.

We may exhibit the quantity of heat radiated from the sun in another way. Let us suppose that it is to be entirely applied to the melting of ice, and that this ice is disposed in a shell closely enveloping the whole sun. Even if the ice had a thickness of 48½ feet the radiation would be sufficient to reduce it all to water in one minute. Statements like this give some conception of the profuse expenditure with which the sun pours forth its stores of heat; they also raise a desire to study the method by which the exhaustion that would seem the obvious consequence of such monstrous extravagance can be avoided.

In the first place it should be noticed that the enormous size of the sun is a very important element in the inquiry. A large body cools much more slowly than a small one. The loss of heat by radiation takes place chiefly, if not wholly, from the surface of the heated body, and the heat from those parts which are not on the surface can only be dispersed by radiation after it has travelled by conduction from the interior to the exterior. Such at least would be the case if the body were a solid one; if, however, it were either wholly or partly in a liquid or in a gaseous condition, as the sun appears to be, then the mode by which the heat would pass from the interior to the exterior would be correspondingly modified. There would, doubtless, be currents of convection in the solar materials just as there are currents of convection which distribute, throughout the bulk of the liquid, the water that has been heated at the bottom of a kettle placed on the fire. This does not contradict the statement that we have made as to the necessity for the arrival of the heat from the interior at the surface before it could be dispersed by radiation. The mode of conveyance of the heat must be different in a fluid from what it is in a solid, but the general principle remains unaltered. The spots on the sun are doubtless connected with the circulation of the heat between the interior and the surface. The character of these remarkable features on our great luminary is well shown by the reproductions of the Rev. F. Howlett's photographs of spots in 1882, 1883.

The extraordinary profusion with which heat is poured forth from every square foot of the sun's surface may perhaps be explained by the following illustration. Suppose there are two concert-halls, built from like designs, but with every dimension in one of the buildings double that corresponding in the other. The area, for instance, in one hall is twice as long and twice as wide as in the

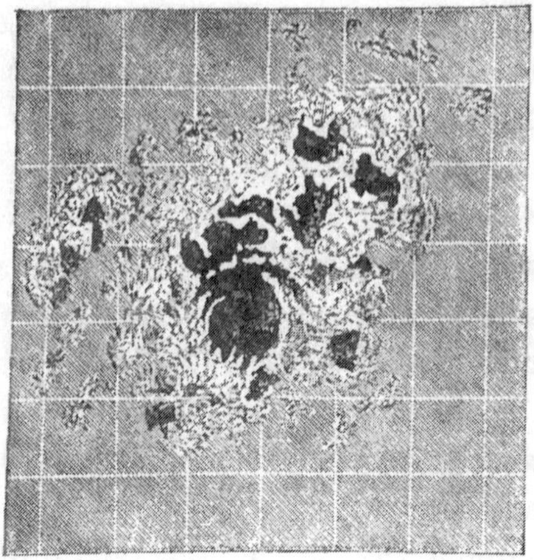

November 19, 1882.

Area of spot about 3,462,750,000 square miles.

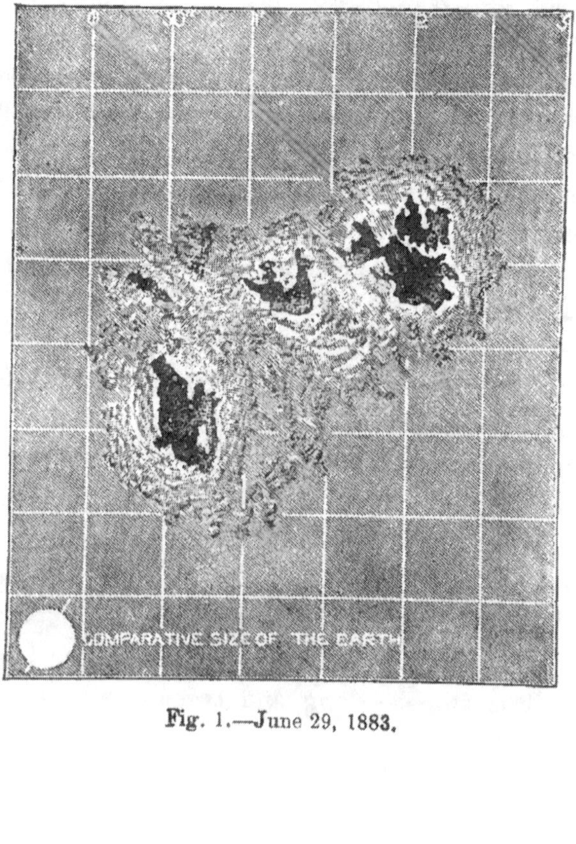

Fig. 1.—June 29, 1883.

lesser hall. There will be twice as many rows of seats in it, and each row will contain twice as many chairs. Accordingly four times as many people can be accommodated in the large hall as in the small one. The buildings being after the same design the number of exit doors will be of course the same in both halls. Each door of the large hall will, in conformity with our supposition, be double as wide and double as high as the corresponding door in the small one. Let us now suppose that both these halls are filled to their utmost capacity, and that in each of them a panic breaks out among the audience from an alarm of fire, or from some similar cause. Would the facilities of escape be equal from the two buildings, and if not, which of them would have the advantage? Considering that the two buildings have been erected from the same designs, it might at first appear that the facilities for a rapid emptying of the buildings should be equal in both; but this is not the case. No doubt the larger building has double the width of door exit possessed by the small one, but, on the other hand, four times as many people have to push through these doors, and consequently the crowding at the exits of the large room would be double as great as at those of the small one. In a precisely similar way it would appear that if one of the buildings had ten times the linear dimensions of the other, it would have ten times as many rows, and each row would have ten times as many seats, so that the whole audience contained in the large hall would be a hundred-fold that contained in the small one. The width of door exit would, however, be only ten times as great, and consequently the crushing and crowding and the difficulty of exit would be ten times more perilous in the larger building than it would be in the smaller one.

This illustration will show the contrast between the escape of heat from a large body and the escape of heat from a small one. For the purpose of our argument, the

Fig. 2.—The Solar Prominences.

sun's diameter may be represented as one hundred times that of the earth. The surface of the sun will exceed the surface of the earth in the proportion of 10,000 to 1, and the volumes of the two bodies will be in the proportion of 1,000,000 to 1. If the two bodies possessed originally the same temperature, and were composed of the same materials, the sun would possess a million times

Fig. 3.—The Solar Corona.

as much heat as the earth. If this heat is to be lost it must be by passing out through the surfaces of the bodies. The sun's surface is no doubt ten thou and times that of the earth ; but, on the other hand, there is a million times as much heat to pass through the sun's surface as through the earth's surface. Hence it follows that one hundred times as much heat must emerge through every square foot on the sun's surface as through every square foot on the earth if the two bodies remain at equal temperatures.

The surface of the sun is in a state of the most tremendous agitation. Look, for example, at Fig. 2, which exhibits, on a small part of the sun's margin, some of the glowing flames that leap from its surface. These outbursts are often tens of thousands of miles high, and they indicate the fearful tempests with which the fiery globe is convulsed. Such objects are known as the "prominences," but the surroundings of the great luminary include also the corona. This is a faint pearly light extending to a vast distance round the sun, and rendered visible when the moon intrudes between the earth and the sun, so as to form a total eclipse.

CHAPTER II.

EXPENDITURE AND SUPPLY.

NOTWITHSTANDING the sun's great mass and immense store of heat, it cannot escape from the application of those familiar laws of cooling that would be observed in a red-hot poker when taken from the fire, or in a freshly-run casting when drawn from its mould in the foundry. The larger the body the longer is the time it will require before it becomes cold. A knitting needle heated red-hot and withdrawn from the fire will become cold in a few minutes. An iron rail, after it has been drawn red-hot through the rolling-mill, may remain hot for an hour.

Our first surmise might be that the luminary is simply a vast white-hot body, glowing with incandescence and parting with its heat in accordance with the ordinary laws of cooling. On this supposition the fact that the abatement in sun heat was not perceptible in historic times might be accounted for in consequence of the immense size of the body. Suppose, for instance, the sun were merely a globe of white-hot iron pouring forth its heat, could we then explain the maintenance of its radiation for so many thousand years at the same rate as at present?

This is a question which cannot be decided by mere off-hand reasoning; we must submit it to the test of actual calculation. As a foundation for this calculation, we know the quantity of heat that would be contained in a globe of white-hot iron of the same dimensions as the sun. We also know the quantity of heat which represents the sun's daily expenditure. It is therefore a simple matter of arithmetic to find the number of days' supply which a white-hot sun could contain. The result is not a little startling; it demonstrates that to supply the current expenditure of solar radiation at its present rate the temperature of the sun would have to decline through some degrees every year if the constitution of the body were what we have supposed. It seems that if the sun's temperature were suffering an abatement at a rate anything like so fast as this supposition would involve, then the effects of cooling would be perceptible in a continuous fall of the sun's efficiency as a radiator. It is therefore obvious that our first notion, which suggests that the sun is merely a white-hot globe cooling down, must be abandoned.

Another conceivable origin of the sun's heat must also be considered for a moment before receiving its dismissal as utterly incapable of affording a solution of the problem. As heat is generated by the consumption of fuel, it might seem not unreasonable to suppose that there may be some process analogous to combustion at present in progress in the sun on a scale of sufficient magnitude. But there are insuperable difficulties about such a view, which will become apparent when we call to mind the actual nature of combustion. The coal which is glowing so cheerfully in the fireplace is the seat of a vehement chemical action. The carbon which constitutes a great part of the coal is uniting with the oxygen of the air, and as an incident of the chemical union between these two substances heat in large quantities is evolved. Hydrogen is another important ingredient in the composition of ordinary coal. When ignited hydrogen combines with the oxygen which the air so plenteously supplies, the union of the two gases produces the vapour of water, and the process is accompanied by the liberation of large quantities of heat. Thus the radiation of warmth from the fireplace is the direct consequence of a chemical union between different elements. It is, therefore, proper to inquire whether the heat of the sun may not be sustained by a somewhat similar action. Can it be that there is some mighty combustion of fuel perennially in progress in the sun, and that continuous radiation of heat is the consequence? This is a question which it is difficult to answer in a simple manner. There can be no doubt that chemical activities of the highest order must be in incessant operation in the sun, but it seems impossible that any appreciable proportion of the sun's radiation can be maintained by chemical action.

Indeed we can show conclusively that no attainable amount of chemical action could be adequate for the maintenance of the sun's expenditure at the rate which has been current for so many centuries. In the first place it is necessary that the two elementary bodies should be both present in sufficient abundance, and that their combination should take place with such uniformity that the daily radiation shall be preserved at a nearly constant rate. We are aware that ingenious machinery is often applied for the purpose of stoking the fires under steam boilers. It is claimed for these machines that they administer the coal to the fire so regularly that the production of steam is carried on with all desired uniformity. If there were sufficient fuel in the sun for the maintenance of its radiation, and if there were gas or other material suitable for union with that fuel in sufficient quantity to generate the necessary heat, it seems difficult to imagine by what arrangements the combustion of the two elements eager for union could be so controlled that the supply of heat produced should remain practically constant. How are we to suppose that the gas and the fuel can be continuously brought together in the duly regulated quantities? These considerations alone suffice to render it highly improbable that chemical union could afford an effective explanation of sun heat.

There is a still more insuperable objection. Careful experiments have taught us the precise quantity of heat that can be extracted from a ton of coal when combined with the requisite quantity of oxygen for combustion at the best possible advantage. We are, therefore, able to compute how much coal would have to be consumed every day to generate enough heat for the maintenance of solar radiation. We can show that the sun's daily expenditure is so enormous that the supply of fuel that would be necessary places this view of the origin of the sun's heat altogether out of the question. Suppose that the whole sun from its surface to its centre were a solid globe of coal. Suppose that from some source or other a supply of oxygen were available which was adequate for the combustion of this globe. Suppose that enough of this coal were to be burned every day to supply a quantity of heat equal to that poured forth by the sun in the same time. It is then a matter of simple calculation to find how long a sun so constituted could last as a source of light and heat. It can be easily shown that on this supposition and at the present rate of expenditure all power of radiation would be totally exhausted in about three thousand years. We have, however, the best reasons for knowing that the sun has already dispensed his beams for a far longer period than that just stated. Hence we learn that the supply of the sun's heat cannot be due to the combustion of any substance with a composition similar to coal.

It is, however, a reasonable question whether there may not be some extraordinary, and to us unknown, elements present in the sun which in the course of their chemical union generate far more heat than those elements with which we are acquainted, so that by the combustion of these materials the solar energies might be recuperated. From all we know of the composition of the celestial bodies, it does not seem in the least degree probable that any materials exist which possess the necessary qualities. In fact, it is one of the triumphs of modern science to have identified to a considerable extent the materials of which the sun is composed with the familiar elements in our earth. By the aid of spectrum analysis it has been discovered that upwards of thirty of the elements on the earth are present also in the sun. Among these we may specially draw attention to iron, which appears to be one of the most widely distributed of all the elementary bodies. Some hundreds of lines in the solar spectrum have been demonstrated to be connected with this element. I should, however, say that it has by no means been proved that there may not be some elements in the sun of a different kind from those we find on the earth. There are indeed many lines in the solar spectrum which have not up to the present been identified with those arising from any terrestrial element. There are, however, so many difficulties attending the identification of lines under widely varying conditions that it would be rash to pronounce emphatically as to whether all the ingredients in the sun may be in some shape or other known to us on the earth. The constitution of the great luminary does not, however, give any encouragement to the suggestion that the source of his heat may be attributed to combustion in the ordinary meaning of the word. Indeed, the difficulties attending such a view seem so overwhelming that we may withdraw this doctrine from any further consideration.

We have thus shown not only that the sun's heat would be insufficiently explained by supposing the great globe to be a cooling body, but also that the phenomena of combustion offer no adequate suggestion towards the explanation of the difficulty.

Our search for the source of sun heat must therefore be conducted in some other direction, and, strange to say, we shall find that source to be not in any immediately available heat, but rather in the transformation into heat of something which was originally of a mechanical nature.

When a shooting star dashes into our atmosphere its course is attended with an evolution of light and heat owing to its friction through the air. We are thus able to account for the enormous quantity of heat, or of what is equivalent to heat, which exists in virtue of the rapid motion of these little bodies. It is true that we only see meteors at that supreme moment of their dissolution when they dash into our atmosphere. It is, however, impossible to doubt that, besides the meteoric streams with which we are acquainted, there must be many shoals of meteors which never collide with our earth. The other great globes in our system must, like our globe, absorb multitudes of meteors which they chance to encounter in their roamings. The numbers of meteors gathered by a globe will be doubtless greater the larger and more massive the globe is, and this for a double reason. In the first place, the dimensions of the atmospheric net which the globe extends to entrap the meteors will, when other things are equal, increase with the size of the globe. But there is also another reason—the more massive the globe the more vehement will be its power of attraction, and the greater will be the number of the meteors that are drawn into destruction in its atmosphere. Of course this reasoning applies in a special degree to the sun. We shall probably be correct in the assertion that for every meteor that descends upon this earth, thousands, if not millions of meteors will plunge into the sun. As these objects pierce their way through the sun's atmosphere light and heat will of course be evolved. It has been conjectured that the friction of the meteors which are incessantly rushing into the sun may produce light and heat in sufficient quantity to aid in the maintenance of the sun's ordinary expenditure by radiation. It has been even supposed that the quantity of energy thus generated may supply all that is wanted to explain the extraordinary circumstance that from age to age no visible decline has taken place in the intensity of the solar radiation. Here again is a question which we may submit to calculation. We have first of all to determine the heat which could be generated by a body of, let us say, one pound in weight, falling into the sun after having been attracted thither from a very great distance. The result is not a little startling; it shows us that such a body in the course of its friction through the sun's atmosphere might generate as much heat as could be produced by the combustion of many times its own weight of coal consumed under the most favourable conditions.

The stern rules of arithmetic enable us to pronounce decisively on the issue as to whether the influx of meteors can be entertained as an adequate source for the supply of sun heat. We can estimate the quantity of heat which would be contributed by a single meteor a pound in mass. This determines the total mass of meteors that would have to be entrapped in the sun's atmosphere every day if the current expenditure of sun heat had to be defrayed from this source alone. We are able to avoid expressing the answer in millions of tons by the fortunate circumstance that the moon happens to present a unit of suitable magnitude for the purpose.

Suppose that the moon were to be entirely crushed into fragments, which were permitted to rain down upon the sun after the manner of meteors, then it can be shown that the total quantity of heat generated by this influx would be sufficient to maintain the sun's expenditure at the present rate for about a year. Stated in this way, we are enabled to decide at once as to the plausibility of the supposition that the meteoric source of supply is sufficient for the sun's wants. If every year the sun devoured a quantity of meteors whose collective mass would form a globe equal to our moon, then the quantity of meteoric matter roaming about our system must be enormously greater than seems likely to be the case. Indeed, it can be shown that if so mighty a mass of material is absorbed into the sun in the course of twelve months, the dynamical conditions of the solar system would be widely different from what we find them. A quantity of matter so distributed that the sun could daily abstract a supply sufficient for its wants would undoubtedly affect the movements of the other heavenly bodies. Were there such an abundance of substance in the vicinity of the sun, the perturbations of Mercury and of the other planets arising from this cause would be assuredly appreciable. As we do not find that the movements of the planets are so affected to the necessary extent, it is incumbent on us to conclude that the quantity of loose material in our system cannot be nearly so great as this doctrine of sun heat would require. We are hence forced to take a modified view of the capacity of meteors to supply the solar radiation. It may possibly be true, nay, doubtless must be true, that the meteors do contribute, to some small extent, to neutralize the sun's perennial losses; but it is wholly impossible that they can contribute in any substantial degree to the solution of the problem as to how the loss of heat by the sun does not become apparent.

Three suggested sources for the sun's heat have been tested and found wanting. We have first considered it as a mere glowing globe, gradually cooling and dispensing its heat by radiation. This will not answer, for the sun would have become cold and dark ages ago if it had no further heat than this supposition implies. We then investigated whether there could be any sufficient supply of something analogous to fire, so that the sun's heat could be maintained by combustion. This, again, will not stand the necessary test: it is wholly impossible that material of the required character should be forthcoming in sufficient abundance. Finally, we have examined the notion that the sun's heat may be produced by the friction of meteors which dash into his atmosphere. This source of supply may be a small rate-in-aid of the sun's current expenditure, but cannot explain how the bulk of that expenditure has to be provided for.

We have now to set forth the true explanation, which has been universally adopted whenever the evidence in its favour has been duly considered. The question is by no means an easy one, but I shall strive to make it as clear as circumstances will permit. A multitude of observations point irresistibly to the conclusion that the sun is not a *solid* body. In this respect we may contrast the sun with the moon. Our satellite is eminently a solid as opposed to a gaseous object; every feature on the moon is permanent and definitely marked, and can be observed from year to year in the same place and with the same surroundings. But there seems to be no permanent object whatever visible on the sun. In fact, it would be a great convenience to astronomers if there were some solid mountain peak which would mark one definite locality on the sun's globe. We are sadly in want of some such definite feature to serve as an origin from which the longitude of spots or other objects on the sun's globe could generally be estimated. Nothing of the kind can, however, be discerned. We are obviously only looking at vast masses of glowing cloud suspended in gaseous matter. The solar vapours have but little more permanence than the unstable clouds of our own atmosphere.

Our knowledge of the interior of the sun is necessarily very imperfect, but there seems no reason to think that the luminary is, even in any part, what may be regarded as a solid body. There is, in fact, a strong presumption in the opposite direction. To explain this it is necessary to contrast certain characteristics of our earth with the corresponding characteristics of the sun. Our globe, for instance, is constituted from materials which are on the whole so heavy that the earth weighs over five times as much as would a globe of water of the same size; whereas the sun is hardly one and a half times as heavy as a globe of water of equal volume. Thus we learn that the sun is composed of materials which have about one-fourth of the density of those of the earth. This points to the conclusion that the materials of the sun are much less closely compressed, and that even the sun's interior can hardly be regarded as consisting of solid substance.

When, therefore, we discuss the loss of heat from the sun by radiation we ought not to compare it with that of radiation from a solid globe; we must rather take it to resemble radiation from a gaseous globe. At first, perhaps, the profound difference between the two cases may escape attention. Indeed it is only in comparatively recent times that the remarkable laws by which a globe of gaseous matter parts with its heat have been thoroughly explained.

CHAPTER III.

HOW THE HEAT IS KEPT UP.

It will be necessary for me, at this part of my subject, to recall to mind a few points in the doctrine of heat. In ordinary language we occasionally employ the words heat and temperature indifferently, but when we are considering such a question as that now before us we must be more particular about our words. The heat contained in a body is one thing, and the temperature shown by that body is a different thing; in fact, it may well be that of two bodies, the one with the higher temperature contains less heat than that which shows the lower temperature. You might take a pound of iron and a pound of water, each at the same temperature, and then give them both equal additions of heat. The iron will rise to a temperature far higher than the water. A foot-warmer filled with hot water will give out far more heat than if it contained merely the same weight of iron heated to the same temperature. A pound of mercury and a pound of water at the same temperature, as shown by a thermometer, would contain very different quantities of heat, the difference being very much in favour of the water. If equal weights of mercury and water had very unequal temperatures, and you stirred the two together, the mixture would assume nearly the temperature of the water, whatever that of the mercury may have been. If the pound of water was cold and the pound of mercury hot the mixture would be nearly cold. If it were the other way, and the pound of water was hot and the pound of mercury cold, the mixture would be nearly as hot as the water.

These illustrations suffice to show that the quantity of heat in a body and the temperature which that body exhibits are not related in any very obvious manner. Especially is this true in the case of gaseous bodies; indeed, the connection between the temperature of a gas and the heat it contains presents sometimes the startling anomaly that while the gas is losing its heat it may be, nevertheless, gaining in temperature. Once we take into view that the sun is, to a large extent at all events, composed of gaseous material, the difficulties as to the supply of the heat necessary for its daily radiation vanish.

The other suggested sources of sun heat which we have already discussed had to be rejected, for the very simple reason that they failed to explain why the sun did not seem to get colder. Now we shall be able to account for the fact—the strange fact, some may certainly think—that the loss of heat does not necessarily involve a fall of temperature. Indeed, it seems just as likely that if the sun's temperature is changing at all at the present time it may be rising instead of falling, though no doubt the alteration must be extremely slow.

A fundamental doctrine in the theory of heat tells us that when heat is imparted to a body it expands. There are no doubt certain exceptions, but they need not here detain us. We have also the correlative truth that if a body loses heat by radiation it follows as a necessary consequence that it must be contracting in dimensions; of course it may usually be added that the body is also losing temperature, but this is not invariably the case. After heat has been lost by radiation without being compensated by an accession of heat from some external source, the total supply of heat, or of what is equivalent to heat, is of course lessened. Owing, however, to the shrinking of material which has taken place the quantity of heat which remains in the body is distributed over a lessened volume. It may therefore conceivably happen that though a body is losing heat, and therefore contracting, yet that, as the heat which remains is concentrated within a diminished bulk, it may actually show a higher temperature than the body had before the heat was lost.

The point I am here trying to explain may be illustrated as follows. Suppose that a man maintains a very large establishment in town, with troops of servants and a stable full of horses, a yacht, a place in the country, a shooting-lodge in the Highlands, and a villa in the south of Europe. He must have a very large income to maintain his position in this fashion, and the income is provided by a fine estate. Suppose that by some reverse of fortune the man loses a part of his property, his income is diminished in corresponding proportion, and he at once begins to curtail his expenses. He sells his yacht, lets his Highland shooting, throws up his villa, reduces his hunters, dismisses half his servants, and curtails his establishment in many other directions. He so lessens the area of his expenses that he has brought them into conformity with his income. If, indeed, he be a wise man he will take the opportunity of carrying on his retrenchments to such a point that his expenses shall be even more conveniently within his income than they were in the original days of high living. With his moderate establishment, and with an income which is abundant in comparison with that establishment, the owner may feel a comfort and enjoy a genuine prosperity which he never knew in those bygone days that seemed more splendid. He may actually have more money in his pocket and be in a more satisfactory financial condition.

In like manner when a great amount of sun heat has been radiated into space and lost for ever, the sun accommodates itself to the altered circumstances by shrinking inwards. Like the prudent man who has suffered a reverse of fortune, the sun when it does shrink takes the opportunity of so far reducing its bulk that, even though it has less heat than it originally possessed, yet that heat so shows itself on the reduced bulk that the orb of day may be a more genial body than ever it was, notwithstanding its apparent losses.

Matter in the solid state undergoes only a comparatively small diminution of its volume by its loss of heat. For example, when a cannon-ball heated to redness cools down through 100 degrees of temperature, the shrinking of its volume amounts to but little more than a thousandth part of the whole. No doubt in some small degree the quantity of heat left in the cannon-ball does show to slightly better advantage in the reduced bulk than it would have done had the body remained at its original dimensions. The gain, however, in temperature from this source is not at all sufficient to counteract the direct loss from radiation, and consequently the temperature falls and the cooling of the body progresses.

But now let us suppose the case of the cooling of a globe of gas. No doubt the condition supposed is one that we can hardly reproduce in our laboratories, but we can imagine a globe of gas in space not enclosed in any envelope, but merely taking the shape that is given by the mutual attraction of its particles. We can indeed see bodies apparently of this description in our telescopes, and we call them planetary nebulæ. Imagine a globe of this kind to be dispensing its heat by radiation. In conformity with the general law, the loss of heat must be accompanied by contraction. It is in the nature of a gas to contract for a given fall of heat, through a much greater range than that through which a solid contracts. The consequence is that though the globe has undoubtedly parted with some heat by radiation, yet the diminished bulk of the contracted gas displays to such advantage the heat still remaining, that the temperature of the mass actually rises instead of falls!

This seems a proposition so remarkable that one may well hesitate before accepting it. There can, however, be no doubt of its truth, and it leads to a very remarkable result. Suppose a great volume of gas were permitted to part with what heat it had by radiation. If the volume were large enough, and if the gaseous bodies of which it was composed were of a nature that would admit of their condensation, then the following is the course which events would take. I am first supposing that the temperature of the gas is but little above that of the surrounding space. The loss of heat will therefore be at first a very slow process, each loss involves a corresponding contraction of the volume, and as we have already pointed out, this contraction must be attended with a rise of temperature. As the temperature of the mass increases the rate at which it parts with its heat will increase also; it follows that the contraction of the volume will proceed at an accelerated pace, and that consequently the rising of temperature will go on with increasing rapidity. We thus find that though the temperature of the gas may have been at first extremely low, yet, that as the loss of heat proceeds the temperature may gradually ascend, until at last it becomes sufficiently high to render the gas visible by actual incandescence. As the process advances still further the body may pass from a mere nebula into a starlike object. With the increase of contraction the pressure also increases, and materials which were originally gaseous will assume more and more a density resembling that of solid bodies.

Here is indeed an astonishing result. We have found that a nebula which may have been originally only a single degree of temperature above the surrounding medium has by the mere fact that it is losing heat grown to the lustre of a star, and may have acquired the heat-diffusing power of a sun. Of course, the capacity for radiation depends on temperature rather than on amount of heat.

The limit to this remarkable evolution has, however to be stated. When the condensation has progressed sufficiently for the body to have become transformed from the gaseous state into a condition resembling that of a liquid or a solid, the foundation of our argument slips from us. It only applies to bodies so long as they remain in the gaseous state, or, at all events, so long as they conform to the laws which gaseous bodies follow, in so far as the present matter is concerned. Once the condensation has brought the bodies originally gaseous into a solid form, then the ordinary laws of cooling for a solid regulate the further changes. Loss of heat will then entail a loss of temperature, consequently the ultimate future of such a body would be that after ages of perhaps nearly stationary splendour the brilliance would begin to wane, the vivid white would be succeeded by hues that indicated a lesser temperature, and ultimately the globe would subside into one of those dark masses with which we know that space is largely tenanted.

This explanation will have prepared the way for the reception of the true theory of the source of solar heat. There can be no doubt that the sun is still largely, if not wholly, of the gaseous or vaporous character. It follows that the process of cooling is still guided by the general principle, that though there may be loss of heat by radiation, yet the temperature of the body, ever lessening by contraction, may show no perceptible abatement. Thus we explain how the sun continues, from age to age, to diffuse a warmth around which shows no evident symptoms of decline. It is unquestionable that the sun must be parting unceasingly with its capital of heat, but by the operation of the laws we have set forth the inevitable loss of heat need not at present involve the loss of temperature.

We can submit this doctrine to the same numerical

test that we have applied to the other explanations which have been offered of the source of sun heat. When we do so the figures supply abundant confirmation of its truth. Suppose that the sun were to pass by loss of heat and consequent contraction into a globe which was less than its present size by one ten-thousandth part of its diameter. Such a change would, no doubt, be considerable if we merely regarded its absolute dimension in miles. It would amount to a shrinkage in the sun's diameter of 87 miles. But on so mighty a globe this alteration is relatively insignificant; indeed no measurements that could be made at our observatories would be sufficiently delicate to detect a change of this magnitude. Helmholtz has, however, shown that if the sun were to undergo even this small diminution of volume the quantity of heat that would be thereby liberated for the purposes of radiation would supply the sun's current rate of expenditure for nearly two thousand years.

This point is so important, that for the sake of further illustration, I shall present it from a somewhat different point of view. Imagine two suns of similar materials and of equal temperature, but so that the diameter of one was a ten-thousandth part greater than that of the other, which latter was as big as ours. Then, although these two suns would be practically the same as far as sensible warmth was concerned, and although the difference between their dimensions would be too insignificant to be appreciable to measurements, conducted from such a distance as that at which we are placed, yet, nevertheless, the larger of these two suns would possess an excess of heat, or its equivalent, over that contained in the smaller, sufficient to supply its entire radiation for two thousand years.

If it be the case that the sun's temperature does remain absolutely constant, then it would seem to follow that the diminution of one ten-thousandth part of its diameter takes place every two thousand years. We have no means of knowing at present whether the actual contraction of the sun takes place at this rate or at any other rate, either somewhat higher or somewhat lower. If the contraction goes on faster than we have stated, then the temperature of the sun must be rising; if slower, then the temperature must be falling.

Here, then, we have a completely satisfactory explanation as to how the sun is able to continue from age to age its beneficent radiation. So long as the body is sufficiently gaseous, so long will it obey the laws of cooling we have indicated, and so long may the amount of its radiation be undiminished. We have seen, however, that there must be some limit to this process. As the contraction of the sun's volume proceeds, the density of the body will increase to such a degree that the luminary is less and less to be regarded as a gaseous mass. At length the time will come when the sun shall have parted with so much heat that it passes to a large extent into the solid condition. There can be no doubt that when this state of things has arrived the heat-dispensing power of the sun will be seriously impaired. The radiation from a solid, as we have already had occasion to show, could not be protracted with sensible uniformity from age to age. We thus have no assurance of the ultimate permanence of the sun as a source of heat to our system. Indeed we may rather anticipate that the character of the sun as a dispenser of heat cannot be eternal. Doubtless the orb of day contains a magnificent supply of either actual heat or potential heat adequate for all the requirements of life for a cycle of ages that must be reckoned by millions of years. It is, however, impossible to overlook the fact that this excessive expenditure must at length produce its natural consequences, and that a bankruptcy of sunbeams is the inevitable destiny of our system. I say inevitable of course with this proviso, that the ordinary conditions of nature as we now find them shall continue to exist.

Seeing that the sun must ultimately become a dark globe, with no higher temperature than that of the surrounding space, it is needless to add that life must ultimately vanish from this earth. We, therefore, learn as a simple consequence from the laws of science as we now find them, that the duration of our earth as the abode of organized beings has a term beyond which it cannot extend.

It would be interesting to inquire whether some confirmation of these views may not be obtained from other parts of space. We remember that cardinal doctrine of astronomy which asserts that our sun is only a star; and as there are millions of stars, it is natural to compare the present phase of our sun with the phases through which other suns are passing. We may for the moment liken the development of a sun to the growth of a tree, which, after passing through every grade of youth, of maturity, and of decrepitude, is finally overthrown to return to the dust from whence it came. In a similar way our sun, which is at present at the height of maturity, is destined to pass into the decrepit state when its powers of radiating heat and light have become greatly impaired before it passes finally into the death-like condition in which it will have no longer any stores of light and heat to dispense. When we look at a forest we see there are a multitude of trees in every stage of development. There are some which are still only young seedlings; there are others which are vigorous saplings; there are a few splendid trees of ample dimensions, and there are others whose mighty trunks show symptoms of decay, while some have already succumbed and are found prostrate and lifeless. These several stages can be witnessed in a glance through a forest glade. In a similar way when we look up at the starry heavens we see a vast multitude of suns in every phase of development; there are some still in the entirely gaseous state, they merely appear as stains of light on the sky; they are what we call the nebulæ. There are others again in which the gradual condensation of the gas has so far advanced that a central and brighter part can be distinguished. In other nebulæ this brighter part has become starlike, and in yet others the transformation has proceeded so far that the nebula seems merely a glow of gaseous atmosphere around a brilliant star. In continuing our search we find others in which the nebula has entirely vanished, while the brilliant star which remains is a striking illustration of the doctrine that the intense fervour of sunlike bodies is due to their contraction from an original gaseous form.

Thus we find the stars furnish us with many excellent illustrations of epochs in the sun's history up to the present time in which the sun has assumed the definite form of a star without being surrounded by a nebula to any considerable extent. The aspect of the heavens will also offer us many suggestions as to the future course of the evolution through which the sun appears destined to pass. There are many stars whose lustre seems declining from what it must once have been. We are acquainted with some stars which radiate quantities of light and heat quite inconsiderable in proportion to their masses. Such bodies as these have evidently advanced towards the conditions of mere red-hot globes of solid matter, and their further decline and ultimate extinction appear to be impending. Unfortunately, however, our observations of stars in stages still further advanced must necessarily be of a very incomplete nature. Once a star has parted with its lustre and become a mere mass of non-luminous matter we are unable to see it. Of course I am speaking here of stars properly so called and not of planets, which are visible not from any light of their own, but in consequence of the sun's light which falls upon them. The stars are, however, usually speaking, millions of times as far from us as are the planets. The beams of our sun are utterly incapable of penetrating to the depths of space with an intensity which would be sufficient to render dark bodies visible. Our sun would, in fact, shed no more light on a dark globe near the star Vega than Vega now sheds on us. To *see* the dark stars is, therefore, impossible, but we are not left entirely destitute of information in respect to them. The dark stars, though invisible, are often very massive; they have the power of attracting objects in their vicinity. It sometimes happens that the movements of a bright star are influenced by the attraction of a dark star which lies near it. When, therefore, we find a difference between the place of a bright star, and the place in which it ought to lie in conformity with calculation, we can attribute the discrepancy to the attraction of some dark star. We are thus able to learn something about these dark stars, which, though never themselves seen, are *felt*, so to speak, by their action on stars that can be observed. The more we meditate on this subject the more probable does it become not only that dark extinguished suns exist, but that they abound in immense numbers; in fact it might be fairly argued that these dead stars vastly exceed in number the bright and living ones. Matter only becomes visible to us across the abyss of stellar distance during those episodes in its career, be they few or many, in which it happens to be at a temperature of incandescence. When the temperature has waned, so that the globe ceases to glow, it may reasonably be held that the body has "joined the majority."

I have been stating merely the results of calculations, and I have made little or no attempt to indicate the processes by which those calculations must be conducted. It is therefore only right that I should refer the inquiring student to some reliable work where he may be able to find the principles on which such researches are made fully set forth. The book I would suggest is Williamson and Tarleton's "Dynamics," at the end of which will be found an instructive chapter on this subject. I shall here extract an interesting numerical fact, for the proof of which reference to this book may be made. Let us suppose that the materials of the sun were originally distributed in a nebulous form, throughout the length, breadth, and depth of space. If these materials were drawn close together in virtue of their mutual attraction, a quantity of heat would be developed in accordance with the laws we have already explained. It is this quantity of heat for which we desire to find an illustration. Imagine a globe of water so vast that its mass shall be equal to that of the sun. We can attach a perfectly definite idea to the quantity of heat which would be required to raise this globe of water from the temperature of ice to that of boiling water. It can be shown that the quantity of heat generated in the contraction of the nebula from dimensions infinitely great down to the dimensions of a sun would be not less than two hundred and seventy thousand times as great as that which would be required to raise to boiling heat an equal mass of water. The result is a remarkable one. It clearly demonstrates that in the transposition of the materials so large a quantity of heat is liberated as to amount to several thousand times as much as the sun now contains. Need we wonder that this mechanical explanation of the source of the sun's heat now finds almost universal acceptance?

CHAPTER IV.

WHAT WE OWE TO THE SUN.

SOME of my readers may think that the subject on which we have been engaged is rather abstruse, and they will perhaps be willing to meditate a little on the simpler matter as to what the sun actually does for us.

A few years ago it was my privilege to deliver at the Royal Institution of Great Britain a Christmas course of lectures addressed to an audience consisting mainly of juveniles. In discoursing of the sun I endeavoured to set before them the many indirect benefits which we derive from his beams, and as an illustration taken from domestic affairs I dwelt on the kindly providence with which the sun ministers to our tea-table. I showed how the heat of the fire came ultimately from sunbeams, how the tea was wafted from China by the sun, how the water for the kettle was brought into our house by solar rays, how the flour was grown and ground by the same agency. I even pointed out that it was the sun which gave whiteness to the tablecloth and bright colours for the ladies' dresses. I do not now refer further to these matters, for they have been recently set forth in my little book called

"Star-Land," in which these lectures have been published. There are, however, one or two points which seemed more advanced than would have been suitable for the readers of "Star-Land," and which I did not accordingly there enter upon. These are of such importance that I am glad to take this opportunity of alluding to them.

It will be remembered that in Gulliver's renowned Travels he visited the Grand Academy of Lagado. The first professor into whose laboratory Gulliver was conducted had been engaged for eight years upon "a project for extracting sunbeams out of cucumbers, which were to be put in phials, hermetically sealed, and let out to warm the air in raw inclement summers. He did not doubt that in eight years more he should be able to supply the governor's gardens with sunshine at a reasonable rate." This is not the only occasion on which Dean Swift has, consciously or unconsciously, given us profound scientific truth under a guise of absurdity. Within a page or two of the passage we have quoted is the announcement of the discovery of the two satellites of Mars by astronomers on the flying island of Laputa. To this we shall return in a later part of this book. The myth of the Lagado professor about sunbeams and cucumbers is allied to a truth still more remarkable.

It is perfectly certain that in the growth of the cucumber plant the leaves do lay hold of the sunbeams, extract the heat from them, and lay up that heat or its equivalent in the fruit which is produced. It is equally certain that the heat of the sunbeams could be extracted again, could even be stored in phials hermetically sealed, and be utilised when occasion might require. There is in fact only one weak point in the scheme of the Lagado professor: its economical aspect is unsatisfactory. The heat of the sunbeams could only be recovered from cucumbers at an utterly prohibitive cost. Nevertheless, the heat is there, and in plants of other growths it becomes quite possible not only to extract the latent sunbeams, but even to do so with the highest profit and advantage. Sunbeams may shine on a tree for a few decades, the leaves may each summer garner the sunbeams which fall on them and incorporate those sunbeams in the solid trunk of the tree. In due time the tree is felled, logs of it are thrown on the fire, and pleasant light and warmth radiate from the hearth. It is not a mere flight of poetical fancy to regard the light and heat from a fireplace as the sunbeams retransformed to the active state from a condition of inertness. It is an undoubted scientific truth.

Let us ponder on the character of the process by which the leaves of a plant contribute so largely to the building up of its solid stem. Wood consists chiefly of the element carbon in association with small quantities of mineral ingredients. The growing tree draws its supplies of the necessary material partly from the earth and partly from the air. The earth provides, speaking generally, the mineral constituents; but carbon, which is the essential characteristic of wood, and which is the principal source of the heat-giving qualities of a log fire, is chiefly obtained from the air.

The atmosphere contains a certain proportion of carbonic acid gas, which is composed of the element carbon in combination with oxygen. To understand what takes place by the action of the growing plant on the carbonic acid of the air, we should note the circumstances under which this gas is ordinarily produced in the combination of oxygen and carbon. In the act of formation quantities of heat are evolved; in fact the production of heat in an ordinary fireplace is the immediate consequence of the combination between the carbon in the coal with the oxygen of the air. The difference, then, between a quantity of oxygen and carbon separately and the same quantity of the two substances united in the form of carbonic acid, simply is that the separate materials have the power of producing not alone the carbonic acid, but of evolving a quantity of heat during the process of combination. If it be required to separate the carbon and the oxygen already united in carbonic acid, then heat must be applied during the process exactly in the same amount as would be given out during the combination of the two elements. The leaves of the tree have to extract carbon from the carbonic acid in the atmosphere around them; to do this they require heat and light, and these they find supplied by the beams from the sun. Each leaf of the plant is a chemical laboratory in which sun heat is applied to the splitting asunder of the atoms of carbon and oxygen held so tightly in combination. It is the carbon that the leaves want; this material is transmitted to the growing trunk in which the results of the operation are accumulated. The oxygen not being required by the necessities of the plant is returned to the atmosphere. It is well known that the operation I have here indicated is a beneficent one, not only to the plant which requires air for its growth, but also to the animals, including man himself, to whom respiration is a necessity. Animals absorb the oxygen and give off carbonic acid, while plants remove this gas, which is pernicious to animal life, abstract from it the carbon they want, and restore the invigorating oxygen.

Thus the growing tree absorbs heat from the sunbeams, and is enabled to acquire from the air that quantity of carbon which is essential for its increase. Afterwards, when the tree is burned in the fire, the carbon returns again to carbonic acid, and in doing so radiates forth again the heat which had been absorbed in its manufacture.

This process becomes particularly interesting when viewed in connection with our supply of fuel in the form of coal. It is well known that coal is the remains of a splendid vegetation, which from time to time has been permitted to clothe large tracts on our globe. No one can venture to express the thousands of years or the millions of years that have elapsed since the last coal forests flourished. Certain it is that the period was long ere man came on this globe. The sun must have shone in those ancient days as he does at present. His genial beams were not, however, lost even so far as man was concerned. The leaves on the great carboniferous forests captured those beams, utilised them on a stupendous scale for the production of carbon, and thus manufactured mighty seams of coal. When we now put this coal on our fires, the heat which it discharges is none other than that sun heat which was laid by in the time of those primeval forests. The light from our gas-burners is of course directly derived from coal, but we may speak of it really as well as figuratively as artificial sunshine; indeed, we might even go further, and show that almost every source of heat and every source of light may ultimately be traced back to sunbeams in one form or another.

Let us take as a splendid example the electric light, which as ordinarily produced is ultimately due to sunbeams. No doubt it is immediately derived from a pair of carbon points, but the current necessary for the purpose is obtained from a dynamo, which must be driven by some source of power, usually a steam-engine. It follows that the power of the steam-engine is the source of the electric light; but the steam-engine is driven by steam, and the steam is made from water, and the water is heated by coal: thus it is coal which actually generates the electric light—the boiler, the water, the steam-engine, the dynamo, the wires, and the carbon points are merely appliances by which something which has been stored in the coal is applied to the particular purpose of generating light. The coal, as we have seen, has derived its potency from the sunbeams which shone on the ancient forests at the time of the formation of the coal measures. Our electric lights to-night may be regarded as a resuscitation on a feeble scale of sunbeams emitted from the orb of day millions of years ago.

In such a case as that just considered, we seem to be drawing on an accumulated hoard of sunbeams stored away in the earth's interior; but we can also utilise what we may describe as the present radiation of the sun from day to day for the production of artificial illumination. For the prodigious energy of modern civilisation the Falls of Niagara have to be rendered serviceable, even though the process involves a lamentable sacrifice of their beauty. The power of those Falls suitably applied to water-wheels could be made to turn dynamos to generate electricity enough for the wants of a mighty people. It is easy to show that even in such a case also sunbeams would be unquestionably the effective agents. Niagara is supplied by the rain which falls over a vast tract of country; that rain is brought thither by the action of warm sunbeams, which beat down on the oceans, evaporate the water, and raise it aloft; then the winds waft the vapour over the globe until it again descends in the form of rain. Thus we learn that the power of Niagara, no less than the efficiency of the coal-fields in the production of heat and light, is to be attributed to the sun, the difference being that in the one case we are utilising the sun's ancient beams, and in the other the power is provided from the radiation of the sun at the present time.

One more question may be briefly discussed. It will be remembered that in what we have here said we are merely discussing the natural consequences of those laws of nature which are in operation around us. We are tempted to push the inquiries back a stage earlier, and examine how the materials of the sun came into the nebulous state from which they have gradually become transformed to the sun that we now have. It is quite evident that the nebula cannot have existed from all time, for were this so the sun must necessarily have long since passed into that cold and inert condition which at present is looked forward to in the dim future. It is, therefore, interesting to inquire whether by the operation of natural laws a vast glowing nebula could have been called into being at some period not infinitely remote from the present day. There is a possible, indeed a highly probable, explanation of such an occurrence. Suppose that two bodies, each dark and cold, were to strike together in space with such velocities as are ordinarily possessed by celestial bodies, then a vast generation of heat would be a consequence of the collision. Each of the bodies possesses a certain quantity of energy in virtue of its motion; but an important law of mechanics tells us that, though the motion may seem partly or wholly annihilated by the collision, yet the energy is not lost; it must reappear in one of the other garbs which energy can so rapidly assume. In such a case as this it will immediately take the form of heat, and the two bodies will be heated by the blow. Other things being equal the quantity of heat that will be produced depends upon the speed with which the two colliding objects rush together. With high speeds the heat that can be thus generated is much greater than when the speeds are low. Thus, for instance, if the speed be doubled the heat that would be generated by the collision is increased fourfold; or if the speed of approach be increased tenfold, then the consequent production of heat is made ten times ten, that is, one hundredfold. Speaking generally, we might say that the heat generated by the collision is proportional to the square of the relative velocity with which the two bodies fly together.

Considering the enormously high velocities with which the heavenly bodies are animated, it is obvious that in the possibility of collision we have a source of heat adequate for the production of the most gigantic phenomena. For example, let us take our own earth, which has at present a speed of eighteen miles a second. Suppose that in the depths of space it should happen that two globes, each as large as our earth and each having a velocity of eighteen miles a second, rushed into direct collision; it can be shown that the energy which would be transformed by the shock would be adequate, when converted into heat, to raise the two bodies not merely to incandescence but even to transmute them into a gaseous nebula. Here then we have a possible explanation as to how the nebula from which our sun has been developed was originally formed. It may have been produced, and most likely was produced, by the collision between two other bodies. In the same way it may yet conceivably happen that after the sun shall have grown condensed and cold, and is journeying on with enormous velocity through space, it may again come into collision with some other body, and the transformation of the energy from motion into heat may again generate another nebula, and set in progress yet another evolution like that through which we are at present passing.

CHAPTER V.

THE CONSTANT FACE OF THE MOON.

THE myriad bodies that adorn the skies are of varied degrees of brilliancy and of the widest range in dimensions. It seems a reasonable question to ask which of all the celestial bodies is the smallest. I speak not now of telescopic objects, I am only alluding to those which can be seen by unaided vision. Many of the stars which lie on the verge of visibility seem extremely minute, but then we have the best reasons for believing that this apparent smallness is merely a delusion. The stars, so far as they are known to us, are found to be bodies far exceeding the earth in size, so much so that many of them are comparable with our sun itself. The planets are smaller than the more important stars, notwithstanding the fact that the apparent lustre of Venus or of Jupiter under favourable circumstances exceeds that of any star. It is, however, somewhat surprising to learn that, so far as is at present known, the very smallest of all the orbs visible to the unaided eye is our satellite, the moon. Seeing that the illumination dispensed by the moon is greatly in excess of that sent to us by all the other heavenly bodies put together, the sun alone excepted, we may well pause before admitting the truth of the somewhat startling fact that each of these stars and planets, dim though they admittedly are, must still be intrinsically larger and heavier than the moon.

No doubt the telescope discloses to us multitudes of celestial objects many of which do not possess one ten-thousandth part of the bulk of the moon. But those objects are all so faint that good instruments are required to make them discernible. As to the real dimensions of the moon I may as well mention, once for all, the few facts that will be important for us. The diameter of our satellite is rather more than one-fourth the diameter of the earth. To express it a little more precisely, we may say that the moon's diameter is two thousand one hundred and sixty miles, that is to say about as far as from London to the Caspian Sea, or from the Straits of Gibraltar to the Crimea.

It is instructive to open a map of Europe and then draw with a pair of compasses a circle representing the size of the moon on the same scale as that of the map. This circle will enable the dimensions of our satellite to be properly appreciated. The British Islands are of comparatively insignificant extent if placed in the centre of the figure.

In the figure on the opposite page we have indicated the circle so as to include the larger part of Europe. From the Ural Mountains the circumference passes north into Sweden and Norway, then traversing the North Sea it just touches the eastern parts of England. There it crosses the Channel, and after passing through the centre

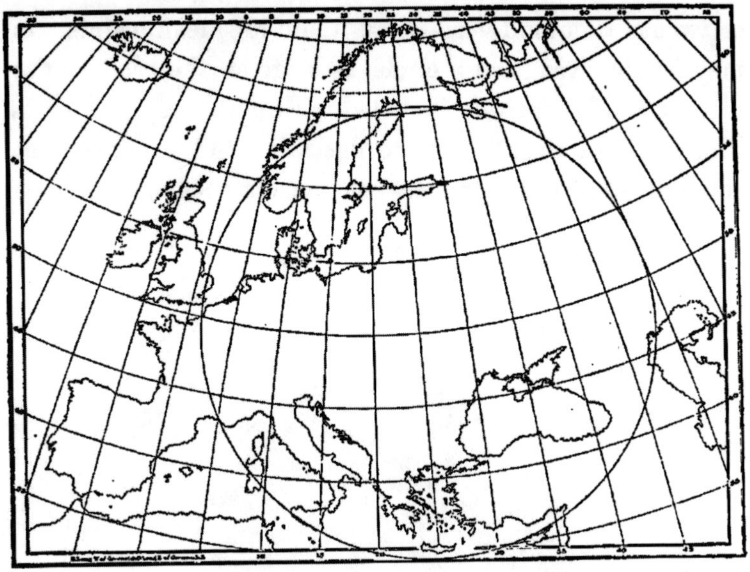

Fig. 4.—The Lunar Disc shown against the Map of Europe.

of France enters the Mediterranean. Bisecting Sardinia and grazing the south of Sicily the circle then keeps well to the south of the Grecian Archipelago, shoots beneath Asia Minor, and touches land again in Palestine. Here it rises towards the north, including the Black Sea in its ample interior, and just cutting off a corner of the Caspian. Finally, the curve bends towards the Ural Mountains, and completes its circuit of the Continent. This little sketch will also show that when we look at the full moon the objects there so conspicuous must be as large, say, as Spain or the Black Sea.

The distance of the moon from the earth is, in round numbers, two hundred and forty thousand miles; however, it varies somewhat, so that in extreme cases the moon's distance may be twenty thousand miles more or twenty thousand times less than its mean value. It may be observed that a circle as large as the orbit of the moon could be entirely included within the sun. This is illustrated in Fig. 5. If we desire to find a convenient standard of comparison between the distance of the moon

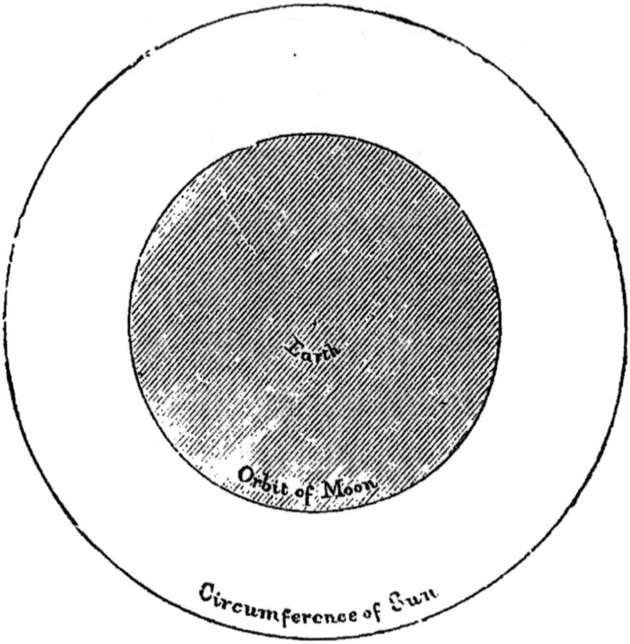

Fig. 5.—To compare the orbit of the moon with the size of the sun.

and the size of the earth, let us think of a cord wrapped ten times round the earth at the equator, this would be long enough to extend from the earth to the moon.

One of the earliest facts that any observer will notice, is that the moon always turns the same face towards us. The simplest observations suffice to give assurance on this point. There are large and conspicuous marks on our satellite which have been observed from all antiquity, and whenever the surface of the moon can be seen, the same marks are always discernible. I ought, however, to qualify this remark by saying that the face of the moon is sometimes tilted a little, so that the objects found close to the edge are not always unchanged. Speaking generally, however, there is hardly a more striking fact in the celestial movements than the constant face of our satellite. We have little doubt that the moon, like the other heavenly bodies, is globular in its form, but we have never been actually able to see that the opposite side of the moon has the hemispherical shape that we find possessed by the side which is presented to us. As we have not the means of holding up a looking-glass behind the moon there seems to be no possibility of learning what is at the other side.

We may perhaps emphasize the remarkable attitude of the moon towards the earth, by contrasting it with that of some of the other celestial bodies. Consider, for instance, the corresponding circumstances with regard to the sun. It is true that our great luminary exhibits to us no permanent features like those which are engraved on the moon's face, but the spots on the sun, transient though they doubtless are, still endure long enough to testify con clusively that the sun rotates on its axis. We learn in fact from a vast accumulation of observations specially directed to this one point that the period of the rotation of the sun is certainly more than three weeks, and certainly less than four. Hence that side of the great luminary which is directed towards the earth must be constantly changing. If we look on one hemisphere of the sun to-day, then a fortnight ago it was the opposite hemisphere that was turned towards us, and in about another fortnight we shall have the original hemisphere restored. Each side of the sun is thus equally accessible to our observations; there is no region withheld from our scrutiny as is the case in the moon.

Similar language may be used with regard to the attitude of the planets towards the earth. Mars is so much farther from us than the moon that we cannot scrutinize his ruddy globe so minutely as we are able to do that of our own satellite; but Mars turns round on his axis once every twenty-four hours and a half, so that we are able to form maps of his entire surface, and whatever incompleteness those maps may possess arises from such causes as the imperfection of our instruments or the distance of Mars; for we cannot assert that the movements of the planet are such as to prevent our examination from being extended over the whole of his globe. The giant orb of Jupiter revolves with rapidity on its axis. Suppose an astronomer looks at the great planet at eight o'clock in the evening, observes the belts and other configurations of its surface, and turns to other work until about one o'clock in the morning; if he now directs his telescope again to Jupiter the panorama is entirely changed. The belts and marks which he saw in the earlier observations have vanished, they have in fact retired to the opposite side of the globe, while all the objects that he sees in his second observation were on the distant side of the globe at the time of the first observation and were consequently invisible. Should his ardour be equal to that of some famous astronomers, as, for instance, to that of Sir William Herschel, whose hours of observing were from dusk to dawn, our observer might then, if the season were suitable, look at Jupiter again at six o'clock; in this case the hemisphere he last saw would have vanished, while that presented to him at eight o'clock on the previous evening would have been restored. He would again find the same belts and marks as those he saw on the first occasion, altered only by such intrinsic changes as may have actually taken place on the planet in the interval. These illustrations will suffice to indicate how different are the circumstances of the moon's motion from those that we find in the other celestial bodies.

If I were asked to offer a conjecture as to what the other side of the moon may be like, I should not hesitate to reply that in all probability it would present features of a similar character to those on that side of our satellite with which we are so familiar. The study of the sun and planets shows that they are, generally speaking, symmetrical in form, and the circumstance that we happen to be prevented from viewing one side of the moon does not impair the analogy between it and the other orbs of heaven. We should therefore expect to find on that distant side of the moon indications of the same volcanic and other phenomena that our telescopes show on that surface which we actually see.

We have mentioned the case of other globes which revolve on their axes, the revolution being conducted in such a manner that the entire surface is more or less known to us. The moon also revolves on its axis, the peculiarity, however, consisting in the circumstance that the time taken for the rotation about its axis is equal to that of its revolution round the earth. An old paradox is connected with this question, for as the moon does not change its aspect towards us, it has been sometimes argued that it cannot be turning round. The difficulty, such as it is, resolves itself more into a matter of words than of actual fact. Let me try to explain it as follows.

Suppose a horse is galloping round a circular course, then a spectator at the centre of the course will have one side of the horse turned towards him, while the other side of the horse is invariably turned away. To this extent therefore the movement of the horse round the course is analogous to the movement of the moon around the earth. When the horse has completed his circuit it will be found that he has not only performed a revolution around the course, but he has also rotated once in the same period. It is obvious that the horse must at one moment or another of his journey have faced every part of the horizon successively. No matter how the course be placed there must have been one point so situated that while passing it the horse was going directly towards the north, while when he has reached the opposite point of the circle he is galloping towards the south. At one intermediate point he is for the moment bound towards the east, but at the point diametrically opposite his flight is towards the west. It is clearly impossible that the horse can have faced north, south, east, and west, without performing a movement of rotation. Unless he rotated he would necessarily be always journeying towards the same point of the compass. Suppose that, at the moment when he was facing due north, his right side being turned towards the spectator in the middle, we bring him to the opposite side of the course, and again place him facing due north. It is clear that the left side of the animal will now be towards the spectator. In such a case it is plain that the movement has not been at all like that of the moon, the characteristic feature of which is that the same face is always directed towards the earth.

It will not be a sufficient explanation to say that if the moon rotated on an axis at all it must rotate in some definite period, and if so, why should not that period be identical with the revolution of the moon round the earth? Would it not be, it might be urged, as likely to be that period as any other? This will not satisfy the student of nature; the coincidence between these periods is so perfect that the chances are many millions to one against its occurrence if there were no physical reason for its existence. It is now well known that there is such a reason, and as it affords an instructive illustration of the mutual relations between the earth and her satellite, I propose to enter into the matter with some little detail.

I must ask you to think of a very ancient epoch; how ancient it is to be I cannot express by the use of ordinary chronology; it must have been hundreds of thousands of years ago, probably many millions of years ago. At this period, however, the moon was not like the object that we know so well. Her surface now seems to be composed of rocks or stone, or at all events of materials which are hard and solid. But this was not always so. There are abundant traces of the remains of past volcanoes on the moon; their craters are no longer active, but some of them once had dimensions and energy transcending any of the volcanoes on the earth that are now known to us. It is thus certain that at some former time the moon must have possessed stores of internal heat by which these volcanic eruptions were produced. It therefore follows that even if the moon be now entirely cold, it must once have been heated. No one is likely to dispute this, but yet the full consequences of such an admission are not always readily perceived. For if the moon were once hot it is plain that earlier still it must have been yet hotter, and therefore the farther we look back into the depths of time past, the hotter and hotter do we see that the moon must have been. At last we discover an epoch, how remote I do not pretend to say, when our neighbouring globe, instead of being the quiescent object that we now see must have contained many active volcanoes indicative of an interior containing volumes of molten lava. Earlier still we perceive the moon ever hotter and hotter, until at last we seem to discern a time when it must have consisted of a globe, partly, or even wholly, molten. This seems an inevitable deduction from the fact that the moon bears traces of having once possessed internal heat. Such a view of the early condition of our satellite will explain many of its characteristic features. At present, however I am only concerned to account for the fact that the moon now always turns the same face towards the earth.

Every one is familiar with the fact that the moon raises tides on the earth; these tides ebb and flow along our coasts, and in virtue of them the satellite exercises a certain control on the movements of our globe. If the moon had liquid oceans on its surface there cannot be a doubt that the attraction of the earth would generate tides in the oceans on the moon just as the attraction of the moon generates tides in the oceans of the earth. But there would be a fundamental difference between the two cases; the shores of the lunar seas would be periodically inundated by tides far vaster than any tides which the moon can create on the earth. But it may be said that as the moon contains no water it seems idle to talk of the tides that might have been produced in oceans if they had existed. It is no doubt true that the moon contains no visible liquid water on its surface at the present time; it is, however, by no means certain that our satellite was always void of water; it is not at all impossible that spreading oceans may have once occupied a large part of that surface now an arid wilderness. The waters from those oceans have vanished, but the basins they presumably filled are still left as characteristic features on our satellite. For our present argument, however, it is really not material that the moon should ever have had oceans as we understand them. Have we not seen that there was a time when the very mass of the moon itself appears to have been largely, if not wholly, liquefied? The water at those remote periods must have been suspended in the form of vapour around the more solid parts of the glowing globe. But tides can be manifested in other liquids besides that which forms our seas. In fact if the basins of our great oceans were filled with oil or with mercury, or even with molten iron instead of water, the moon would still cause tides to ebb and flow, no matter what the material might be, so long as it possessed to some extent the properties of a liquid. It need not be a perfect liquid, for any material which is in some degree viscous, like honey or treacle, would still respond to tidal influence, though not, it may be well believed, with the same alacrity and freedom of movement as would a fluid of a more perfect character. In the molten moon itself, throughout the very body of our satellite, the tidal influence of the earth must have been experienced in these primitive ages.

We can hardly describe the tides in such a case as producing actual currents like those which our sailors know so well; they must rather be regarded as throbbings or heavings throughout the mass of the moon which would originate deformations of its constitution. Whenever movements of this kind are produced *friction* must inevitably result, and it is characteristic of friction to act in such a way as tends to check the movement by which it is caused. The effect of the tides in the wholly or partially fluid moon would therefore incessantly tend to adjust the moon's movement in such a manner that the tides should not further disturb it. There would, no doubt, be a high tide on two opposite meridians of the moon and low tide in the intermediate regions, but those conditions would be permanent. To take the simplest supposition we may regard the high tide as present on the central meridian on that side of the moon turned towards the earth, and as that side remains constantly directed towards the earth during the moon's monthly movements, the high tide remains always at the same lunar locality There is no ebb and flow, there is no distraction of the material of the globe, which, having become once adjusted to this condition, remains without future tidal change.

There cannot be a doubt that in ancient days when the moon was sufficiently fluid, the action of the tides tended without ceasing to the establishment of such an adjustment between the rotation of the moon around its axis and the revolution of the moon around the earth, that the two should be brought to have equal periods. Friction would incessantly operate until this adjustment had been effected, and owing to the preponderating mass of the earth such strenuous tides must have been evoked in the moon that our satellite was brought under tidal control with comparative facility. Hence it arose that in those early days the habit of bending the same face incessantly towards the earth around which it revolved was established on our satellite.

Time passed on, the moon gradually dispensed its excessive heat by radiation into space, and it gradually became transformed from a molten globe to a globe with a solid crust. It may be that the water was condensed from vapour and then collected together into oceans on the newly formed surface ; if so, these oceans would not have any ebbing tide or flowing tide, for it would be constant high tide at some places and constant low tide at others. Such a state of things would at all events endure so long as the adjustment of equality between the moon's rotation and its revolution continued. In fact, should any departure from this adjustment have manifested itself corresponding tides would have begun to throb in the lunar oceans, and their tendency would be to restore the adjustment which was disturbed. This arrangement between the two movements was necessarily stable when tidal control was always at hand to check any tendency to depart from it.

It may be that the moon has now cooled so thoroughly that not only is it hard and congealed on the exterior as we see, but it seems highly probable that the heat may have so entirely forsaken even the interior that there is no longer any fluid in the globe of our satellite to respond to tidal impulse. There is, therefore, in all probability, no longer any actual tidal control. On the other hand, however, there is nothing to disturb the adjustment. It was, as we have seen, caused by the tides which have done their work; the consequences of that work are still exhibited in the constant face of the moon, which, now that it has been brought about, seems likely to exist permanently as a stable adaptation of the movement.

CHAPTER VI.

THE MOON'S HISTORY.

THE doctrine which I shall here endeavour to set forth is mainly due to the labours of Sir George H. Darwin of Cambridge. I have mentioned how the tendency of the tides on a tide-disturbed globe is to adjust the movements of that globe in such a way that the tides shall no longer ebb or flow, but that permanent high tide shall be established in some places and permanent low tide in others. If the rotation of the body be not fast enough the tide will pull the body round in order to effect this object. If the rotation of the body be too rapid then the influence of the tide will tend to check the movement and bring down the speed of rotation until the desired adjustment is obtained. At present the earth is spinning too fast to permit the high tides to remain at permanent localities, and consequently tides are applied with the effect of checking the rotation. The earth is, however, so vast, and the tides generated by so small a body as the moon are relatively so impotent, that their effects in reducing the speed of the earth's rotation are insignificant. Nevertheless, small though they are, they unquestionably exist, and there cannot be a doubt that to some extent the earth is affected by the unremitting action of the tides; the consequence is that the rapidity with which the earth rotates upon its axis is gradually declining.

One result of this can be stated in a very simple manner. The length of the day must be increasing It is true that this gradual stretching of the dav is very slow; it is indeed quite inappreciable in so far as our ordinary use of the day as a measure of time is concerned. The alteration almost eludes any means of measurement at our disposal. Even in a thousand years the change is so small that the diminution in the length of the day is only a fraction of a second. We can doubtless afford to disregard so trifling a variation in our standard of time so far as the period contemplated in mere human affairs is concerned. In fact the change is absolutely devoid of significance within such periods as are contemplated since the erection of the Pyramids, or indeed since any other human monument has been reared. We must not, however, conclude that the change in the length of the day has no significance in earth history. Of late years it has become known that this alteration in the day is connected with an important chapter in the remote history of this globe. In fact there is hardly a more interesting doctrine in modern science than that which deals with this subject. I have explained the phenomena somewhat fully in my little volume entitled "Time and Tide," in which I have endeavoured to sketch the remarkable evolution through which the earth seems to have passed. I must, however, here give a few of the leading features in the story, for it would be quite impossible to exclude it altogether when the subject of our satellite is under discussion.

The significance of the gradual elongation of the day by the tides arises from the circumstance that the change always takes place in one direction. In this form of effect the tide differs from other more familiar astronomical phenomena which sometimes advance in one direction and then after the lapse of suitable periods return in the opposite direction, and thus restore again the initial state of things. But the alteration of the length of the day is not of this character, it is not periodic, its motion is never reversed, is never even arrested. Only one condition is therefore necessary to enable it to obtain tremendous dimensions, and that is sufficient time in which it can operate.

There are many lines of reasoning which show the extreme antiquity of our globe: the disclosures of geology are specially instructive on this head. Think, for instance, of that mighty reptile the Atlantosaurus, which once roamed over the regions now known as Colorado. The bones of this vast creature indicate an animal surpassing in proportions the greatest elephant ever known. No one can count the æons of years that have elapsed since the Atlantosaurus, whose bones are now to be seen in the museum at Yale College, breathed its last. A still more striking conception of time than even the antiquity of this creature affords is derived from the consideration that his mighty form was itself the product of a long and immeasurable line of ancestry, extending to a depth in the remote past far beyond the limits of computation. I have mentioned this illustration of the antiquity of the earth for the purpose of showing the ample allowance of time that is available for tides to accomplish great work in earlier stages of our globe's history.

As the evidence of the earth's crust proves that our globe has lasted for incalculable ages, it becomes of interest to think how far the gradual elongation of the day may have attained significant proportions since very early time. It may be that even in a thousand years the effect of the tides is not sufficient to alter the length of the day by so much as a single second. But the effect may be very appreciable or even large in a million years, or ten million years. We have the best reasons for knowing that in intervals of time comparable with those I have mentioned, the change in the length of the day may have amounted not merely to seconds or minutes, but even to hours. Looking into the remote past, there was a time at which this globe spun round in twenty-three hours instead of twenty-four; at a still earlier period the rate must have been twenty hours, and the further we look back the more and more rapidly does the earth appear to be spinning. At last, as we strain our gaze to some epoch so excessively remote that it must have been long anterior to those changes which geology recognises, we see that our globe was spinning round in a period of six hours or five hours, or possibly even less. Here then is a lesson which the tides have taught us: they have shown that if the causes at present in operation have subsisted without interruption for a sufficiently long period in the past, the day must have gradually grown to its present length from an initial condition in which the earth seems to have spun round about four times as quickly as it does at present.

We should, however, receive a very inadequate impression of what tides are able to accomplish if we merely contemplated this change in the length of the day, striking and significant though it doubtless is. The student of natural philosophy is well aware that there is no action without a corresponding reaction, and it is instructive to examine in this case the form which the reaction assumes. Our reasoning has been founded on the supposition that it is the attraction of the moon on the waters of our globe that gives rise to the tides. It is, therefore, the influence of the moon which checks the speed of the earth's rotation and adds to the length of the day.

As the moon acts in this fashion on the earth, so, by the general law that I have mentioned, the earth reacts upon the moon. The form which this reaction assumes expresses itself in a tendency to allow the moon gradually to move farther and farther away from the earth than the earth's attraction would permit if our globe were a solid mass void of all liquid capable of being distracted by tides. It is, therefore, certain that the distance of the moon, which is at present about two hundred and forty thousand miles, must be gradually increasing; but we need not look for any appreciable change in the moon's distance arising from this cause when only an interval of a few centuries is considered. We need not expect to measure the difference due to tides between the size of the moon's orbit this month and the size of the orbit last month. In fact, there are so many periodic causes of change in the dimensions of the moon's orbit, that it becomes impossible to detect the tidal influence even in the course of centuries. Here, again, we have to remember that in dealing with the history of our earth, as such history is contemplated by the astronomer, we are to consider not merely the thousands of years that include the human period, not merely the millions of years that are required by the necessities of geology, but also those unknown periods anterior to geological phenomena to which we have already referred.

In the course of such vast ages the reaction of the earth on the moon's orbit has not only become perceptible, it has become conspicuous; it has not only become conspicuous, but it has become the chief determining agent in making the moon's orbit as we find it at the present day. We have seen that as we look into the past the length of the day seems ever shorter and shorter; and concurrent with this decline in the day is the diminution in the moon's distance from the earth. There was a time when the moon, instead of revolving at a distance of two hundred and forty thousand miles, as it does at present, revolved at a distance of only two hundred thousand miles. As we think of epochs still earlier we discern the moon ever closer and closer to the earth, until at last, at that critical time in the history of the earth-moon system, when the earth was quickly revolving in a period of a few hours, our satellite seems to have been quite close to the earth; in fact, the two bodies were almost in contact.

The study of the tides has therefore conducted us to the knowledge of a remarkable configuration exhibited in the primitive earth-moon system. The earth was then spinning round rapidly in a day which was only a few hours long, whilst close to the earth, or almost in contact with it, the moon coursed around our globe, the period of its revolution being shorter to such an extent that the satellite completed its circuit in the same time as the earth required for one turn round its axis. We cannot indeed say that the earth and the moon in this wonderful condition bore much resemblance to the earth and the moon as we now know them. Even if the bodies had by that time assumed the globular form, it seems certain that they must have been composed of wholly or partially molten material, very unlike the rigid globes that the earth and moon now appear to be.

Up to this point our reasoning has been based on the results of mathematical investigation. It is characteristic of such investigations that they leave no loop-hole for error when the conditions have been properly stated. We are naturally anxious to push the research one step farther and to learn how it was that the moon happened to be found in such a remarkable situation in the immediate vicinity of the earth. At this critical stage mathematics seems to withhold its guidance, but at the same time does not forbid an attempt to penetrate the mystery of the moon's origin. The reasoning that has hitherto guided our inquiries becomes no longer available, and anything which we can add to the sketch already given of earth-moon history must therefore be received on authority possessing a different value from that which has characterized the former stages of the inquiry. It is, however, almost impossible to resist the conjecture which naturally arises when we endeavour to form a mental picture of the condition of the earth and moon at this most interesting epoch.

We must remember that the materials destined to form the pair of allied planets did not then form two solid bodies as they do at present; they were both, in all probability, incandescent masses glowing with fervour, and soft, if not actually molten, or incoherent, or even gaseous. These aggregations were close together, and one of them was whirling around the other in a period of a few hours, the duration of that period being equal to the time in which the larger mass revolved on its axis. In fact, the two objects, even though distinct, seem to have revolved the one around the other as if they had been bound together by rigid bonds. The rapid rotation with which they were animated suggests a cause for this state of things. It is well known that a fly-wheel, when driven at an unduly high speeed, is liable to break asunder in consequence of its rapid motion. If a grindstone be urged around with excessive velocity the force tending to rend the stone into fragments may overcome its cohesion, and it will fly into pieces, often projected with such violence that fearful accidents have been the consequence.

Viewing the earth as a rotating body, it must be subject to the law that there is a speed which cannot be exceeded with safety. With the present period of rotation of once in every twenty-four hours the tendency to disruption is but small and consequently the earth retains its integrity, though no doubt the protuberance at the equator is the result of the accommodation of the shape of the globe to the circumstances attending its revolution. But let us suppose that the length of the day was greatly diminished, or, what comes to the same thing, that the speed with which the earth rotates on its axis was greatly increased; it is then conceivable that the tension thus arising might be too great for the coherence of the material to withstand. We believe that the earth could turn round with double the speed that it has at present before this tension approached the point at which disruption would ensue. But supposing the day were to be so much shortened that the period of rotation was only a very few hours instead of twenty-four, there is then good reason to know that the tension in the earth arising from this rapid rotation would be so great that a rupture of the globe would be imminent.

Provided with this conception, let us think of the initial stage when the moon was quite close to the earth. Our globe was then, as we know, spinning round so rapidly that its materials were almost on the point of breaking up in consequence of the strain produced by the rotation. It is interesting to note that the tidal action of the sun would also conduce to the rupture of our globe in the critical circumstances we have supposed. It seems hardly possible to doubt that such a separation of the glowing mass did actually take place, a small fragment was discarded, and gradually drew itself by the mutual attraction of its particles into a globular form and thus became the moon.

Such is the view of the origin of the moon which is suggested by tidal evolution. Similar deductions from the theory of the tides will enable us to offer a forecast of the future career of the earth-moon system. Let us transfer our attention from the remote past and endeavour to think of the distant future. So long as the solar system shall last without the intervention of other agents than those known to us by the law of gravitation, it seems certain that the progress of the earth-moon system must be in substantial accordance with the principles here laid down.

We have seen that at the present moment the day is becoming gradually longer and the moon is steadily receding farther and farther from the earth. At present these changes take place with extreme slowness, but in the primitive periods of which we have already spoken, the changes in the length of the day, and the changes in the distance of the moon, proceeded at a rate far more rapid than at present. As the moon has receded farther from the earth its efficiency as a tide-producer has declined, and consequently the rate at which the consequences of tidal action have proceeded is continually lessening. It must therefore be expected that the progress of tidal evolution in the future will be ever getting slower and slower, so that the periods of time required for the further development of the phenomena far exceed those which have elapsed in the course of the history already given. We can, however, foreshadow what is to happen in the following manner. The length of the day will slowly increase; and we can indicate a state of things in the excessively remote future towards which it may be said the system is tending. The day will grow until it becomes not merely twenty-five or twenty-six hours, but until it becomes as long as two or three of our present days. In fact, as we stretch our imagination through ages so inconceivable that I forbear to specify any figures which might characterize them, we seem to discern that the length of the day may go on ever getting longer and longer until at last a stage is reached when the day is about fifty or sixty times as long as our present day.

All this time, in accordance with the general law of action and reaction, the moon must be gradually retreating; the orbit of the moon is destined to grow ever wider and wider; the distance of our satellite from the earth becoming ever greater and greater until at last the period is reached to which we have already referred, when the day is some fourteen hundred hours long. As the orbit of the moon is gradually enlarging, the time that the moon takes to revolve around the earth must be continually on the increase; from the present month of twenty-seven days the length of the month will gradually augment as the ages roll by until at last when the moon has reached a certain distance the period of its rotation will have become double what it is at present, or indeed rather more than double, and we shall have the day and the month equal, each being about fourteen hundred hours long. When this state of things is reached, the earth will always turn the same face towards the moon, just as the moon at present always turns the same face towards the earth.

We have already explained how the constant face of the moon can be accounted for by the action of tides raised in the moon by the attraction of the earth. Owing to the small size of the moon the tides have already wrought all that they were capable of doing, and have compelled the moon to succumb to the conditions they imposed. Owing to the great mass of the earth and the comparatively small mass of the moon the tides on the earth raised by the moon have required a much longer period wherein to accomplish their effects than was the case when the earth raised tides on the moon. But small though our satellite may be, yet the tides raised on the earth have incessantly tended to wear down the speed of our globe and reduce it to conformity with the law that the two bodies shall bear the same face towards each other. At present the earth turns round twenty-seven times while the moon goes round once, so the tides have still a gigantic task to accomplish. With unflagging energy, however, they are incessantly engaged at the work, and they are constantly tending to bring down the speed of the earth; constantly tending towards that ultimate condition of things in which the earth and moon are destined to revolve in a period of fourteen hundred hours as if they were connected with invisible bonds.

If such a state of things as this were established then it is plain that tides would no longer ebb and flow, that is, at least, if we exclude from our consideration the intervention of any other body. High tides must prevail at some parts of the earth, and low tides at other parts, but the position of these tides will remain fixed. Where it is high tide it will always be high tide; where it is low tide it will always be low tide. When this state of things is reached, the moon will be constantly visible in the same part of the sky from one half of our globe, while the other half of our globe will never be turned towards the moon. In fact, the moon would always appear to us in a fixed position as the earth would always appear to be if viewed by an observer stationed on the moon. If there were any Lunarians whose residence was confined to the opposite side of the moon, they could never see this earth at all, while those who lived on this side of our satellite would always be able to see the earth apparently fixed in the same part of the sky. An observatory located at the middle of the moon's disc, say near the crater Ptolemy, would always have the earth in its zenith or very near thereto, while the astronomer, let us say, in the Mare Crisium, would always find the earth low down near his horizon.

In order to facilitate our reasoning I have assumed that the moon is the only tide-producing agent; this is, however, not the case. No doubt the ebb and the flow around our coasts is generated mainly by the attraction of the moon. It must not, however, be forgotten that a portion of the tide is originated by the attraction of the sun. These solar tides will still continue to ebb and flow quite independently of the lunar tides, so that even if the accommodation between the earth and the moon had been completed some further tidal disturbance would not be wanting. The effect of the solar tides will be to abate still further the velocity with which the earth turns round on its axis, and consequently a time must ultimately arrive when the length of the day will be longer than the time which the moon takes to revolve around our earth.

It is here interesting to note that an adaptation of a somewhat similar kind has already been detected in another part of the solar system. Our neighbouring planet Mars is attended in its revolution around the sun by a pair of small satellites. The inner of these little moons presents features unlike those to be seen in any other part of our system at present, but resembling in a marked degree the future which we may venture to prognosticate for our earth-moon system when sufficient ages have elapsed. Mars rotates on its axis in about half an hour longer than our present day. The interior satellite to which we have referred courses around the planet so quickly that it completes a circuit in about seven hours and a half, so that the Martial moon revolves three times round its primary in the same time that Mars requires for a single rotation. In the case of this planet and his satellite the dimensions and the masses involved are much smaller than are those in the case of the earth-moon system. It seems, therefore, that we have in the adjustment of Mars and his moon a sort of miniature representation of the state of things to which the earth-moon system tends in the excessively remote future.

CHAPTER VII.

THE LUNAR WORLD.

THE genuine man of science can never approach the study of the moon without recalling that the orbit of our satellite is a precinct specially associated with the name of Newton. It was obvious to the clear vision of the great philosopher, that some power resided in the earth by which the famous apple was pulled down. The existence of this power was, however, not Newton's discovery; many a previous investigator, while pondering on the fact that bodies fall downwards to the earth, perceived the obvious analogy to the attraction of a piece of iron by a magnet. To demonstrate the mere existence of that force which we call the attraction of gravitation did not require the intellect of a Newton. One of the discoveries which have given immortality to the name of the great philosopher was connected with the moon. He soared in thought far above the apple-tree, and he asked himself whether the motion of the moon may not be due to the same force as the fall of the apple. When he had solved that problem, the scheme of the universe lay open before him.

Let us consider this question of falling. Objects dropped

from a balloon which has ascended two or three miles into the air will duly fall to the earth. A meteorite, which is often a lump of solid iron, may tumble down here from an altitude of unknown miles. The tendency to fall to the earth certainly exists at a height of ten miles, or fifty miles, or hundreds of thousands of miles. Why, then, does not the moon fall? There is assuredly no material structure to keep it up, no scaffolding to enable the moon to resist the earth's attraction; why, then, does it not tumble down? We feel pretty confident that it is not falling down, for the moon is not nearer to the earth now than it was a twelvemonth ago; for hundreds of years, or thousands of years, our satellite has approached no nearer to the earth. In fact, we have already seen that in so far as there is any difference at all, the moon is getting farther away from us instead of coming nearer. Nor can we suppose that at the great distance of the moon, the tendency to fall earthwards ceases to operate. No doubt our satellite is a quarter of a million miles away, but it is not that circumstance which preserves its position. If a stone or a world or anything else were taken up a quarter of a million of miles and simply let go, it would unquestionably tumble down on the earth. In the fall of a body from the height of the moon to the earth, it would move very slowly at first; so slowly indeed that the movement performed in the first minute would not exceed that fallen in the first second, where the body was let drop near the earth. As the journey proceeded, the pace would gradually mend, would gradually become rapid and ever increasing; the body would at last crash down on the earth, after a journey lasting altogether about five days.

But why does not the moon do this? Or rather why has not the moon done it ages ago? By what spell is that body poised aloft in seeming defiance of the attraction by which mother earth seeks to gather together all exterior objects into her bosom? We have read how the coffin of Mahomet was poised without support in the mosque of the faithful, from which all unbelievers were so rigidly excluded; no material support was necessary to sustain the remains of the prophet, the body itself seemed ever on the point of following the departed spirit to the realms of bliss. A perennial miracle was indeed necessary to sustain the revered sarcophagus in space. The infidel, no doubt, is somewhat sceptical about this marvellous phenomenon, but now, as ever, truth is stranger than fiction. Far over our heads there is a vast globe larger and heavier than millions of sarcophagi; no material support is rendered to that globe, yet there it is sustained from day to day, from year to year, from century to century. What is it that prevents the moon from falling? That is the question which now lies before us.

It is assuredly the case that the earth continually attracts the moon. The effect of the attraction is not, however, shown in actually drawing the moon closer to the earth, for this, as we have seen, does not happen, but the attraction of the earth keeps the moon from going farther away from the earth than it would otherwise do. Suppose, for instance, that the attraction of the earth were suspended, the moon would no longer follow its orbit but would start off in a straight line in continuation of the direction in which it was moving at the moment when the earth's action was intercepted. What Newton did was to show, from the circumstances, the moon's distance and movement, that it was attracted by the earth with a force of the same description as that by which the same globe attracted the apple; the difference being that the intensity of the force becomes weaker the greater the distance of the attracted body from the earth. In fact, the attraction of the earth on a ton of matter at the distance of the moon would be withstood by an exertion not greater than that which would suffice to sustain about three-quarters of a pound at the surface of the earth. I do not, however, now enter further into the subject, but in my little volume of lectures entitled "Star Land," I have endeavoured to explain the movement of the moon under the action of gravitation in as simple a manner as possible.

The moon is entirely dependent upon the light from the sun for her illumination. This is now well known, but the ancients seem to have had the impression that the moon must be self-luminous, at all events to a certain extent. Nor can it be denied that a plausible reason for such a supposition may be offered. The simplest considerations suffice to show that the phases of the moon, those interesting changes by which its light increases from the faint crescent up to the half moon and then to the full moon, are due to the aspects under which the sun-illuminated hemisphere is turned towards us. There is, however, one condition in which the moon seems to present a justification for the belief that it contains some intrinsic light. In the early stages, while our satellite is still a crescent, the larger part of its disc can be seen to glimmer with a pale ashy light. This could not have come directly from the sun, and hence it was supposed that it was

Fig. 6.—View from the Surface of the Moon.

provided by the moon itself, and that therefore our satellite could not be a wholly non-luminous object. But this inference is not a correct one, and to prove this to be so, it is only necessary to imagine yourself for a moment an inhabitant of the moon at the time when this phenomenon is witnessed. To the Lunarian the earth would then present much the same aspect as the full moon does to us. There would, however, be one important difference, for the full earth would present to the moon a disc thirteen times as large as the full moon exposes to us. The intrinsic brilliancy of the two lighted surfaces being the same, it therefore follows that the Lunarian illuminated by a "full" earth would find the country around him thirteen times as brilliant as this earth is at night, when the full moon is above the horizon. Here then lies the explanation of that phenomenon which is often spoken of as the old moon in the new moon's arms. It is indeed produced by sunlight, only that sunlight has not shone directly on the moon, but has been reflected there from the earth. We have, in fact, sufficient reasons for knowing that the moon exhibits no light of her own, and would necessarily be wholly invisible were it not that light is provided from another source.

There is perhaps no more interesting question suggested by the results of astronomical research than that as to whether the other worlds around us are inhabited. These worlds exist in teeming myriads, they are of all sizes, and in every stage of development. Some of them are no doubt smaller than our own, but many of them are far greater and more splendid. As our globe is clothed with verdure, and swarming with living creatures, it is surely of much interest to inquire whether some of these other globes may not also be tenanted by organic life. To solve this question we naturally turn first to the globe which is most easily accessible to our instruments; of course, this is the moon, which is always at a distance of less than a hundredth part of that of any other globe in the sky. The results of a telescopic investigation, conducted from this point of view, are, however, somewhat disappointing to those who would expect to find inhabitants elsewhere. We cannot detect on our satellite the slightest trace of organic life. Further reflection will, however, show that little more could have been expected. Even if the moon had contained living objects resembling those on the earth, no telescope could reveal them, for though it is no doubt true that the moon is our closest neighbour in the celestial host, yet we must recollect that it is still two hundred and forty thousand miles away.

A moderate telescope will show the moon as if its distance were only a tenth part of its actual amount. A good telescope might reduce the apparent distance to about one hundredth part, while when we employ one of the greatest instruments to scrutinise our satellite we are able to see it as if it were brought within a thousandth part of that distance, by which it is actually separated from us. An instrument capable of achieving so much lends greatly augmented power to human vision. Each thousand miles seems thus reduced to one mile, but as there are two hundred and forty of these thousands in the distance of the moon, the fact still remains that the utmost efforts of the most potent lenses known to the astronomer can only reduce the apparent distance of the moon to about two hundred and forty miles. It follows that no object can be visible on the moon even from our greatest observatories unless it be large enough and distinct enough to be visible with the unaided eye at that same distance of two hundred and forty miles.

This at once shows that we need not expect to see any objects on the moon, even with our best telescopes, unless those objects have dimensions that must be veritably colossal. An elephant could hardly be seen, even under the most favourable circumstances, at a distance of more than a couple of miles, so that the biggest elephant would be utterly invisible on the moon, unless our telescopes were a hundred times more powerful than any instrument that has ever yet been constructed. In fact, with our present appliances, no object would be visible on our satellite unless it were as large as some great building like a cathedral or town-hall. The loftiest trees could not be discerned if they grew on the moon, though it must be admitted that were there vást forests on our satellite, which shed their leaves periodically, the varying hues in the different seasons would doubtless be detected. But phenomena of this kind have never been fully established, and hence we are obliged to conclude that, so far as direct telescopic observation goes, the evidence as to the existence of organic life on our satellite must be esteemed entirely negative.

There is, however, another way in which the question can be studied, and which will suffice to show that, in all probability, life of every type with which we are acquainted must be almost certainly absent from the moon. Every kind of life, whether animal or vegetable, requires both the presence of air and the presence of water; we do not of course say that in other parts of the universe there may not be types of life for which neither air nor water is essential; nothing is, however, more clear than the evidence which we are able to produce with reference to the presence on, or absence from, the moon, of the substances we have named. First, with regard to water. I have already had occasion incidentally to allude to this subject; there are, no doubt, some reasons for thinking that there may have been at one time water on the moon, but it is now certain that there is no liquid on its surface, nor indeed can I find much reason to believe that there is even frozen water there, as has been sometimes supposed. It is certainly a singular fact that two constituents which are so abundant here should seem to be entirely wanting in the moon, and it is an interesting speculation to consider what has happened to the water on the moon if it once existed there.

It is generally believed that as our satellite cooled down the water penetrated into the interior, and was there seized upon by the minerals which required water in order that they might assume their appropriate crystalline forms. The water on the moon has therefore, according to this view, become transformed into a solid and incorporated with the bodily texture of the globe. It has even been surmised that a similar destiny awaits the oceans on our own globe; broad and deep though they are, they yet may be inadequate to quench the thirst for water possessed by so vast a mass of crystallizing minerals as must exist in the interior of the globe. But whether this be the explanation of the absence of liquid water from the moon or not, the fact of that absence cannot be questioned. The moon has been subjected to careful scrutiny for centuries, yet no one has ever seen any genuine ocean or sea, no one has ever seen any indication of the present existence of water, and we are entitled to assert that water, in a liquid form, is absent from the surface of our satellite.

On the allied question as to the existence of air around the moon something must now be said, and here let us understand distinctly the problem which awaits solution. I do not here enter on the vexed question as to the nature of the boundary which separates the higher limits of our atmosphere from the emptiness of space; it is quite sufficient for our present purpose to remark that the great mass of the encompassing air lies within a few miles of the earth's surface, though no doubt the more attenuated portions extend with ever-declining density to a distance above the surface which appears at present indeterminate. It is, however, certainly known that an atmosphere is found in the vicinity of many of the other globes in the universe besides our earth, though there is the widest difference both in its density and extent, as well as in its material composition. The sun, for instance, is encompassed by a stupendous atmosphere comparable in depth and density with his tremendous mass. Similarly the other planets have gaseous envelopes. There is Mars, the world that seems most like our own in other respects, and it too is encompassed with an atmosphere of some sort, though we have no reason to think it resembles in any degree the atmosphere which is suitable for our respiration. Nor are Venus and Jupiter void of that gaseous vestment which seems appropriate to every planet.

Here again our satellite the moon stands in striking contrast with the other globes that are accessible to our observation. If the moon ever possessed an atmosphere, and this is a point on which we cannot feel any certainty, it has at least now vanished. I should perhaps qualify this statement with the remark that acute observers have detected occasional indications of some gaseous material on the moon in extremely limited quantity confined to certain valleys or depressions. At first sight it may perhaps seem difficult to imagine that the telescope could be invoked to study the question as to whether there was atmosphere on the moon; for atmosphere seems so transparent, and is indeed so invisible, that we might naturally ask, how is it to be observed? No doubt if there were water on the moon, we might reasonably expect to see clouds or vapours if air existed in which those vapours could be suspended. But the air itself we could not expect to see; how then can its absence be demonstrated by the telescope? It may be true that we never could observe material quite translucent, but what we might expect to see are certain indications that would be perceived if the atmosphere were present, and as we do not find them we infer that the atmosphere does not exist.

The simplest method of demonstrating the absence of atmosphere of sensible amount surrounding the moon is by observing the phenomenon presented in what is called the occultation of a star. As the moon wends its way over the starry heavens it sometimes passes between the earth and a star, and the phenomenon is often one of considerable interest. With the aid of a good telescope the moon is observed to approach close to the star, and then to pass in front of it, whereupon instantly the star is extinguished. The sudden character of this phenomenon is that which generally strikes the observer, for he can, in fact, observe with accuracy the second of time when the extinction of the star takes place. This particular class of observation can be made with such definiteness and with such precision that it becomes of much value for the determination of the position of the moon itself. If, however, the moon were surrounded by an atmosphere, it is quite clear that the phenomenon attending the occultation of a star would be something wholly different from that which we actually find it to be. In proof of this we need only refer to the circumstances which can be observed here when a star is in process of setting. As the star gets lower and lower it gradually becomes fainter and then passes to extinction. Indeed, though we talk of the star "setting," no one has ever yet seen a star "set," the fact being that the star has become quite invisible long before it apparently reaches the horizon. If there were an atmosphere surrounding the moon at all comparable with that surrounding our earth, the occulted star would gradually decline in lustre and be extinguished long before it reached the edge of the moon. Even with a lesser degree of atmosphere the place of the star as well as its appearance would be largely affected by refraction, and this could not fail to be noticed by the discrepancies it would produce in the position of the star.

From these various considerations it becomes certain that there is no atmosphere surrounding the moon, which

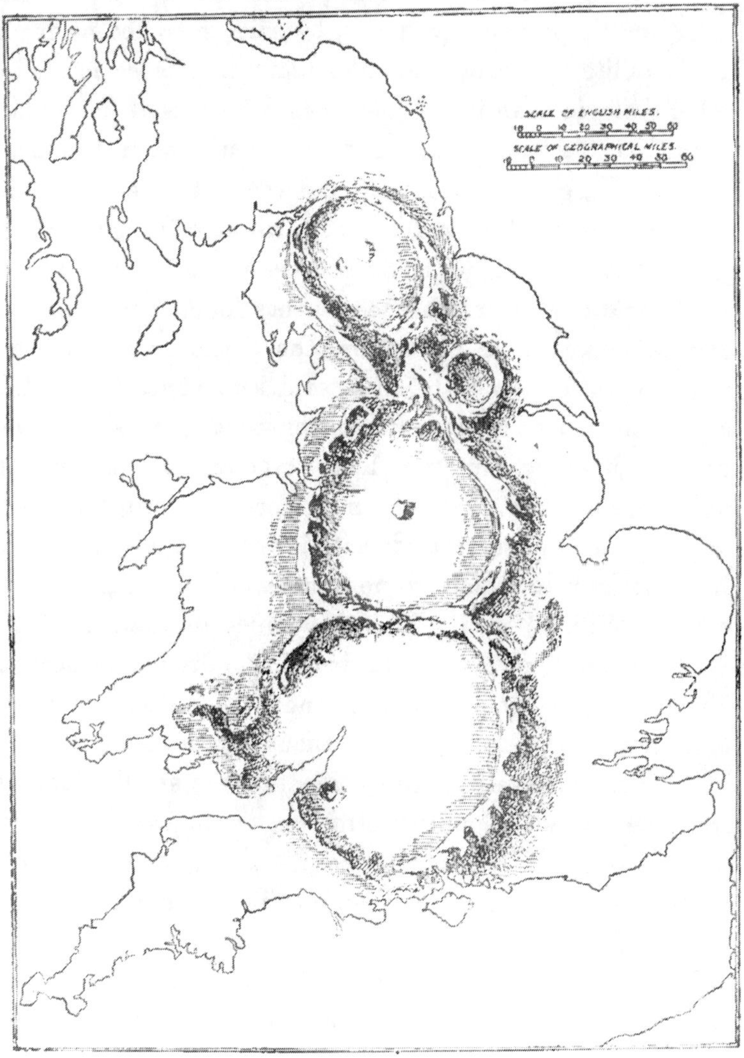

Fig. 7.—Lunar Craters compared with area of England.

Ptolemæus, diameter 115 miles; Alphonsus, diameter 83 miles; Arzachel, diameter 65 miles.

is even a thousandth part so copious as the atmosphere surrounding the earth. Seeing then that air and water may, for all practical purposes, be said to be absent from our satellite, it becomes at once plain that those forms in which life is manifested here must be absent from our neighbour. Strange indeed to us would seem the conditions of a globe without air and without water. Let us try for a moment to realise what we should find such a a world to be like if we could procure the means of getting there, and if we were able to dispense for once with such a primal necessity as air to breathe. The surface of the moon would appear to be an utter desert, at least in so far as the absence of organic life is concerned; we should see around in every direction huge craters, the remains of ancient volcanoes that are now never in eruption, but which in the days of their activity sculptured the moon into the form in which we now see it. Some of these vast craters (Fig. 7) would be many miles in diameter, the larger of them, in fact, upwards of a hundred miles across. They would be generally surrounded by a range of lofty cliffs, a mile or more in height, though on account of their large size relatively to the comparatively small globe of the moon, these bounding cliffs or "ramparts" as they are generally called, would be often below the horizon of the observer who was standing in the middle of the crater. Then, too, we should occasionally see great ranges of lofty mountains comparable with our Alps in altitude; they would, however, like all other lunar features, possess a ruggedness and a sharpness transcending anything to be found in the wildest regions on our globe.

All over this earth there are agents in operation

tending to wear down and reduce the asperities on its surface. Water in its varied forms is constantly acting in this way; the rains trickle down the slopes of the mountains wearing down the materials and gradually tending to smooth away irregularities. Frost is also a potent disintegrator of rocks. It finds its way into their crevices and with irresistible power the rocks are riven asunder by the expansion which the water undergoes when it passes into the form of ice; thus great blocks of rock are loosened from their sites, and the other agents effect their complete disruption. The inveterate action of streams and rivers is gradually transforming the appearance of our globe, and in the course of ages a stream will cut a deep valley through the hardest rocks. In fact, there is scarcely a spot on our globe in which the features of the landscape have not been largely affected by water and weather in some of the numerous ways in which they operate. Of course all such agents are absent from the moon, and hence it is impossible for us to see on our own earth any tracts of country really resembling the lunar surface.

It is true that we have volcanic districts and we have rainless districts, but we should require a district not only entirely volcanic, not only entirely rainless, but even devoid of air itself, to reproduce the phenomena that we find in the moon. There are no doubt some localities on our globe which seem to suggest the mode in which some of the characteristic lunar features may have arisen. We have, for instance, in the Sandwich Islands the great crater of Kilauea: at this wonderful spot the traveller will see a large basin of molten lava surrounded by a range of glowing cliffs; if we could extinguish the internal fires, by which at present this mighty cauldron is kept incandescent, the floor of lava would become congealed, and we should then have a plain surrounded by a ring of cliffs, and offering a resemblance to those objects which are seen by hundreds on the moon. There are other localities in the Sandwich Islands in which the fires have apparently ceased, and where the craters now look as little liable to eruption as are the extinct volcanoes in the moon. The absence of air and water has had a distinctly preservative effect so far as the features of lunar scenery are concerned. As the volcanoes sculptured our satellite into form countless ages ago, so it has retained that form to the present day.

If a building were once erected on the moon, it hardly seems conceivable that it should ultimately fall into ruins, if purely volcanic agents are wanting. Without atmosphere and without water, what harm can time do to the fabric? In fact, with the exception of the expansion and the contraction by the alternation of heat and cold, it does not seem that any agent of destruction can exist. We find it difficult to realise the circumstances of an airless globe. Fires could not burn, for there is no air to support the flame; winds could not blow, for of course wind is only the passage of air from one place to another; there need be no windows in the building, for there is no air to keep out; there need be no roof, in so far at least as a roof is required as a protection against rain. Two out of the five organs of sense with which we are endowed operate solely by utilising certain properties which air possesses. Our ears are exquisite contrivances by which we are enabled to receive and to interpret the undulations which are transmitted through the air. On an airless globe our ears would be almost useless; we could hear no sound transmitted as those sounds are which usually reach us. I ought, however, to add that certain audible waves admit of being transmitted through other materials besides air, and consequently in some exceedingly imperfect and indirect method a sense analogous to that possessed by our ears might be rendered available on an airless globe. The other sense which would be useless to any inhabitants who might dwell on our satellite or other airless globe would be that of smell. Although much less is known about this sense than about either the sense of vision or that of hearing, yet it seems certain that our nasal organs receive extremely minute particles, and when these come in contact with our olfactory nerves the sensation appropriate to those nerves is occasioned. Whatever may be the mechanism of this process, it can hardly be doubted that air is the vehicle by which these particles, so minute and so imponderable as to elude entirely all our other senses, are wafted from their source. The sense of smell would apparently be impossible on an airless globe like the moon.

There is, however, another wholly different class of sensations which would be experienced by a denizen of this earth if he were translated to a small globe like the moon. We must remember that in every fibre of our constitution we have been specially adapted to the life on this particular sphere. We have already seen how our senses are adjusted in harmony with the particular atmosphere with which the earth is surrounded: we have now to notice another point, in which the texture of our bodies is arranged to suit the material contents of this globe on which we dwell.

It may seem strange to learn that the strength of our bones and muscles has been adjusted not solely with regard to the size of our bodies or the quantity of matter they may contain, but with reference to the dimensions and mass of the earth. Even though on another globe there was an atmosphere exactly like our own both in density and in composition, even though it was supplied with water as ours is, even though it provided us with abundance of suitable food and had a climate agreeable to our constitution, yet it might be wholly impossible for us to exist there by reason of an incompatibility between the strength of our frames and the mass of the globe on which we stood. Thus, to take the case of the moon, which only weighs about one-eightieth part of the earth; the gravitation with which the moon would draw all bodies towards it would be much less than the similar gravitation on the earth. The weights of all objects would be reduced to about one-sixth part of that which we find them to possess here. The buoyancy of our bodies would be so great that athletic feats would be easy on a body the size of the moon, which could never be attempted on this globe by beings with muscles like ours. If a man of twelve stone were to be transferred to the moon, the weight of his body would be reduced to about two stone. If his muscles and his frame remained the same it would seem as if he would be able to jump over a wall twelve feet high on the small globe without any greater exertion than would be required to clear a wall two feet high on the earth. Looked at from every point of view, it seems hardly possible that there can be any life on the moon resembling the life that we know of on the earth.

But though the want of atmosphere surrounding the moon may deprive it of some features of interest, yet to the user of a telescope on this earth the airless nature of the moon is a distinct advantage. Suppose, for example, that a Lunarian were to endeavour to study our earth with the telescope, he would see little, comparatively speaking, of the actual surface, for our atmosphere itself, so closely enveloping the earth, would obstruct his vision, while the clouds with which so large a part of our atmosphere is often charged would form an impenetrable screen. It would be only in a very imperfect fashion that the dweller on the moon would be able to make out the features of the globe to which the moon is a satellite. But the terrestrial astronomer experiences no such difficulties. It is true that our own atmosphere often interferes with us in a manner with which every astronomer is only too painfully familiar, but by suitable choice of opportunities these disadvantages may be largely obviated and beautiful pictures of our satellite may be obtained. The want of atmosphere on the moon enables us to see its features with exquisite clearness and sharpness, and the shadows are cast with a definition which we never find in terrestrial scenery.

There is another circumstance which makes the moon an attractive and easy subject for the telescopic inquirer. Owing to the constant face of the moon, he always finds the craters in nearly the same position, and as our satellite courses through her monthly vicissitudes the observer learns to watch for the reappearance of the same object in much the same position, just as in a garden we love to watch for the blossoming of our old favourites as the spring comes round. It is also a great advantage that the moon is sufficiently near us to be well within the reach of telescopes of moderate pretensions; even a little instrument that may be held in the hand will with the help of a map of the moon afford much interest to the beginner in seeking out the different craters and learning to identify them by name.

CHAPTER VIII.

A VISIT TO AN OBSERVATORY.

It is well known that in the United States there are many more opportunities for educated women to gain useful and remunerative employment than are found in Great Britain. I was particularly struck with this when I saw American ladies employed in doing work in the astronomical observatories of their country, which on this side would be almost exclusively performed by men. The work they had to do was eminently suited to ladies; it required neatness and care, and a conscientious determination to perform it with unremitting accuracy and attention. How successful they have been is known to all astronomers who have made themselves acquainted with the great volume of excellent astronomical research that flows from the American observatories.

I was much interested and entertained lately by reading a paper written by one of the American astronomers to whom I have referred. Two years ago a new astronomical observatory was opened at Carleton College, Northfield, Minnesota, and at the laying of the foundation-stone an appropriate—a most appropriate—address was delivered in celebration of the auspicious event. When I add that this address was given by a lady it will, I think, show that America, in respect to such performances, is much in advance of the countries on this side of the Atlantic.

The address was published in the *Sidereal Messenger*, and has been copied into the *Observatory* for December, 1886. It is signed Mary E. Byrd, and is well worth reading. It admirably expresses the wide divergence that there often is between the presumed nature of the work that is performed in an observatory in the popular imagination, and the routine of somewhat prosaic detail that is the actual fact.

I cannot resist quoting a passage from this address as the best introduction to our present subject.

"It is commonly fancied that there is a great deal of poetry and romance within the walls of an observatory. All have read the ancient legend of Tycho Brahe, how he went to the observatory in robes of state, as if the presence of the stars was the presence of princes. And people fancy that here at midnight, in starlit domes, you almost hear the music of the spheres. They picture to themselves the observer seated at his telescope hour after hour looking down, down, into deep lunar craters, feasting on delicate nebulæ and swift-flying comets, or revelling in gorgeous star clusters. Here, they think, night after night before his rapt vision there passes all the panorama of the heavens multiplied and glorified a thousandfold by his powerful lenses. I have sometimes wished that it were so; but it is *work* that goes on in an observatory, work as stern as that of the factory."

The actual fact is, indeed, widely different from that

supposed view of the duties of the astronomer which are here so humorously portrayed. The popular notion of the way in which astronomical discoveries are made is often very wide of the truth. It seems sometimes to be thought that the astronomer in search of some crowning triumph sits gazing with ecstatic rapture through the tube until suddenly some majestic, and hitherto utterly unheard of, celestial body soars into his view, and he immediately records an immortal discovery. The fact is that when an astronomer goes into his observatory for his night's work he finds it usually convenient to leave all the ecstatic and most of the poetic portions of his constitution outside. He arrays himself in costume, not with a view to the sublimity of the universe, but to the effectual keeping out of the cold. It is not the stupendous size of the celestial bodies that so often appals him; he is rather straining his attention to the effort of hiding a tiny star behind the spider web of his micrometer.

But though it may be generally true that the work of the observatory is essentially a routine almost of a prosaic character, yet the astronomer must indeed be of a callous nature who does not feel the noble character of the occupation to which his nights are devoted. I propose in these pages to give a sketch of what the visitor to the observatory may reasonably expect to see, if his or her visit be appropriately timed. It must be remembered that the celestial objects are not always to be observed. It is no doubt true that Saturn or the great nebula in Orion are like the Matterhorn or the Falls of Niagara, always to be seen if the visitor could only go to the right place. But very often no terrestrial observatory can be the right place for seeing either of the objects named, and this for various reasons. In the first place, it may be that the season of the year is wrong. There is, for instance, no use in going to look for the great nebula in Orion in summer, nor is there any possibility of seeing Saturn when, as happens every year, he is situated near the sun on the surface of the heavens.

Then, too, it must be remembered that some objects never rise at all in our latitudes. You need never expect to see the Magellanic clouds by going to any observatory in England. Nor can the astronomers in Australia ever observe the companion to the pole star through the great reflector at Melbourne. Even when the body you want to see is "up," it may be in a very unfavourable condition for making observations. If it be the moon that you wish to see, and even if it be up, and high up, it may be quite unsuited for telescopic scrutiny from the simple fact that it is "full"; a condition in which the varieties of light and shade which give to the moon-pictures their beauty and their instructiveness are altogether wanting.

The planets, too, will often be accessible to the telescope, but still be very unfavourably placed for disclosing their real beauty as compared with the seasons when they can be observed to advantage. The ring of Saturn may be presented under an aspect in which it is too much foreshortened, or the opposition of Mars may be one in which his distance from the earth is too great to admit of a truly effective telescopic picture being produced. It will thus be obvious that to observe any of the celestial bodies effectively not only must good instruments be available, but a careful forethought must be exercised in choosing the appropriate times for each object. But even when the best moment for observation has arrived, and we are quite ready to secure the examination of the celestial body under the most favourable auspices, there is still the very important consideration of the weather. For astronomical work a clear sky is indispensable. When we find that a cloud or two can obscure from us the direct image of the sun, we need hardly expect that stars or planets or objects still fainter and more delicate will be perceived through a dense curtain of watery vapour. Fogs and mists, no less than more extensive clouds, must be absent, and even nights that seem tolerably clear to the ordinary spectator may, from atmospheric causes alone, be very ill-adapted for any careful astronomical work.

From all these reasons it will be seen that the hours in which really excellent work can be done in an observatory are but few in comparison with the whole number of hours in the year. When such hours do arrive astronomers greatly prize them, and it may be readily believed that during the time for which they have waited so long they are often not too well pleased to be disturbed by visitors who come on a star-gazing expedition.

Of all the impediments to astronomical work those produced by the atmosphere are the most vexatious, because they do not admit of being predicted. The astronomer may sometimes have even gone to the other side of the earth to observe some rare phenomenon like a total eclipse of the sun, or the still more occasional transit of Venus across the sun. The time when such an event will occur admits of actual prediction; all may be in readiness. when the incalculable clouds overcast the sky, and the whole object of the enterprise is frustrated.

But even when not charged with clouds the atmosphere is baneful to the practical astronomer, for air when clearest and purest still obstructs a great deal of light. It makes the stars appear fainter than they would otherwise be, while rays from very small stars are extinguished by it, though those rays would have been quite sufficient to render their source perceptible in our telescopes if we could observe without the intervention of the atmosphere.

An airless globe like the moon would, for merely telescopic purposes, present the most favourable condition conceivable, though how it would fare with the astronomers involves questions of a different character. We have not only the imperfect transparency of even the purest skies to contend with, but there are other difficulties. Even under the stillest and clearest sky it is of the essence of the atmosphere to distort the places of the celestial bodies. To see a star we have to point the telescope, not at the real position of the star, but in a somewhat different direction. Astronomers speak of this derangement as refraction ; they are obliged continually to bear it in mind, and their observations have to be corrected for it so as to place the star in its true instead of its apparent position. The amount of the displacement of a celestial object depends, among other things, upon the temperature of the air. If the temperature changes the amount of the displacement will change. While, therefore, there is any fluctuation of temperature the place of the star will appear to be continually disturbed. The astronomer will say that "the stars are very unsteady to-night." As long as this lasts the value of his observations is appreciably impaired; sometimes the unsteadiness is so great that he must desist from working altogether.

To escape from the pernicious influences of the atmosphere is at present the pressing need of practical astronomy. In this respect of course there will be great differences between one climate and another. But the best method of evading the severe tax which the atmosphere imposes on every astronomer's time and the injury that it inflicts upon his measurements is to carry his observatory to the top of a lofty mountain.

The ocean of air that lies over our heads is perhaps one hundred miles or more in thickness. It is, however, in the lowest mile or so that most of the mischief is done of which the astronomer so sadly complains. A lofty mountain peak which reared its head a mile above the earth's surface would protrude through the most troublesome portion of the atmosphere. An observatory perched on the summit of this mountain will therefore be in a position to observe the stars almost free from the atmospheric anxieties of the astronomer at the bottom of that turbid atmospheric ocean on which the mountain astronomer can now look down.

At the present moment the attention of the astronomical world is largely fixed on the bold experiment which has been made in America to locate a telescope of perhaps unsurpassed optical perfection on the top of a mountain in one of the most exquisite climates on the globe.

Mr. Lick, a Californian millionaire, committed to the

care of the Lick Trust a great sum of money, and directed them "to erect a powerful telescope, superior to and more powerful than any telescope ever yet made, with all the machinery appertaining thereto, and also a suitable observatory."

To carry out this trust a careful search was made to obtain the most suitable locality, and an expedition was sent to the top of Mount Hamilton, near San José, in California. The observations showed that the air was remarkably steady, and that there was a continued succession of perfect nights. Then, too, it was found that observations of objects very low down in the sky were practicable to a far greater extent than in other observatories in similar latitudes. Mr. Burnham, a distinguished American astronomer, who conducted these preliminary tests of the capabilities of Mount Hamilton, made many valuable discoveries of new double stars, many of them being exquisitely beautiful and delicate objects, during the six months that his stay lasted. These trials having proved eminently satisfactory, Mount Hamilton was decided upon as the seat of the Lick Observatory. Then commenced the arduous task of constructing and equipping a vast astronomical establishment on the summit of a mountain four thousand feet in height, and twenty-six miles distant from the nearest town. With true American energy these difficulties have been severally vanquished. The county of Santa Clara provided, and now maintains, a magnificent road, which runs by a gentle slope the whole way from San José to the top of Mount Hamilton. Then the top of the mountain had to be cut off to make a level platform large enough for the buildings. To do this no less than seventy thousand tons of material had to be removed. When the question arose as to the erection of the telescope, the first point to be settled was whether it should be a reflecting telescope or be a refractor,—that is, whether it should, like the great telescope of Lord Rosse at Parsonstown in Ireland, consist of a large and brilliant mirror at the end of a long tube, from which the rays of light from the stars were to be reflected; or whether it should be founded on the more familiar principle of refraction, in which powerful glass lenses are made use of to concentrate the light and render faint objects visible. There was much to be said on both sides, but finally the trustees, after taking counsel with the wisest astronomers all over the world, decided to erect a great refractor.

The preparation of the object-glass was the next great work to be accomplished. It was to consist of two pieces, one of crown glass and the other of flint glass, and it was to have a diameter of the unparalleled length of thirty-six inches. The fabrication of the actual pieces of glass on which the opticians could work was a matter of the greatest difficulty, and sorely tried the patience of all concerned; to obtain the rough discs of glass alone no less than six years were required, and they were only finally adopted after twenty unsuccessful trials. At last, however, when Messrs. Alvan Clark, of Cambridgeport, Massachusetts, did obtain suitable pieces of glass whereon to employ their optical skill, another year of assiduous work was necessary to give to the glasses the exact shapes that would render the vision through them perfect. For the execution of this great object-glass the Lick trustees paid to Messrs. Alvan Clark a sum exceeding £10,000. The length of the tube in which this pair of lenses had to be mounted was adapted for a focus of fifty-six feet two inches. On the 1st June, 1888, the celebrated Lick Observatory was formally pronounced ready for work, and handed over to the charge of the regents of the University of California.

I take these particulars from the first volume of the publications of the Lick Observatory. The charges of the future publications will be generously provided by the State of California, while the United States has presented the site. With consummate astronomical equipment, with a staff of practical astronomers that cannot be surpassed in the world, we may confidently hope that the Lick Observatory will fulfil the generous intention of its founder; indeed, we have already in some exquisite photographs and in other ways received earnest of its success.

I have entered thus fully into the account of the Lick Observatory, partly on account of its novelty and its importance, but also because in one aspect of its work it suitably illustrates the title at the head of this chapter. Professor Campbell, the accomplished astronomer who presides over the Lick Observatory, has arranged that the resources of the great telescopes shall, under suitable regulations, be available to those visitors who may spend an evening at the Lick Observatory.

I propose to mention some of the objects which a visitor to an astronomical observatory should specially wish to see. He will first of all desire to learn by actual examination something of those marvellous instruments by which the astronomer has detected the movements and learned the actual character of the heavenly bodies. He will see the fundamental weapon with which inaccuracy is driven

Fig. 8.—The Meridian Circle.

from the field of astronomy. That weapon is the transit instrument, or rather the more complete apparatus which is found in all our modern observatories, and is known as the meridian circle. This consists of a telescope of considerable but not of the largest dimensions, mounted in a particular way for a particular purpose. A view of the meridian circle at Dunsink Observatory is given in the adjoining sketch. The telescope is attached to an axis about which it can revolve, just as a cannon can be turned up or down in its bearings. The axis carries two large circles. On these the utmost refinements of mechanical skill must be exercised. The circles in the instrument at Dunsink Observatory, the establishment over which I have had the honour to preside, are about three feet in diameter. There is a rim of silver let into the margin of the wheel; this silver is graduated by fine marks—marks indeed so fine that they require a microscope for their detection. When the telescope is pointed to a star, the position of the marks shows the elevation of the instrument, and thus the height of the star above the horizon is determined. The telescope is carefully adjusted so as to move in the plane of the meridian. It can be pointed to the due north, then it can be raised up to the point of the heavens vertically overhead, then it can be turned downwards to the south. But it is of the essence of the meridian circle that it admits of no other movements; it cannot be turned to the east or to the west in the slightest degree.

A star or a planet, the sun or the moon, can therefore only be observed with the meridian circle at the very instant of crossing the meridian. In fact, one of the purposes of observing with the meridian circle is to determine the time at which the celestial body is on the meridian. To obtain the requisite accuracy, it will not be sufficient merely to observe the star in the field of view of the telescope—we must have some means of readily indicating the precise line down the field which represents the meridian ; a thread or wire has to be stretched across for this purpose. The magnifying power of a large meridian circle is, however, so considerable that any ordinary thread would look like a coarse rope, and would be utterly unsuited for work requiring nicety of observation. We must therefore employ some fibre which shall be extremely fine, and which shall yet be strong enough to admit of being stretched into a perfect straight line, while a certain degree of elasticity is also requisite in order to preserve the straightness of the line with any permanence. These various conditions are most completely complied with by the beautiful thread of the spider. It is a somewhat delicate task to stretch one of these exquisite filaments properly over the little circular framework at the eye-end of the telescope, but when it has once been done the web of the spider is sufficiently durable to fulfil many years of service.

The method of observing the transit of a star will consist of noting the time by the astronomical clock when it passes behind the spider web. The due estimation of this time taxes the skill of the practical astronomer; it depends on the appreciation of the fractional part of a second at which the transit takes place. Here, as in so many other departments of science and of the arts, the aid of electricity is invoked to give a subtleness to the work that cannot otherwise be obtained. As the star passes behind the spider web the astronomer taps a key which closes the current, and impresses a mark on a revolving cylinder.

Thus a record is obtained which makes the closest approach to absolute precision.

But for the purposes of the continuous observation of a celestial body the meridian instrument is quite unfitted. It merely gives us a flying glimpse of the object as it hurries through the field; a glimpse sufficient for the determination of the place of the object, but quite inadequate to enable us to examine the object with any close attention. A totally different form of mounting for our telescope is now required, which shall enable us to follow the object persistently for hours together. Of course the facility of movement in the telescope which this implies can only be obtained by the sacrifice of some other qualities. The equatorial—for so this form of mounting is termed—is quite unsuited for the rigidly accurate purposes of measurement, which it is the sole object of the meridian circle to obtain. In the stand of the equatorial clockwork is placed, by which the instrument, after it has been once pointed to the star, is constrained to move so that the object under examination shall continue steadily in the field of the observer's view.

It is the equatorial that we are to visit when we come to spend our evening at the observatory. We shall find ourselves usually in a circular room covered by a dome. This dome reposes on wheel work, so that it can be made to revolve. In it is a shutter, which can be opened so as to allow the telescope to be pointed to the sky. There is, of course, no glass window in the opening; even the most transparent plate glass would impair the perfection of the image. Nor will it be allowable to have the building warmed by artificial heat. If the temperature inside were raised appreciably above that which is found outside, the heated air from the interior would pour out through the opening, and the disturbance thence arising would produce a mixture of air of different degrees of density, which would be quite sufficient to impair the delicacy of the telescopic images. Wind, if unattended with clouds, is, as a rule, not injurious to good seeing, though the comfort of observatory work is greatly promoted by a tranquil atmosphere.

And now as to the objects which the visitor to the observatory should specially ask to see. It must be borne in mind that many of the most interesting objects to the astronomer are almost completely devoid of effectiveness from the merely spectacular point of view. A grand nebula, for instance, will often have portions so faint, that however we may find it necessary to represent them in drawings, they are in the field of the telescope only to be seen by most assiduous attention with an eye especially trained for such work. The visitor will hardly feel contented if he be desired to look at something which he may only have a chance of seeing after he has steadily gazed for several minutes at one place. There are, however, some splendid objects in the sky against which no objections of the kind can be alleged, and it is to these that we specially commend the attention of a visitor who is anxious to see some of the wonders of the heavens.

The celestial objects which I have now specially in view are three: they are the planet Saturn, the star cluster in Perseus, and the great nebula in Orion. Any one who has had the gratification of witnessing these objects on a cloudless sky, and through a telescope of adequate dimensions, will have obtained a fair notion of the glories of the heavens. Nor is it often possible to compass all these objects during a single visit to the observatory. The moon, as if jealous of the other celestial bodies, drenches the skies with such a flood of light that the glories of the lesser bodies become well-nigh invisible. In fact, just as the sun at midday prevents us from seeing any of the stars, so the beams of the moon pale the smaller stars to invisibility, and largely detract from the lustre of the brighter ones. Some description of these objects will occupy us in the following chapter.

CHAPTER IX.

AN EVENING WITH THE TELESCOPE.

The opportunities for observing the planet Saturn are not nearly so frequent as those in which the moon may be advantageously observed. We must choose the time when Saturn comes nearest to the earth. This will take place when the earth lies nearly between Saturn and the sun. Supposing that such an occurrence is now taking place, the earth will in a short time have moved away from the best position, and the distance from the earth to the planet will be on the increase. When a year has elapsed the earth will have returned to its original position, but it will not then be exactly between Saturn and the sun, for the great planet has moved. Like the earth, Saturn also revolves round the sun, but the magnitude of his orbit is much greater than that of the earth, and consequently the time that Saturn requires to complete a single revolution is about twenty-nine and a half of our years. Hence it follows that Saturn will have moved in the course of the year, so that the earth must pursue its journey for another twelve or thirteen days before it will again have resumed its position between the planet and the sun.

Saturn, like our earth and like the moon, is entirely indebted to the sun for its supply of light. Bright as the planet may seem, it has no intrinsic luminosity—all we see is merely the reflected solar beams. Its globe is of noble proportions. Were that globe divided into six hundred equal parts, and were each of those parts rolled

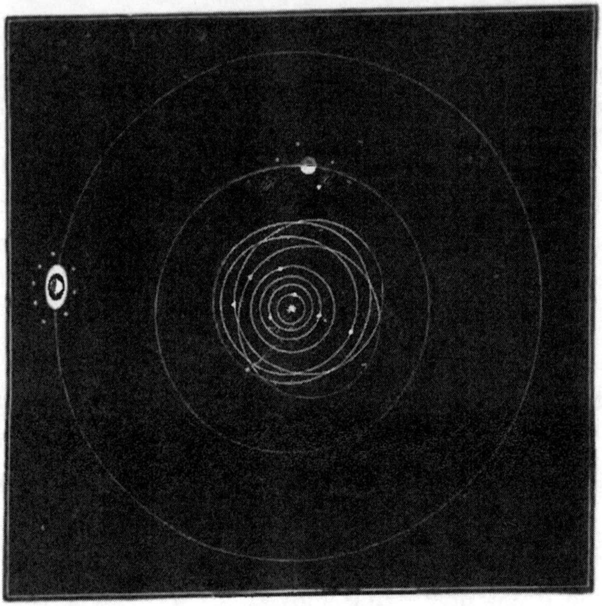

Fig. 9.—The Sun and its Attendant Worlds.

into a globe, it would be a larger ball than this earth of ours, eight thousand miles in diameter. A view of this orbit of Saturn, as well as of some of the other planets, is shown in the adjoining figure.

This mighty globe also revolves on its axis, but its day is much shorter than ours, as each revolution of Saturn is accomplished in ten hours and fourteen minutes. Owing to its higher speed of rotation, the bulging out at the equator of Saturn is much larger than in our earth; in fact the elliptical form of Saturn is so evident as to be at once detected without any delicate telescopic measurements. The surface of the globe presents but few features of interest, and indeed there is little on it which can be depicted in a drawing. It is of a nearly uniform whitish yellow colour, occasionally, however, marked over with faint bands. It is obvious that what we see is merely the outside of a great casing of cloud, in which the entire planet is shrouded. In fact it seems very doubtful whether Saturn bears any resemblance to a solid body at all. Our first impression might perhaps be that the planet was a sort of rigid globe like our earth, covered by a coating of cloud, much deeper and denser, and more uniformly distributed than the somewhat intermittent clouds of which we on the earth have so often to complain. But it is not easy to see how far the interior of Saturn can, with propriety, be likened to a dense globe like ours, and for the following reason:—our earth is composed of rocks and metals, and the entire weight of the globe is above five times the weight that a globe of equal bulk of water would have. It may seem a very difficult problem to weigh the planet Saturn, and so to compare its mass with that of an equal globe of water, but the task is not beyond the resources of the practical astronomer. Whenever a planet is provided with satellites, or little attendant moons, it is possible to put the great globe into the weighing scales and to determine how heavy it is. I cannot here delay to explain fully the details of the process; suffice it to say that it can be done with great accuracy, and the result in the case of Saturn is truly astonishing.

We learn that the globe has so little resemblance to our earth that it is actually lighter than a vast globe of water would be were its dimensions the same as those of Saturn itself. Indeed, if we could imagine a model of the planet just as large and just as heavy as the planet actually is, and if that globe were cast into a great ocean of water of suitable dimensions, the mighty planet would float buoyantly on the surface. It seems hard to reconcile these facts with the belief that there can be much solid matter in the interior of the planet.

It is impossible in any picture to represent the exquisite delicacy of Saturn as revealed in a great telescope, but to make our description plain we have to present a sketch which will at least give a general notion of the ring system, and may perhaps stimulate the reader to secure some opportunity for observing these objects in a telescope.

We must notice that the rings are not fastened to the globe. There is a tendency for them to fall down on the globe of the planet, but that tendency is neutralised by their rapid rotation around the globe. The rings are shown slightly turned towards us in the picture. Were we able to look squarely at them they would be circles; when we view them edgewise they are found to be so extremely thin that they elude our vision almost entirely, except in powerful instruments. We speak of them as rings in the plural, because it will be seen that they are threefold. The two outer are separated by a broad line of demarcation which can be traced the entire way round. These two outer rings are apparently of the same general nature, and there are some other dark lines or divisions of a somewhat fainter description, of which one at least, in the outer ring, is a permanent feature of the system.

To see the most delicate part of this beautiful structure requires a telescope of considerable power ; it has only been discovered in comparatively recent years, and is the third ring of the system. It extends from the inner margin of the second ring, half-way in towards the globe of the planet. The name assigned to this mysterious but lovely object is the *crape* ring, and the appropriateness of the designation will be apparent when the hue of the object as well as its curious semi-transparency is noticed.

The structure of the rings of Saturn suggests problems that have exercised the profoundest mathematicians. It was speedily seen that the rings could not be thin plates of solid material. No doubt a superficial glance at their appearance will suggest that such is their nature. However, it can be demonstrated by mechanical principles that the very existence of the rings would be impossible if they were what this notion implies. In this instance, as in many others, the pen of the mathematician has proved a more potent instrument than the telescope. What the astronomer could hardly expect to find out in his observatory has been demonstrated by actual calculation made by pen and paper. It has been proved that this wondrous set of rings consists of a multitude of small objects, each pursuing its own voyage round the planet like a little moon. These bodies are so numerous and so close together that the most powerful telescope can hardly be said to recognise their individual existence, though occasionally no doubt the rings do seem subdivided in a way which renders to the true view of their nature some degree of telescopic confirmation.

It is only in this way that we can offer any reasonable account of the semi-transparency of the crape ring. The little moonlets (if I may for the moment coin a word) which go to make up the rings are, in the outer of the structures, so close together that they reflect what is generally seen as a continuous sheet of light; but in the crape ring the moonlets are either not so numerous or not so large as in the outer rings: the consequence is they do not appear as a continuous sheet of light; we are able in some degree to see between them, and this is how we explain the semi-transparency of the crape ring.

Nor is the Saturnian system wanting in other attractions which would render it of great interest, even were the supreme feature of the ring system absent. The planet is attended by no fewer than eight moons, some of which are easily visible in the most modest telescope, while others demand the employment of exceptionally powerful instruments.

I hope that every one of my readers will obtain some opportunity of observing Saturn at a suitable time and with a telescope of sufficient power; assuredly they will be delighted and fascinated with the spectacle. But I ought also to add a word of warning. I have before now met with people who were woefully disappointed with the planet, even when the circumstances were most favourable.

I remember many years ago taking a bright little boy of six to the Dublin Zoological Gardens. It was his first visit, and all the way he prattled to me delightfully of what he expected to see; the principal object of his desires being an eagle. Perhaps he had been duly instructed in the semi-fabulous stories of children being borne away by eagles; probably he was also acquainted with the adventures of Sinbad the Sailor and the Roc; at all events, we made our way to where there was a large cage con-

Fig. 10.—Saturn and his Rings.

taining several fine sea eagles. I awaited his rapturous delight, but in vain. I saw the poor little fellow assume a crestfallen aspect. "They are so small," was all he said, but I could easily divine that he had expected to see something about twenty feet high, and that one of his pretty childish idols had been smashed to pieces.

On a more recent occasion I visited the Falls of Niagara. When we reached the station in the middle of the night, one of my fellow-passengers, who was not by any means a child, remonstrated with the conductor, who came round to tell us that we were at Niagara Falls. "That cannot be," said the individual in question, "for I know two things—first, that the station is not two miles from the falls; and secondly, that the noise of the falls can be easily heard twenty miles away, and as I hear nothing I know that this cannot be the station." But it was nevertheless. The conception of the thunders of Niagara in the mind of the tourist bore no more relation to the actual fact than did the Roc which the boy expected to the actual eagle which was all I could show him. Nor did I fail to observe the utterly disgusted and disappointed demeanour of my unhappy fellow-traveller the next day, when he perceived the contrast between the wretched trickle of the real Niagara and the splendour of that ideal cataract which all this journey had been taken in the hope of seeing. Had the Atlantic Ocean been seen pouring down from the moon it would not have done more than realise the expectations of volume and altitude which so ruthlessly collapsed before the fact.

It is obvious that properly to appreciate natural scenery persons must either be naturally gifted with intuitive taste, or else they must wait until experience has taught them what to see, and what it is reasonable to expect to see. Let not any one, therefore, be disappointed if their first glimpse of Saturn falls far short of what they anticipated, the beauties of it are not so glaring that they can be discerned without nice and careful observation. Remember that the crape ring is so subtle an object that multitudes of astronomers gazed at Saturn for ages and never saw it at all. Even the immortal William Herschel, with his excellent instruments and with his indefatigable perseverance, never noticed the crape ring. Let the casual visitor bear this in mind, and not expect to see Saturn exhibited as a vast panorama which he that runs can read; let him rather expect to find an exquisitely wrought miniature, which will demand the closest attention, but which will reveal ever new beauties to those who know how to woo the real loveliness of nature in the only way in which it can be won.

Widely different, indeed, are the attractions of the next object we have to mention from those of which we have just been speaking. Saturn is a planet lighted by a sun, while the globular cluster of stars in the constellation of Perseus is itself a group of suns.

Girdling the entire heaven is that beautiful but somewhat irregular band of light, the Milky Way. It is composed of myriads of stars, too small and too faint, by reason of their vast distance, to be severally visible; but their different rays unite to give us the beautiful "Via Lactea." This is a star cluster on the grandest scale, but the several components are too much scattered to furnish us with a brilliant or effective telescopic picture.

In the sword handle of Perseus there are two densely-packed groups of stars, which form the two celebrated clusters. They are visible to the unaided eye as faintly luminous spots, but in a grand telescope they unfold into spectacles of the most gorgeous sublimity. Each of the two clusters—and they lie close together—is sufficient to crowd the field of view with a multitude of brilliant stars, in which the curious eye will find charming configurations; in one of these clusters notably a horseshoe, in the other a beautiful system of triangles. Many of the stars are of a ruddy hue, and as contrasted with other clusters the smaller and inconspicuous stars are comparatively absent. We can, as it were, see right through the entire group at every part to the space beyond. Such a collection of gems, and so exquisitely set, will extort admiration from everybody; I do not remember to have seen any one disappointed at this spectacle. But it requires some previous acquaintance with a few facts in astronomy to fully realise all that the picture represents. Unhappily we are not able to supply the most important piece of information which will naturally be asked: we are not able to give the actual dimensions of this system. The case is in this respect very different from that of the moon or of Saturn. There the arts of the astronomer have been successful in the attempt to measure and even to weigh; but in the stellar regions proper our knowledge of the weights and the distance is always scanty, and not infrequently entirely wanting. This is so in the case of the cluster in Perseus. We do not know the distance by which it is separated from us. The methods which astronomers are in the habit of using in such investigations have, I believe, never been yet applied to the cluster in Perseus. The belief no doubt exists that the only methods available would be inapplicable to such an object.

In seeking the distance of a fixed star, the ordinary method is to select some other star in the neighbourhood apparently, but which is really very much farther behind, though in the same line of sight. By a careful series of measures made in the course of an entire year, there is an apparent displacement of one of these stars relatively to the other, caused by the fact that the earth has been ever changing its position in the course of its annual revolution around the sun. The method fails if the star's distance be beyond a certain limit, as it actually is with the great majority of the bodies to which the method has been applied. The difficulty of applying this process to the cluster in Perseus is, that we have no clue to guide us in the choice of the pair of stars which would be suitable; one of them must lie in the cluster, the other must be far behind it. If we had any means of identifying a pair of stars which were certainly so situated, the inquiry would be certainly undertaken; but it would not improbably happen, if a pair of stars were chosen at random, that they would be both in the cluster, and thus the attempt would be abortive. It is doubtless this feeling which has prevented astronomers from devoting their attention to an arduous and protracted series of observations, of which the result would not improbably be futile.

CHAPTER X.

NOTES ON NEBULÆ.

I AM attempting in these pages to give a conception of the varied nature of the objects which the skies offer to our contemplation. In the moon we have a body of the most solid description, evidently cold and hard. We then saw that Saturn was entirely destitute of those rigid features which gave the moon its beauty. The charms of Saturn lie in quite another direction. Then we passed from these sun-illuminated bodies to a group of suns themselves in the glorious star cluster. Now we look to an entirely different class of objects.

The telescope, ever an ally in the study of the heavens, is in this part of the science absolutely indispensable. In other branches of astronomy we can learn something without its aid. Indeed, many great astronomical discoveries were made long before the telescope was invented. But ere this memorable event in the history of science it was impossible for us to know anything of the existence of the nebulæ. It is indeed true that there is one of these objects which can be just detected by the naked eye. It lies in the constellation of Andromeda, where, on a clear and dark night, a faint spot of light can just be discerned by a good eye. But a mere glimpse gives us really no adequate notion of the true character of the object. It might only, so far as the naked eye discloses its nature, be a cluster of stars like that we have already discerned in Perseus, or like the similar group that, under the name of the Beehive, is comparatively familiar in the constellation of Cancer. With the single exception of the nebula in Andromeda, all the objects so called are entirely telescopic, yet how important a constituent the nebulæ form in the contents of the heavens will be shown by a look at some of the lists of these objects. There are now several thousands of nebulæ known, and their positions in the sky, as well as the details of their appearances, are set forth in the catalogues.

It will therefore be proper that during our evenings at the observatory more opportunity should be taken to examine these mysterious nebulæ. An exceptionally fine night should be chosen for this purpose. The sky should be clear and bright, and the moon should be absent. Indeed, when the moon is present the light it scatters over the sky is sufficient entirely to extinguish the faint nebulæ, and greatly to impair the lustre and the beauty of the brighter ones. A good test of the suitability of a night for such purposes is found in the visibility of the Milky Way. If it be seen clearly spanning the sky, then the night will usually be favourable for such observations. From the same considerations we may infer that it will not do to choose nights in the middle of summer. Then the twilight glow over the sky in our northern latitudes

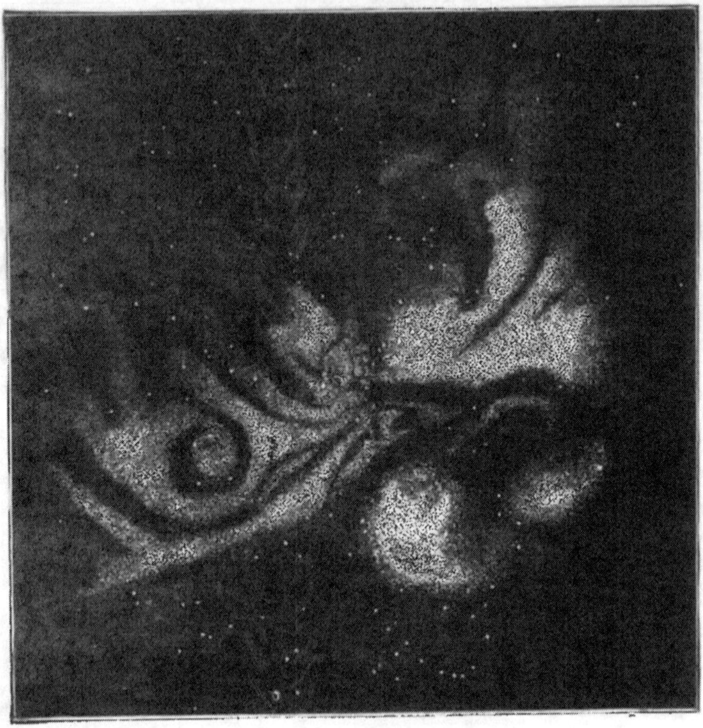

Fig. 11.—The Great Nebula in Orion.

has a similar effect to the moonbeams, in so far as it greatly detracts from the telescopic effectiveness of the nebulæ. In fact, these objects are most of them so faint that the caution I have already given as to the liability to disappointment must be especially remembered. Many of them can only be made out by careful watching, and for the fainter ones an eye specially trained to such work is required. It is for nebulæ that the leviathan reflectors have been chiefly constructed. The great mirrors are specially adapted to grasp all the feeble rays of light that these objects diffuse, and concentrate them so as to produce an image bright enough to admit of being observed.

The most glorious constellation of stars in the firmament is undoubtedly that of Orion. This splendid group is seen in the south during the winter months, and towards the close of January it is situated in a very convenient position for observing early in the evening. The group is specially characterized by the number of unusually bright stars which it includes, and the three stars in the centre, forming the so-called Belt of Orion, is as well known a celestial figure as the sky contains. Directly under the belt are three much smaller stars nearly in a line, which points straight upwards to the middle star of the belt. These three lower stars are usually known as the sword handle of Orion, this being the position which they occupied in the fanciful old sketches of the constellation. The three stars of the sword handle of Orion are plunged in the Great Nebula. This object cannot be seen by the unassisted eye, though doubtless around the central star a little haziness is perceptible, and even the slightest telescopic aid will suffice to indicate that the central star of the sword handle is attended by a surrounding glow of light, which renders it quite unlike other stars. This can indeed be sufficiently shown with an ordinary opera-glass, one glance through which will awaken in the beholder a keen desire to study the object under more favourable conditions. But to do justice to the object, telescopes of large power are desirable.

To realise fully the magnificence of the Great Nebula, the observer who is being introduced to the object for the first time should not, strange to say, direct the telescope at the nebula; the instrument should rather be pointed at the heavens, just a little to the west of the nebula. The clock driving the equatorial should not be started, and the observer should take his seat and look through the eye-piece before the nebula has entered the field. He will see, no doubt, a few stars on the black background, which gradually pass in procession across his field of view. This is merely the ordinary diurnal journey of the heavens, by which all the objects move slowly from east to west; I ought rather to say *appear* to move, for of course the motion on the heavens is only apparent, the fact being that it is the earth which is turning around.

After the observer's eye for a minute or so has become familiarised with the dark aspect of the heavens under ordinary circumstances, he will begin to perceive on the eastern side (it will appear in the telescope no doubt as on the western side) a faint dawn of light. Gradually there will steal across his field of view a sort of ghostlike luminosity that is in marked contrast to the darkness in the rest of the field; as the seconds move on, this object will disclose itself until the full splendour of the Great Nebula comes into view; then the entire field will be filled with the light, and then it will gradually advance and gradually pass away again to emphasize the contrast between the brilliance of the nebula and the darkness of the sky. Unless this method is adopted, the full interest of a telescopic view of the Great Nebula is not attained, for when the entire field is full of the glow the beginner will hardly recognise the nebula. He will be apt to think that the fainter part of the field he sees is the ordinary groundwork of the sky, and this illusion can only be dispelled by enabling him to witness the actual contrast in the way I have described. The central portions of the nebula are, however, so brilliant and so wonderfully marked with interesting detail, that even a small instrument will suffice to reveal much of its beauties.

In the centre of the nebula is the star known to astronomers as Theta Orionis, the most prominent star of the sword handle. To the eye this looks like an ordinary star, but the telescope speedily dispels that notion. Theta Orionis is found to consist of four, or rather six, stars all so close together that the unaided eye fails to distinguish them separately. A structure so complex gives to this star quite a special, indeed a unique, interest, wholly apart from the marvellous nebula of which it is the focus. We must dwell a little on the peculiarities of this star. We are familiar with stars which are called double; there are indeed some ten thousand objects so designated known to astronomers and duly registered in catalogues. Some of these are no doubt only casual doubles. It happens that two stars lie nearly in the same line of vision: they are thus found to be very close together in the heavens. Such objects are merely said to be optically double, and so far as their physical nature is concerned they are of comparatively little interest, though their practical utility in facilitating the discovery of the distance of the nearer of the pair ought not to be overlooked. It will, however, often happen that two stars are not merely apparently near each other on the sky, but are actually quite close together, in comparison, that is, to the immense distance at which they are both separated from our system. This we know because we often see the stars actually revolving one around the other, not, it is true, with any very rapid motion, in the ordinary acceptation of the word. One of the stars may require many years to complete a revolution around the other, but the fact that such revolution has been noticed is sufficient in the cases where it occurs to prove the connection existing between these stars. We must also, of course, remember that these stars are suns of stupendous magnitude, and from a view of our own system, in which the great planets take many years to complete one of their mighty journeys around the central orb, it is not in the least to be wondered at that the periods of revolution of these double stars should demand no less intervals of time.

Many of these double stars are objects of extreme telescopic beauty; sometimes they offer to our admiration a delightful contrast of colours; perhaps one will be topaz colour and the other bluish, or on rare occasions a pair of emerald gems will be seen with an invisible band of mutual connection. Sometimes triple stars are found, in which three stars are obviously in alliance; but multiple stars of greater complexity are comparatively rare; and so marvellous a spectacle as Theta Orionis, in which no fewer than six stars are obviously an allied group, is almost unique. It is not a little remarkable that we find the most exquisite multiple star which the sky can show, beautifully framed or set in the centre of the grandest of the nebulæ. Of course it might conceivably happen that the apparent concourse of these objects was fortuitous. The actual phenomenon could be accounted for by the belief that the Great Nebula was either very much nearer or very much farther than the multiple star, and that they chanced to lie in the same line of sight, and had no other connection. But to me it appears that this view is quite at variance with every reasonable probability; that the most wondrous multiple star should have happened to lie in line with the very centre of the most wondrous nebula, would have been a coincidence, against the occurrence of which the probabilities were almost infinite. There can scarcely be any doubt that the multiple star and the Great Nebula are part of the same system, and that the star is, in truth, placed in the middle of the nebula, as it actually appears to be.

And now as to the composition of this mysterious object. Here, indeed, the terrestrial analogies seem to render us but little assistance. While we were discoursing about the moon, we could appeal to the volcanoes, both active and extinct, on the globe, as offering some clues to the nature of the lunar craters. So also when we were speaking of Saturn we were able to derive some assistance in our attempt to understand the appearance of its globe from the analogy of terrestrial clouds. No similar resource is open when we study the nebulæ; we look in vain for natural phenomena on this globe which shall render the needful clue.

The word nebula means, of course, a little cloud, but the expression is apt to be a misleading one. In a sense no doubt they are little, inasmuch as the patch of the sky which a nebula covers would be small compared with one of our ordinary clouds. Indeed, a nebula which covered as large an apparent part of the sky as the size of the moon would be ranked as a large object of its class, while even the greatest of them is perhaps not more than ten or twelve times as great. Nor is the word cloud, as applied to nebula, an appropriate one. What we mean by a cloud is only a vast mass of watery vapour raised by the sun from the sea, and poised aloft until such time as it shall be again dispersed into invisible water, or until it shall descend to the earth as rain. Such clouds are of course within the limits of our atmosphere, and are rarely more than a few miles above the earth's surface. The light which renders clouds visible only comes from reflected sunbeams, and consequently at night clouds become invisible, though the astronomer is often only too unpleasantly made acquainted with their presence by the opacity with which they shut out the stars from his view.

Utterly different in all respects are the nebulæ. They are not masses of watery vapour. It may no doubt possibly be that water in some form is there, but it is not water which we see. We are looking at some gaseous material of a bluish hue. The light with which it glows is no reflected sunlight. The nebula is indeed indebted to no foreign source for that weird—I had almost said ghost-like—radiance which it gives forth. The light comes from the nebula itself. But how, it may well be asked, should a purely gaseous substance be able to radiate forth light? It is easy for us to comprehend how stars or suns or comparatively solid bodies can, in virtue of their tremendous temperature, glow with heat like red-hot or white-hot iron. It is true that flame is gas in an incandescent state, but in flame a vehement chemical union of oxygen with some other substance is in progress, and this is the source of the heat and the light that flame gives forth. We cannot regard the Great Nebula in Orion as originating in anything resembling flame.

We can, however, in our physical laboratories arrange an experiment which seems to throw some light on the composition of the nebula. Into a glass tube a small quantity of hydrogen gas is admitted, the air having been previously extracted. Then, by means of two wires, one at each end of the tube, an electric current is transmitted through the gas. Here there is no combustion; the gas is merely the vehicle by which the electricity flows from one pole to the other. In doing so the gas instantly begins to glow with an intense bluish light, and a very beautiful effect is produced, which can be renewed or terminated at will by simply making or breaking the electric current. It would seem as if the gas we see in the nebula were in a condition somewhat analogous to the gas in the tube. I do not mean that the passage of electricity through the nebula is the source of its luminosity. There is, indeed, no ground for such a supposition. It is the property of electricity when passing through a conductor to warm that conductor; thus we know that if a powerful current be transmitted through a wire of the most infusible of all metals, platinum, the wire will not only get warm, but it may become red hot, white hot, and even melt under the influence of the heat which is generated. In those beautiful incandescent electric lamps which are now happily coming into such extensive use a current of electricity flows through a filament of carbon, and kindles that exquisite incandescence which is maintained while the current flows. It would appear that so long as the electricity is flowing through the glass tube its action on the gas is to impart a very high temperature. It is in consequence of this temperature that the gas glows. Now we can offer a reasonable account of the luminosity of the Great Nebula in Orion. The particles of gaseous or vaporous material of which it is formed are of an extremely high temperature, sufficient to enable them to glow with the brilliancy which renders them visible.

It is now almost twenty years since a marvellous accession to our knowledge of such objects as the Great Nebula in Orion was made by Sir William Huggins. I have used hydrogen as an illustration in describing the character of the nebula, but I have now to add that the presence of hydrogen is no mere fiction but a substantial verity. Truly we here open up one of the most marvellous chapters which science has to disclose. The chemist can analyse the different substances on the earth with his test tubes, and he can tell the elements of which they are composed. But in this old-fashioned chemistry it was at least reasonable for the chemist to demand a portion of the substance he was expected to analyse. Unless he were provided with a sample, how could it be possible for him to grind it up or submit it to the various operations of his laboratory? In these modern days the chemist can perform operations of which his predecessors never even dreamed. No doubt the old method is still used—nay, is indeed at this moment cultivated with greater skill and means than in any previous age—but side by side with the old method, and as an invaluable supplement thereto, the new method of chemical research, called spectrum analysis, has been created, and has already conducted to many profoundly interesting discoveries in the most varied branches of science.

In the application of the spectroscopic method it is not indispensably necessary that we actually have a fragment of the substance; all we require is a beam of light which that substance can be made to yield when heated to a sufficiently high temperature. No doubt this statement should receive some more precise qualifications, but for our present purpose it will indicate the nature of spectrum analysis with sufficient accuracy.

To begin with a simple case, the colour of a light will often afford an indication of its character. Thus the red light seen in displays of fireworks is due to the presence of the element strontium. The ghastly yellow hue produced by burning common salt with spirits of wine is equally characteristic of sodium. Rarely, however, in nature is a simple unmixed light presented to us, as it is no doubt in the two cases I have mentioned. Suppose that a number of distinct hues are blended into a single beam, we could hardly expect to recognise the combination they produce. We must have some method for disentangling the several ingredients so that they can be tested separately.

The spectroscope gives the means of effecting the required decomposition. A beam of light is passed through a wedge-shaped piece of glass called a prism, or more frequently through a whole series of prisms. If the light under examination be a sunbeam, then the prism unfolds a beautiful series of hues: the red, orange, yellow, green, blue, indigo, and violet forming all the colours of the rainbow. Thus we demonstrate the highly composite character of a sunbeam; but the light from the nebula in Orion, with which we are at present concerned, is of a much more simple character.

When a beam of the nebular light is transmitted through the prisms, it declares at once that the object from which that light has come is totally different from a star like the sun. Instead of the beautifully coloured band, decked in all the glowing hues of the rainbow, the nebular beam is seen to be composed simply of six or seven widely separated strips. It is important to test the character of the light in these strips. Fortunately this can be done in a way that is completely satisfactory. We can produce artificial lights from known sources, and observe them through the spectroscope simultaneously with the light of the nebula.

There are in the composition of this globe some sixty or seventy different elementary substances, and under suitable conditions each one of these substances can afford a perfectly characteristic spectrum. Thus the way of making the comparison with the nebula is to try the different elements one after another, until one can be discovered which pours forth a light that behaves under the prism as does the light from the nebula. Pursuing this inquiry, Sir W. Huggins found that when hydrogen gas was ignited to incandescence by the passage of electricity, it emitted light which, after passage through the prisms, came to coincidence with one of the lines in the spectrum of nebula; and the hydrogen character of two of the other lines has been since demonstrated. It was thus established that hydrogen is one of the constituents of the Great

Nebula in Orion. Further confirmation of this important discovery was forthcoming when the photographs of the spectrum of the Great Nebula were subsequently obtained. On those photographs lines were present which are constituted by light of such a nature as to be wholly invisible to the eye, though perceptible on the photographic plate. It is of the greatest interest to discover that these invisible rays from the nebula are also indicative of the presence of hydrogen. Thus we obtain a beautiful confirmation of the fact that the nebula is partly composed of glowing hydrogen.

There are, however, some remaining lines, the character of which has not yet been ascertained.

It would be a little premature to assert that there must be some substance in the Great Nebula not at present known to us on the earth. This would be, no doubt, one interpretation of the facts. We must, however, admit the possibility of another explanation. It is frequently found that the lines yielded by an incandescent material vary to some extent when the physical conditions of temperature and of pressure are modified. It is, therefore, not impossible that the unknown lines in the spectrum of the Great Nebula may be due to some element known to us, but which has not yet been tested under the conditions which would make it yield the particular rays we are speaking of.

The composition of a nebula as disclosed to us by these researches is very instructive. Here we are looking at an object which seems to lie at the very limits of the visible universe—an object so remote that our attempts to fathom its distance are quite unsuccessful; yet in this inconceivably distant part of our system we find at least one ingredient which we know well on the earth. Previous to actual trial no one would have expected, I think, to find the Great Nebula largely constituted from such a familiar element as hydrogen. This gas enters into the composition of water, and is thus an element of extreme abundance on the earth. That an element so common with us here should also be abundant in these awfully distant regions of the universe is one of the most astonishing facts that modern science has revealed.

As the eye follows these ramifications of the Great Nebula, ever fading away in brightness until it dissolves in the blackness of the sky; as we look at the multitudes of bright stars which sparkle out from the depths of the great glowing gas; as we ponder on the marvellous outlines of a portion of the nebula, we are tempted to ask what the true magnitude of this object must really be. Here, again, we have to confess that science is unable to satisfy this very legitimate curiosity. The only means of learning the true length and breadth of a celestial object depends upon our first having discovered the distance from us at which the object is situated. Unhappily we are, as I have said, entirely ignorant of what this distance may be in the case of the Great Nebula in Orion. Our ordinary methods of conducting such an inquiry are hardly applicable to such an object, and its position so near the equator introduces fresh difficulties into the problem. We shall, however, certainly not err on the side of exaggeration if we assert that the Great Nebula must be many millions of times larger than that group of bodies which we call the solar system.

There are many other nebulæ which would be well

Fig. 12.—The Great Spiral Nebula.

worthy of attentive examination. Here, for instance, in Fig. 12 we represent one of the most famous known as "the Great Spiral," but we must not linger any longer over these objects. A treatise would be necessary to convey what is known about them.

Our evening at the observatory has now been spent: we have looked at the most remarkable objects which the universe contains, and we have, let us hope, acquired a fresh appreciation of the sublimity of that scheme of creation in which our earth plays a small though dignified part.

CHAPTER XI.

VENUS AND MERCURY.

AMONG the planets of our system Venus is one which has always been most tantalizing to astronomers. Notwithstanding the fact that when this beautiful globe is seen at its best it is far brighter than any star or any other planet, yet as a telescopic object Venus is often disappointing. It shows, no doubt, the beautiful crescent which charmed Galileo, when he first directed the newly invented tube towards it, and the crescent of the evening star is still one of the most pleasing telescopic spectacles, which specially delights the beginner who for the first time finds himself in the possession of a telescope. But it is the very brilliancy of Venus which often leads to disappointment. We see a radiant object, a beautiful gem of light, but the brightness tends to prevent us from seeing the actual features on the planet. In this respect we can contrast Venus with another globe, namely, the planet Mars. This body is our next neighbour on the outside, just as Venus is the next neighbour on the inside. It is, therefore, of particular interest for us to learn all we can about the two bodies which are similarly situated with regard to the benefits which the sun dispenses so liberally.

It is well known that we are far better acquainted with the aspect of Mars, in so far as the topographical features of its surface are concerned, than we are with Venus, notwithstanding that Mars is a smaller globe than Venus, and, generally speaking, much farther away. We can even study the surface of Jupiter, with considerable detail, though under every combination of circumstances this great planet is never less than twice as far from the earth as is Venus. It is, however, only proper to add that it is the vast bulk of Jupiter and the correspondingly great size of his features which render him so discernible in spite of his vast distance. We are able to speak of the belts of Jupiter, to talk of the oceans and continents on Mars, and even the "canals" on the latter globe are duly set down on our maps. Many of the features on these two globes can be represented with perfect confidence, and have conveyed to us much valuable information with regard to our neighbours in the solar system.

The case is very different with regard to Venus. The reflected sunbeams which radiate so charmingly from this planet bear to us but little information with regard to the actual details of that globe from which they come. Few astronomers have that confidence in the perfection of their instruments and the accuracy of their eyesight which will enable them to make out recognisable features in the Evening Star. It is true that certain of the older astronomers did indicate the existence of certain discernible marks on the planet. It was sometime thought that darker patches could be observed which were permanent features of the globe. It was also thought that when Venus appeared as a narrow crescent of light, the irregularities near the horns of the crescent could be attributed to mountains on the surface; while some astronomers had the hardihood to attempt to calculate the elevation of the mountains which would give rise to the features that were noticed. It can hardly be said at any time that these observations and inferences commanded any very large degree of credence among those competent to judge. From the facts which have recently come to light, and which form the subject of this sketch, it seems certain that even the small amount of belief which was accorded to these researches must now be almost entirely withheld.

There are many reasons why it should be of special interest to learn all that we can of the topography of this planet, which lies so near us. It so happens that Venus has a bulk which is very nearly the same as that of the earth. It seems also to be quite certain that Venus is clothed with an atmosphere, for it would be otherwise impossible to explain the girdle of light which surrounds the planet when she is in front of the sun's disc. The measures of heat and light from the great luminary which are received by Venus are, no doubt, in excess of those which fall to the earth's share; but still it seems that Venus is a world so like our own in many respects that every element of intellectual curiosity excites us to learn all we can about another world to which we are linked by so many affinities. There seems no prospect that we shall ever perceive the features of the planet as fully and as minutely as we shall learn those of Mars. However, one step has now been taken, and the results are pregnant with interest.

Viewed as a world, there is no more important point for consideration than the length of the day as it would appear to an inhabitant of Venus. This has long been a matter of much uncertainty. The only means we have of determining the period of rotation of a distant globe on its axis is by watching some mark or object on the globe, which we can recognise with certainty, and then observing the time which it requires to go round to the opposite side, and back to where it was originally situated.

On Mars this process presents but little difficulty. There are many features on that globe which possess the desired attributes of definiteness and sharpness; and accordingly the period of rotation of Mars on its axis, or the day of that planet, is known with all desirable accuracy. It is known even to the fraction of a second, and it happens by a curious coincidence not to be very different from the length of our own day. A similar method can be applied to some of the other celestial bodies, though there are individual peculiarities which often give rise to difficulties. For instance, we know that the sun turns on its axis in about twenty-five of our days. This is learned by the observations of those spots by which the surface is frequently marked. As, however, the sun is not a solid body, and as the spots are merely apertures through a covering of luminous clouds, they do not possess either the definiteness or the permanence which would enable us to rely on them for any very minute accuracy. Each spot is also too transient to enable any large number of consecutive rotations to be watched by its aid; and unless a large number of rotations can be included in the observations as in the case of Mars, any very great precision in the determination of the period of rotation is impossible. Indeed, it may be remarked that the sun does not rotate in the same manner as a solid globe would necessarily have to do.

The difficulty about finding the length of the day of Venus simply arose from the fact that the marks on the planet seemed too vague and faint to be relied upon for the purpose. It is true that certain observations of this kind had been made in former years, and it had been conjectured that the length of the day on Venus was about equal to that of the earth. The question would be, of course, settled if there were some great mountains standing out from Venus which every one could see through their telescopes; or if there were any black spot or other unmistakable mark, it would answer the purpose. Unfortunately, there are no such features discernible—none, at least, that are perceptible to ordinary eyes furnished with ordinary telescopes and used in those latitudes on the earth where astronomical observations are most abundant. Much of what we have said with regard to Venus may be applied to the planet Mercury, which lies still nearer to the sun. The period of rotation of both these planets has been until lately a matter of much uncertainty.

We are, however, recently indebted to the keen eyes of Professor Schiaparelli, of Milan, for a minute scrutiny of Mercury, on which he has discerned features sufficiently recognisable to enable him to solve the great problem of the length of the day on our neighbouring world. He has shown that the earlier notions are apparently erroneous. It would have been something to have learned even thus much; but the positive results at which

Schiaparelli has arrived are so striking and full of interest that they constitute one of the most important additions to our knowledge of the solar system that has been brought to light for many a long day. It ought, however, to be added that some competent observers are unable to convince themselves of the accuracy of Schiaparelli's investigation.

Now, however, Schiaparelli has shown that the constant face which the moon turns to the earth seems to have a parallel in the revolution of Mercury around the sun. It is not that Mercury always directs the same face to the earth. That would be utterly inconceivable on any rational hypothesis, and would not be at all analogous to the behaviour of the moon. It is to be remembered that Mercury revolves around the sun. This planet, therefore, stands in the same relation to the sun that the moon stands to the earth. The singular fact to which I desire to call attention is that Schiaparelli's researches show that Mercury constantly keeps the same face directed towards the sun. The period of rotation of Mercury on its axis is, accordingly, of the same length as the period of its revolution around the sun. We never see the other side of the moon, because the moon always moves so as to keep the same face towards us. In a similar manner, only one side of Mercury is ever visible from the sun. The other side is sedulously averted from that luminary.

The side of Mercury which is turned away from the sun is, therefore, eternally in dark night, while the favoured side is perennially suffused with the glory of an unintermittent day, much brighter and hotter than any day we know, inasmuch as Mercury is a planet so much nearer to the sun than we are. Schiaparelli's attention has also been given to Venus. He has certainly shown that the period of rotation of this planet is very much longer than has been hitherto supposed. However, the difficulties of the observations are so great that the results are not so definite as in the case of Mercury. It seems, however, hard to resist the conclusion that Venus, like Mercury, revolves so as always to show the same face to the sun.

But to my mind the significance of Schiaparelli's investigation does not lie so much in the mere perception of certain features in the planetary movements. It is the interpretation of these phenomena which offers the chief points of interest. Indeed, there has never been any time at which these discoveries would have been more acceptable in the scientific world than at the present moment. They furnish us with a vivid and unexpected illustration of the doctrine of tidal evolution, to which we have elsewhere (p. 60) given attention.

We revert to the case of the moon for a suggestion as to the cause of the remarkable peculiarities shown in the movement of Mercury, and presumably true in the case of Venus. We have explained that the constant face of the moon is a monument of tidal action. It would be an infinitely improbable coincidence if there were no physical cause to account for it, and the tides afford a perfectly satisfactory explanation.

In a precisely similar way we can account for the fact that Mercury always bends the same face to the sun. The matter is fortunately not a little simplified by the fact that Mercury is certainly devoid of any considerable satellite, and very likely has no satellite whatever. The sun is the only tide-raising globe that can affect Mercury. We, of course, also experience sun-raised tides on this earth, but to us they seem of comparatively little importance, because they are much less than the tides raised by the moon. There is, however, a double reason for regarding the sun-raised tides on Mercury as of special importance to that globe. In the first place, as there are no perceptible satellite-raised tides, there the solar tides are the determining agents in tidal phenomena, and, secondly, as Mercury is closer to the sun than we are, the sun-raised tides will be much larger and stronger than those which we experience. It seems, therefore, certain that the constant face which Mercury directs towards the sun is a consequence of tidal action. In fact, it might almost have been anticipated from tidal phenomena alone that Mercury would have been found to move in this manner. The solar tidal control on Mercury must be much more vigorous than that on Venus, but any attempt on either planet to escape from the thraldom that requires it to keep the same face constantly to the sun would be checked with exemplary energy.

It will thus be seen that the results of the delicate observations of an Italian astronomer seem to illustrate in a striking manner one of the most interesting of modern astronomical doctrines.

CHAPTER XII.

MARS AS A WORLD.

It is rather curious that the planets should so closely simulate the guise of the fixed stars. Saturn and Mars, two of the most celebrated planets, have often a superficial resemblance to Aldebaran or Betelgeuse. Yet it is difficult to emphasize sufficiently how wide is the actual difference between them. The planets are not self-luminous bodies like the stars; they are merely orbs revolving around the sun, and indebted, like our earth, to the sun for the benefit of his light and heat. These planets are bodies which must be generally, if not always, smaller than the fixed stars; and their apparent brilliancy, notwithstanding their small size and the fact that they exhibit only reflected light, is simply a consequence of their comparative nearness.

The apparent resemblance between planets and stars is quickly dispelled when a telescope is directed towards them. The star, as we have stated, shows merely a bright point of light. It is far otherwise when we look at the planets. Each of them exhibits in any instrument, even of moderate power, a characteristic appearance by which the planet is at once distinguished from the stars, while the several planets can each be discriminated from the others.

There is, however, a crucial test which will detect every object of a planetary nature. The very word *planet* means a wanderer; and the term is appropriately employed to designate the wandering stars which move about over the surface of the heavens. These bodies pass from one constellation to another in the course of their circuits around the sky, and they are thus widely distinct from the so-called fixed stars by which the constellations are themselves formed. In the course of a few weeks, or even less, it will be easy to observe, even without telescopic aid, the actual changes in the positions of the planets; while, with the assistance of a good equatorial telescope, a single hour is usually sufficient to disclose enough movement in a planet to show that the object is something quite different from a star.

It is my object in this chapter to convey a sketch of what is known, or can be reasonably conjectured, with regard to Mars as a world. This globe is of particular interest to us; for it is natural to feel curious with regard to the neighbouring globe, which is in many respects placed in much the same conditions as is our earth. It would seem that our globe occupies an intermediate position, so to speak, in the general system of the planets. I do not now refer only to the fact that there are some planets which are nearer the sun than we are, and that there are others more distant. This is undoubtedly true; but there are other circumstances of a still more significant character. This world is a good deal larger than some of the planets, while it is a good deal smaller than others. We are attended by a single moon; and if in this respect we are disposed to envy the superior endowments of a planet which has two moons, like Mars, four moons, like Jupiter, or eight, like Saturn, we should be consoled by the reflection that though Venus is a globe as large as we are, yet she has no attendant moons at all, and that Mercury is in a similar solitary condition. In physical constitution, also, it will shortly appear how our earth is more solid than this planet or less solid than that; how it has more air and clouds than some of these bodies, and less air and clouds than others; how the earth, viewed as a habitable world, seems to be in the meridian of life, while there are other globes still in the phase of early youth, or in a more advanced old age. All these various circumstances give to the study of the worlds which form the sun's family a quite exceptional interest to us. We may expect to learn from this study some facts which will throw light on that question so pregnant with interest, as to the possible habitability of the other globes in space.

Of all the planets the one that comes into the most favourable position for telescopic scrutiny from the earth is unquestionably that globe known to the ancients by the name of Mars.

Mars revolves around the sun, and accomplishes its journey in a period of 687 days. It moves in a path which we shall not greatly misrepresent if we describe it as a circle with a radius of about one hundred and fifty-one millions of miles. The true shape of the path is, however, oval or elliptical, so that the planet is sometimes about one-tenth of the distance just stated nearer to the sun, and as often the same distance farther from the sun. The orbit of this planet is thus farther out from the sun than is that of our earth; and in the annexed figure (Fig. 13) we have drawn the relative sizes of the two orbits, both represented in their actual form. It will thus be seen how similarly the two bodies are circumstanced, in so far as their relations with the sun are concerned. It is, however, obvious that the earth occupies a more favoured

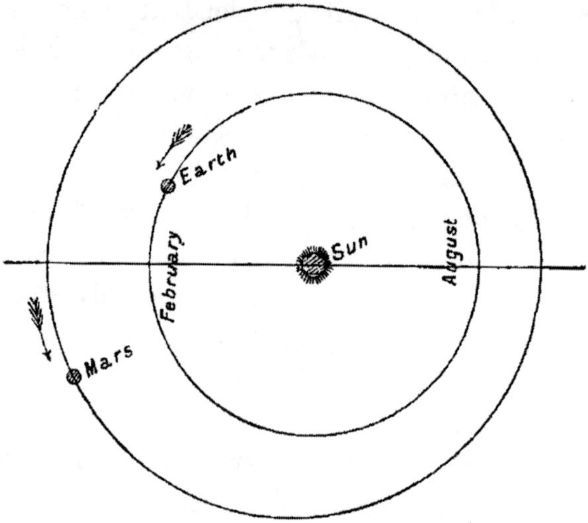

Fig. 13.—Orbits of Earth and Mars.

position for the enjoyment of the light and heat dispensed from the common source.

In another respect also the resemblance between this planet and the earth is very notable. Our globe rotates on its axis, and accomplishes each complete rotation in one sidereal day; that is, in 23 hrs. 56 min. 4 sec. of solar time. In like manner does Mars revolve on its axis. By assiduous watching of the varied points on its surface, which are seen gradually to turn round, to become invisible, and then to reappear, it has been possible to discover the period of his rotation with much accuracy. This period is singularly close to that of our earth; there is not three-quarters of an hour's difference, the duration of the rotation of Mars being the greater, or stated exactly, 24 hrs. 37 min. 23 sec.

It is, however, the telescopic aspect of the planet itself which is especially interesting. With the single exception of the moon, there is no other body in the universe that our telescopes can investigate so closely as they can the planet Mars. It is now more than two hundred and fifty years since it began to receive that assiduous attention from astronomers which has been continued to the present hour. Among the earliest observations we have are those of Fontana, at Naples. His feeble telescope was sufficient to show that on the ruddy face of the planet were certain more or less definite markings.

The nature of these marks on the globe has been now so carefully studied that there can be no doubt that the chief of them indicate permanent features on the planet. In fact, astronomers have prepared several charts or actual maps of the continents and oceans, or rather of the dark regions which are presumably oceanic, and of the more ruddy or often orange-coloured portions which seem to be land.

The entire surface of the planet is in some degree known to us; in this respect there is a notable difference between Mars and the moon. Of the moon we are only acquainted with that face of it which is turned towards the earth, and the other side is eternally secluded. But as Mars rotates, we see now one side of it and now another, and the various features of it are disclosed under every variety of aspect and foreshortening as they advance from the margin, and then cross its surface to recede again from view by the progress of its perpetual rotation. We have not, however, to rely solely on the rotation of the planet to present us with a view of its different aspects. It fortunately happens that sometimes the north pole of the planet and sometimes the south pole is tilted towards us.

To understand the different circumstances under which the planet is thus presented, it will be necessary to enter a little into the nature of its movements as represented in Fig. 13. This drawing shows two orbits which, at a superficial glance, appear to be circles, but which, on a more careful examination, are found to be ellipses. The inner of the two represents the path of the earth, the outer shows the orbit of Mars. At the centre the sun is placed. The earth completes its motion round the sun in 365 days, while Mars requires 687 days for its journey. It will therefore happen, sometimes, that the earth, as it were, overtakes Mars, and comes between the planet and the sun. This phenomenon is called the *opposition* of Mars; and it is on the occasion of an opposition of the planet that the greatest facilities for making a telescopic scrutiny of its surface are enjoyed. This will be obvious from a glance at the figure, which shows that at the moment of opposition the earth must be closer to Mars than the bodies can generally be at other times. Remembering also that our point of view is on the earth, which, in such a case, lies between Mars and the sun, it follows that at the best hours of observation, in the middle of the night, the planet must be on the meridian, and at its highest in the sky.

The oppositions of Mars succeed each other at intervals of 780 days. It therefore follows that about every two years and two months the planet occupies a favourable position for being observed. It must, however, be noticed that all oppositions are not equally advantageous. Owing

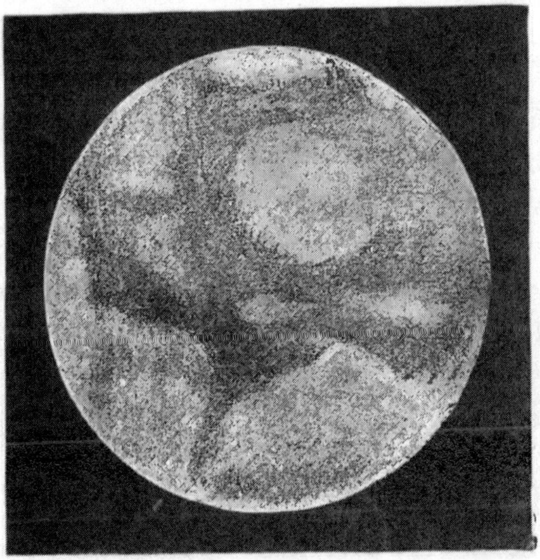

Fig. 14.—View of Mars, Sept. 10th, 11h. 20m., 1887.

to the high eccentricity in the shape of the orbit of Mars it lies in one region of its path much closer to the earth's circuit than it is when elsewhere. To express the results with numerical accuracy, we may take the average distance from the earth to the sun to be about ninety-three millions of miles. Then the distance between Mars and the earth at opposition may sometimes be as much as sixty-three millions of miles, and sometimes may be as low as thirty-four millions of miles. It will thus appear that the best oppositions will exhibit the planet at a distance which is but little more than half that of the unfavourable oppositions. The most convenient method for expressing any particular point of the earth's orbit is by the day at which the earth is annually due there. On August 26th the earth is in that part of its path which lies nearest to the orbit of Mars. If, therefore, an opposition of the planet should occur on or near to that date, the earth and the planet will then be separated by the least distance possible. On the other hand, when the earth is passing through that part of its path which it traverses every February 22nd, the conditions are reversed. Should an opposition of the planet then occur, the distance between the two bodies will attain a greater value than is possible when the opposition occurs at any other date in the course of the year. It therefore follows that the nearer the oppositions are to August 26th, the better they are, and the nearer they are to February 22nd, the worse they are.

It is a noteworthy fact that the relations between the periodic times of Mars and the earth are such that seventeen revolutions of Mars are accomplished in nearly thirty-two years. There is a still more approximate relation expressed in the fact that twenty-five revolutions of the planet are almost exactly completed in forty-seven revolutions of the earth. Hence it follows that the relative positions which Mars and the earth occupy to-day they will again regain in forty-seven years. Thus we see that any favourable opposition of Mars will be succeeded at intervals of thirty-two years and forty-seven years by oppositions which are also favourable. As an illustration of the use that may be made of these numbers, we shall predict the occurrence of an approaching favourable opposition. There was one in 1877, there must, therefore, have been a good opposition thirty-two years previously, that is, in 1845. It must similarly be followed in forty-seven years by another good opposition, which brings us to 1892. We may therefore anticipate in the autumn of 1892 another good view of our neighbouring planet.

We have already spoken of the rotation of Mars, and it follows that this planet has an axis about which that rotation is performed; the planet being in this respect, as in so many others, a body analogous to our earth. The plane of the orbit of Mars is inclined at a small angle to that of the earth. This angle is under two degrees. It varies slightly, and is at present decreasing with extreme slowness. The value for the year 1890 is 1° 51′ 1″, and the decline in its value is at the rate of two or three seconds per century. So far as the mere aspect of Mars from our earth is concerned, this small angle of inclination possesses an inappreciable influence. The case would be very different, however, from the point of view of an inhabitant of Mars. If there were absolutely no inclination between the two orbits, then, whenever an opposition of Mars took place, it would happen that the earth would, of course, be seen actually projected on the disc of the sun when viewed from Mars. As, however, there is some inclination, it will usually happen that the Martial inhabitant will not see the earth in front of the sun during opposition, for the same reason that we do not see Venus on the sun's face every time that she is in conjunction. She is usually either over the sun or under the sun, and only on rare occasions have we the pleasing spectacle of a transit of Venus. So rare, indeed are the transits of Venus, that though the present generation has witnessed two, namely in 1874 and 1882, there can be no recurrence of the phenomenon until the years 2004 and 2012 have come round. The Martial inhabitant will also find that a transit of the earth in front of the sun is an occasional and noteworthy spectacle. It has been pointed out by Mr. Marth that such an occurrence might have been witnessed from Mars on the 12th of November, 1879.

We may, however, for the present purpose ignore this slight inclination of Mars' orbit to our own. But we have now to consider the very different matter of the inclination of the axis about which Mars' rotation is performed to that of its actual orbit. We may here again advantageously refer to the parallel case of our own globe. The earth, in its annual progress round the sun, turns now one pole and now another towards the sun, thus producing the vicissitudes of the seasons. In a similar manner the equator of Mars is inclined to the plane of its orbit, and thus we sometimes are enabled to see one pole of the planet and sometimes another. It happens that when the planet is in opposition in our autumn, the southern hemisphere is turned towards the earth. The planet is then seen under the most favourable conditions, in so far as its apparent dimensions are concerned; for, as we have already pointed out, it is under such circumstances at its least distance from the earth. It thus follows that the most complete series of telescopic pictures of the planet which we possess are those in which the south pole is exhibited.

Many astronomers have given to us carefully finished sketches of the appearance of the planet on such occasions. Among these I now specially invite attention to the remarkable series of drawings obtained in the opposition in September, 1877, by Mr. N. E. Green, who enjoyed the privilege of observing Mars under singularly favourable conditions in the beautiful skies of Madeira. The telescope he employed was a reflector of the Newtonian form, with a mirror thirteen inches in diameter, figured by Mr. With, of Hereford. The magnifying power he most usually employed was one of about 250 diameters. In Mr. Green's memoirs he gives us representations of twelve of his drawings selected from a much larger number. The pictures have been chosen to show the planet at intervals of two hours. This arrangement secures that the plane shall be displayed under every different aspect, for after twelve views at intervals of two hours have been depicted, the thirteenth would merely be a repetition of the first, as the rotation of the planet on its axis is so nearly twenty-four hours. Mr. Green also suggests the caution with which all drawings of planets, and, indeed, all drawings of celestial objects generally, should be received. He truly remarks that "they are necessarily exaggerations. When the eye has been taxed to the utmost to observe the form of some delicate marking, any shade which the hand could apply to a drawing, and which could be trusted to remain as a memento of the observation, would be far beyond the strength of the reality. But the value of the representation need not thereby be unduly depreciated, for if a proportionate amount of force be given to all the details, it is still useful as expressing the general character of the object, and valuable as exhibiting a fair relation between its several parts."

As soon as the prominent features on the planet came to be recognised, it was found necessary to devise means by which their positions on the globe could be conveniently indicated. The analogy of our own earth showed that the proper method of accomplishing this was to adapt to Mars a system of latitudes and longitudes. As to the former, there was but little difficulty. Once the rotation of the planet was sufficiently observed, its axis became known, and also its equator. The latitude of an object on Mars is, of course, its angular distance from the equator. But the longitude presents a difficulty as to the zero from which it should be measured. This difficulty is not exclusively found on Mars. We have it on our own globe. Englishmen naturally measure all longitudes from the meridian of Greenwich; but national susceptibilities arise, which prevent us from actually asserting that all terrestrial longitudes are measured in the same manner that we use.

On Mars the difficulty is of a somewhat different nature. The first essential for the zero of longitude is that it shall be at all events a mark so clearly defined that there shall be no ambiguity. This is the point about which there has been some difference of opinion among astronomers. But I think there can be little doubt that the proposition made by Mr. Knobel, in 1884, is the correct one. He points out that there is on the face of the planet one spot so very clearly defined and so very easily observed with moderate telescopes, that it should obviously be adopted as the zero from which all longitudes should be measured. The nomenclature of the different objects is a little confusing. The zero of the longitudes was called the Oculus by Mädler, the Terby Sea by Green, and the Lacus Solis by Schiaparelli. The zero now mentioned is not that which Mr. Green had employed. Professor Schiaparelli, in his charts of the appearance of Mars in 1881-82, places the meridian of 90° through what he has called the Lacus Solis, and which, following Mr. Knobel, is the zero of longitudes. The Oculus or the Lacus Solis, or the Terby Sea, whichever name be adopted, is to be regarded as the Greenwich on the planet Mars. In my "Atlas of Astronomy" I have given a map of Mars, in which the nomenclature has been détermined from a careful comparison of the different authorities.

Mr. Green has provided us with an excellent reason for referring to his picture of Mars on September 10th. He tells us that it "was without comparison the grandest obtained at Madeira. This drawing also, of all the series, most effectually recalls the impression made at the telescope; this sight of Mars was felt at the time to be a rich reward for every effort, and will remain, while memory lasts, a constant delight and satisfaction."

The interpretation of the various marks which pictures of the planet exhibit involves questions that must still be regarded as of a somewhat speculative character. It is so natural for us to conjecture that the objects on the planet may be of identical nature with the objects on the earth, that we are accustomed to employ language on the subject that is apt to express more than the extent of our information will actually warrant. In the first place, the most striking feature presented in Mr. Green's drawings, as well as in every similar series of pictures, is the remarkable white region near the pole of the planet. In the case before us it is the southern pole that is exposed to view. It does not, however, appear that the white region is situated quite centrally with reference to the axis. Mr. Green gives good reasons for believing that the true south of the end axis of rotation of Mars lies just within the eastern edge of the white cap, as it appeared in September, 1877. The phenomena of our own poles at once suggest an explanation of the presence of these white regions on Mars. Can it be that this planet, which resembles our earth in so many other respects, resembles it also in the possession of polar regions crowned with solid masses of perennial snow and ice? Apart from the argument founded on analogy, the strongest evidence that can be adduced in support of the ice explanation of the white region arises from the undoubted variability of size of the region over which the white fields extend, corresponding with the Martial season.

The existence of an atmosphere surrounding the planet has also been asserted, perhaps I might say demonstrated. It is, however, certainly very much less ample than the atmosphere enveloping this earth in its density and extent. The most reliable indications of air around Mars are afforded by the indistinctness of the planetary features as they approach the margin by the gradual rotation of the planet. In fact, Mr. Green speaks of the atmospheric ring of bluish white surrounding the interior edge of the disc. The atmosphere also sometimes contains masses of cloud, though here, again, the thickest clouds ever seen on Mars fall very far short of the dense cloud masses with which our globe is so frequently shrouded. There can be no doubt that portions of the permanent features on the planet are temporarily obscured by the intervention of clouds. Perhaps it would be more correct to regard these objects in the atmosphere of Mars as rather in the nature of mists or fogs than of clouds in the ordinary sense of the word.

Still greater caution must be used in the attempt to interpret the varied hues of the different permanent features of the face of the planet. The general appearance of the surface of the disc, as represented in Mr. Green's drawings, is of "a warm yellow, heightening into orange" in some of the regions. With these are strongly contrasted the dark portions which Mr. Green well describes as being of "a greenish grey, partly due to contrast with the orange."

It is customary to speak of these latter portions as lakes, or seas, or oceans, according to their size and surroundings; while the yellow and warmer portions generally are spoken of as islands or as continents. There can be no inconvenience in using this language so long as we clearly remember that the distinction between land and water on the planet is purely of a conjectural character.

Those oppositions of Mars in which the northern hemisphere of the planet is turned towards the earth, are, as already explained, of a disadvantageous character for a minute scrutiny of the planet's surface. It is then at an exceptionally great distance from the earth. Mr. Knobel has well observed that, as the planet is then near its perihelion and receiving a larger supply of sun heat, the meteorological condition of its surface may be very different from what is found when the opposition occurs at a different part of the planet's orbit. Still, it is so important to study the aspect of Mars when the north pole is tilted into view, that, notwithstanding the small apparent size of the planet when near its aphelion, such oppositions merit careful attention.

A careful study of Mars was made during the opposition of the planet, in 1884, by Mr. E. B. Knobel, and his drawings are given in Vol. xlviii. of the Memoirs of the Royal Astronomical Society. Although I do not reproduce Mr. Knobel's careful examination of many isolated features on Mars, I give here an abstract of the more general remarks on the planet to which his researches have conducted him. It is impossible to look with care at any of the good drawings of the planet and not be struck with the fact that there is a wide discrepancy between the appearances of the northern and of the southern hemispheres. The various dark markings, the so-called seas, which are so conspicuous and so well marked in the southern hemisphere, become replaced in the northern hemisphere by objects of a much more ambiguous character. Indeed, the only object in the northern hemisphere which can be regarded as thoroughly marked and identified is that portion of the so-called "Kaiser Sea" which extends north of the equator. This remarkable Martial feature is by far the most conspicuous and well-defined marking that its globe presents. Even in quite small telescopes the Kaiser Sea is well seen when hardly any other object of the planet admits of being recognised.

It is shown in Fig. 14 as the dark pointed region extending towards the north pole.

Around the north pole, as around the south, is also to be found the accumulation of white material which so irresistibly reminds us of snow. I have often been struck, when observing Mars with the 12-inch refractor of the Dunsink Observatory, with the extremely sharp boundary line by which this white region is marked off from the body of the planet.

I must now discuss another discovery, the result of the acute observations of Schiaparelli, the director of the Milan Observatory, to whose labours much of our knowledge of the topography of the planet is due.

In September, 1877, when Mars occupied that particular situation relatively to the earth in which the distance between the two globes was almost at its lowest point, and when, consequently, the apparent magnitude of the planet attained its highest value, Professor Schiaparelli, availing himself of the clear atmosphere in which his observatory was situated, made a remarkable observation on the planet. He showed that the regions heretofore spoken of as continents appeared to be intersected by dark streaks, which must have been about sixty miles wide, and which often attained a length of thousands of miles. During the opposition of 1881-1882, Schiaparelli again recognised the presence of the canals, but on this occasion it would seem that a very extraordinary phenomenon was perceived. Several of the canals were observed to be double, that is to say, there were a pair of canals seen separated by an interval of two hundred miles or more, and running parallel to each other throughout their whole course. It is, however, a doubtful point as to the actual nature of these objects. Many assiduous astronomers, who have enjoyed the aid of excellent telescopes, have failed to see them. It would, at all events, seem that there are no permanent markings on the planet which appear like the twin canals. If we admit their existence at all—and this is a point on which some astronomers entertain considerable doubts—they might be regarded rather in the light of certain periodic phenomena connected with the changes of the seasons in the planet than as permanent configurations on the globe.

I am, however, fortunately able to discuss here some observations made by very capable observers during the opposition of 1888. An excellent account of the results which have been thus obtained is found in the *Observatory* for September, 1888, by Mr. E. W. Maunder, of the Royal Observatory, Greenwich. It must first be remarked that the opposition was not a favourable one, in so far as the apparent size of the planet was concerned, but still there were many very interesting observations recorded, and some very beautiful sketches of the planet were obtained. The existence of the canals has been asserted by Dr. Terby and M. Perrotin, and the latter astronomer, provided with a superb telescope at Nice, has also detected the remarkable phenomenon of the double canals. Prof. Schiaparelli himself has again confirmed their existence, and, in the enthusiasm of a brilliant telescopic view, he declares that the Martial canals had all the distinctness of an engraving on steel, with the magical beauty of a coloured painting.

Several theories have been put forward to account for

these extraordinary "canals." We naturally try to obtain from terrestrial phenomena some clue to their explanation. The late Mr. Proctor, to whom we are indebted for the first successful attempt to construct a useful map of Mars, regarded the canals as rivers; but, as Mr. Maunder has so well pointed out, the objections to this view are insuperable. In the first place, they often intersect each other, a phenomenon which is almost an impossibility for two rivers. The curious straightness of the canals is anything but suggestive of the sinuosities of a river. We also frequently find the canals running sheer across the continents, connecting one sea with another. It is needless to say that the rivers on our globe do not display any phenomena of this description. For the present, all we can say is, that the "canals" present problems of a very mysterious nature, which have not yet been solved. We must anxiously await further really favourable oppositions of the planet, in the hope that the quickened attention to the subject, and the admirable optical powers now at the disposal of astronomers, will permit of some satisfactory results being arrived at.

If we have reluctantly been compelled to leave the configuration of Mars' surface in a somewhat ambiguous and unsettled condition, it is satisfactory to turn to the very clear and well-defined discovery of the satellites of the planet. In this we have the pleasure of recording the most interesting of pure telescopic discoveries that have been made during this century. As our earth is attended by one moon, as Jupiter is attended by four, Saturn by eight, while the outer planets—Uranus and Neptune—are also dignified by the companionship of satellites, it seems rather strange that the remaining planets—Mercury, Venus, and Mars—should be entirely unprovided with whatever benefits the possession of attendant moons is competent to bestow. So far as Mercury and Venus are concerned, it may, indeed, be contended that the presumption that they ought to have moons had but little substantial basis. It was obvious that the outer planets had, on the whole, more satellites than the inner planets, and as the earth had only one moon, while Venus and Mercury both revolved in orbits inside that of the earth, it was obvious that there was but slender ground for expecting that Mercury or Venus should be found provided with attendant orbs. But the case of Mars was different. As Mars revolved in a path between that of the earth and Jupiter, and as the earth had one moon and Jupiter had four, it could be plausibly contended that Mars ought to have at least a couple. But before the year 1877 this conjecture was entirely devoid of any telescopic corroboration, and the "moonless Mars" was the phrase in which one of the five great planets of antiquity was somewhat contemptuously spoken of.

While the British Association was holding its annual session at Plymouth, in 1877, a telegram arrived from the United States, stating that Professor Asaph Hall had achieved the superb feat of discovering two satellites to Mars, and had shown that these satellites were objects of the utmost interest. I well remember the enthusiasm which this announcement produced among the philosophers then assembled at Plymouth. Of course we were all impatient to learn the details of the process of search, and the particulars of the observations. These were not long in forthcoming, and Professor Hall himself described his great work in a complete memoir published at Washington in the following year. It is to this paper that we turn for full information on the subject.

It has been often said that the astronomer's best assistant is his wife, but perhaps few of them have the same confession to make as Professor Asaph Hall does when he tells his readers that at first he thought the prospect of discovering new satellites to Mars was very discouraging. Other astronomers, and skilful astronomers, too, had tried to find the satellites, and they had not been successful. Why, then, should he hope to succeed in an enterprise which had been already pronounced desperate? He tells us that he felt this so keenly that he might have abandoned the search had it not been for the encouragement of his wife.

In 1877 the planet approached exceptionally close to the earth, and this it was which indicated to Professor Hall that the right time for making the search had arrived. In this respect he, of course, only enjoyed the same facility which every other astronomer possessed of choosing the most favourable moment for making the attempt.

There were, however, two circumstances which were greatly in favour of the success of the search which Professor Hall was enabled to make. In the first place, the United States Naval Observatory is situated in the pure skies of Washington, and the more northward latitude of the observatory gives it also a distinct advantage over the similar observatories in Europe. Another factor in Professor Hall's success was the use which he enjoyed of a superb object glass, two feet in diameter. This magnificent instrument is one of the very finest in the world; perhaps, indeed, its optical perfection is at this moment hardly surpassed anywhere. Like the great Lick telescope already referred to, it is a monument of the consummate optical skill of the Messrs. Alvan Clark, of Cambridge Port, in Massachusetts.

But though these were necessary conditions in Professor Asaph Hall's work, yet it would be absurd to attribute his success either to the locality of his workshop or to the perfection of his tools. A man's genius is best shown by the right use which he makes of his opportunities. Many faculties are required to make a skilful observer, and those faculties require careful training and long experience before they can be trusted to do valuable and reliable astronomical work. The practical astronomer is, indeed, an artist of a special kind. He must have cultivated delicacy and quickness of perception, he must have a nice manual dexterity, he must conduct his work with much forethought and tact. It must be all carefully organized and planned. He must have anticipated his difficulties, and decided how they shall be overcome or evaded. Unless he possess these qualities, and many more, he will not be a discoverer of the satellites of Mars, no matter how superb the telescope he is provided with, or how glorious the climate in which he is situated.

It was in the middle of August, 1877, when the planet was blazing in the glories of opposition, that Professor Hall discovered the satellites. Tiny objects they indeed were. Their feeble light was so faint that, to render them visible at all, the fiery planet itself had to be moved out of the field of view, or otherwise screened off. At first Professor Hall was greatly puzzled by the extraordinary behaviour of one of these little moons. It first appeared at one side of the planet, and then at the other, in a manner so incomprehensible that Professor Hall began to think there must be two or three bodies instead of a single one.

Nor was such a supposition unnatural. It was, indeed, the only alternative to an explanation which at first seemed wildly improbable. This latter supposition, which ultimately turned out to be the correct one, showed that the inner of the two moons accomplished a feat entirely without parallel in the solar system. It actually completed three revolutions around Mars in less time than Mars required for a single rotation on his own axis. To appreciate the significance of this statement, let us refer to the condition of our own earth-moon system. The moon requires about twenty-seven days to complete its circuit of our earth, so that the revolution of the moon is twenty-seven times as long as the rotation of the earth. In a similar way, though not always to the same extent, the periods of revolution of all the satellites that had been previously discovered were each much larger than the period of rotation of their primaries.

Contrary, however, to the invariable precedent exhibited in the case of every other satellite of our system, the inner satellite of Mars exhibits, to our astonishment, the spectacle of a little moon galloping round the planet three times for every single rotation that the planet itself accomplishes. The outer of the two Martial satellites follows the analogy of the other similar bodies in our system. Its period of revolution is, however, only about a day and a quarter, which is not much longer than the period of rotation of the planet.

The names of the two satellites were suggested by a passage in Homer, where Deimos and Phobos were summoned, as the attendants of Mars, to yoke his steeds, while he put on his armour. Deimos is the outer and more conspicuous of the two, Phobos is the inner and more interesting.

Immediately after Professor Hall's great discovery, the powerful telescopes all over the world were directed to Mars, and many observers were fortunate enough to obtain measurements of the position of the satellites, and thus to contribute to our knowledge of their movements.

One of the functions of the astronomer is to measure and to weigh the masses of the celestial bodies. Now, difficult as it may seem actually to weigh a mighty planet, yet in many cases the task is a comparatively simple one. It is true we do not seek to evaluate the actual mass of the planet in tons. We are at present only striving after a relative knowledge—a knowledge of the mass of the planet as compared with the mass of the earth or the sun. Our task is an easy one when we have to deal with planets attended by one or more satellites. It becomes a very difficult one when the planet has no satellite that can be observed.

Let me endeavour to give some explanation of the method we adopt when we seek to weigh a great planet—such, for example, as our earth against the sun. We shall suppose that the earth revolves around the sun in a nearly circular orbit, and that the moon revolves around the earth in an orbit nearly circular also. We may further suppose, with sufficient accuracy, that the distance between the earth and the sun is 400 times the distance between the earth and the moon. The celebrated law of Kepler tells us that if two satellites be revolving around the same primary, the squares of the periodic times will be proportional to the cubes of the mean distances. I must ask you, then, in order to conduct the calculation, to assume the existence of a fictitious satellite revolving around our earth at a distance which is 400 times as great as that of the moon at present. This would move much more slowly than the moon, and it would require a great many months indeed to complete one revolution. How many months are required can be discovered by Kepler's law just stated. As the moon goes round in one month, the fictitious moon would require a number of months, which is determined by first multiplying 400 by itself twice, that is by obtaining the number 400 × 400 × 400, and then taking the square root of it. We fortunately find that for this particular problem the actual nature of the work is materially facilitated. Each of the several factors, 400, is itself found by multiplying 20 by itself, or as we would say the square root of 400 is 20, hence the square root of the cube of 400 is found by merely multiplying 20 by itself twice over, and that gives us the answer 8,000. Hence we learn that if there were a fictitious moon revolving at a distance 400 times that of our present moon, its periodic time would be 8,000 of our present months.

We have now placed the problem in the following aspect. Our earth revolves around the sun in a year, or, for our present purpose, we may, with quite sufficient

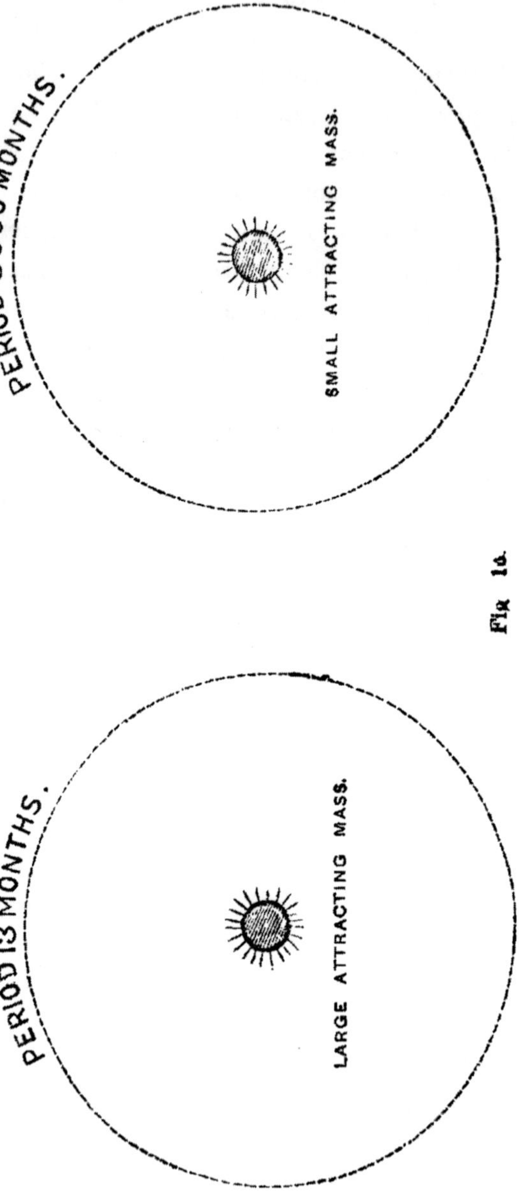
PERIOD 8000 MONTHS.
SMALL ATTRACTING MASS.
PERIOD 13 MONTHS.
LARGE ATTRACTING MASS.

Fig 14

accuracy, speak of the period as thirteen lunar months. We have, therefore, two systems to compare. In one of these the period of revolution is 8,000 months. In the other, the period of revolution is thirteen months. In each case the distance from the central body to the revolving body is the same. The first is, of course, the case of the earth and the fictitious moon, the second is the case of the sun and the earth. The advantage of this method of treatment is that we have by an artifice brought the two distances into equality, so that they need not be further considered.

Look now at the two figures exhibited on the previous page. They represent equal circles. In each case there is a great attracting body in the centre, while the revolving body describes the circumference of the circle. The circumstances, it will be seen, are quite similar, except that there is a marked difference between the periods of the two revolutions. To what can this difference be due? As the distances are the same, the discrepancy in the periodic times can be only attributed to the difference in masses between the central bodies. We can show that the mass or size of the revolving body has no appreciable influence in the matter. At a specified distance from its primary, a satellite will revolve in substantially the same time, whether its mass be only an ounce or a million of tons. Start any object around our earth with the right velocity and at the right distance, and it will perform the circuit in 8,000 months. We have a quite analogous phenomenon on our earth. A heavy body and a light body will fall to the ground in the same time. Take a bullet in one hand and a cork in the other, drop them at the same instant, and you will find that they reach the ground at the same moment. It is true that with very light bodies there is some difference, but this is caused by the resistance of the air. There is no resistance to the motion of satellites in the way we are now considering. It is therefore plain that the masses of the satellites can in no degree account for the huge disparity between the periods of their revolutions. Our search has now become greatly narrowed, for the only remaining point of difference between the two systems is found in the masses of the primaries. To this, therefore, we must look for an originating cause of the differences of the periods of revolution of the two satellites. If the two central masses had been equal, there can be no doubt that the two periodic times would also have been the same. The value of this reasoning consists in the deduction which it enables us to make. We know the periodic times, and from that knowledge we are enabled to calculate the masses of the two central bodies, by which the satellites that were revolving in those periodic times have been controlled.

This point is of such fundamental importance in astronomy, that I feel I must pursue it a little further, so as to enable us actually to solve the majestic problem of weighing our earth against the sun.

In the first place, it can be shown that the greater the mass of the sun, the greater must be the rapidity with which the planet revolves, in order to sustain its position in a circular orbit at a specified distance. The planet would, if unacted upon by any force, pursue a rectilinear path and move on continuously with an unaltered velocity. The presence of a central force constantly compels the planet to swerve from a rectilinear path, and thus constrains it to move in a circular orbit. The more rapid the motion, the more intense must be the force which is continually drawing the planet aside from the rectilinear path, and consequently, the greater must be the mass of the central sun by which the attraction is produced. The proportion is, however, not a very simple one. If the mass of the sun be doubled, the speed of the planet will not be increased in the same proportion. The true law is that the mass of the central attracting body will be proportional to the square of the velocity, or inversely proportional to the square of the periodic time. Hence it follows that if the mass of the central sun be increased fourfold, the speed of the satellite will be doubled, or what comes to the same thing, the periodic time of the satellite will be reduced to one-half.

Returning now to our figure. We have seen that the two bodies revolve in periods of 8,000 months and thirteen months respectively; that their distances from the primaries are equal; and from these data it is required to conclude the relative masses of these primaries. One of these numbers is about 615 times the other. Hence we have to determine the relative masses of two central attracting bodies, such that the relative periodic times of their planets at equal distances shall be 615. We have shown that the masses of the central bodies must be inversely proportional to the squares of the periodic times; hence we learn that the more rapidly moving of these two bodies must be controlled by a central force which is 615 × 615 times greater than that necessary for the slower motion. We have used approximate numbers in making this computation, so that the result thus obtained is rather in excess of what would have been the result if we had retained several small elements in the calculation which we have thought it convenient to discard in such an elementary sketch. The final result, as obtained by the most trustworthy methods, is that it would take 326,800 earths, all rolled into one, to form a mass as ponderous as the sun.

It will thus be seen from this illustration, that the observation of satellites in attendance upon a planet enables us to weigh that planet. Hence we see that the discovery of the satellites of Mars and the observation of their periods, conducted us to an accurate knowledge of the mass of the ruddy planet himself. I say an accurate knowledge, for it must not be presumed that we did not know something of the weight of this planet before. The different departments of astronomy are so closely interwoven, that the influence of each planet is often felt under circumstances that would hardly be credited by one who had not the means of following out the complete details of the subject. Our earth, in pursuing its annual progress round the sun, is, of course, mainly guided by the all-compelling and powerful attraction of the great central luminary. But every planet also draws the earth in some degree. The capacity of the planet to make the earth swerve to the side of its path is dependent on the mass of the planet. If the planet be great, its influence will be correspondingly large. By incessant observations of the sun, astronomers have learned, with the utmost minuteness of detail, the nature of the path which the earth follows. They are actually able to disentangle the marvellous complexities of its motion, and to assign to each of the causes of disturbance its due share of responsibility.

It thus comes to pass that we learn how much Mars affects the path of the earth, and hence we are able to discover the mass of the planet itself. Is not this a marvellously recondite inquiry? Yet it shows the perfection to which astronomy, both theoretical and practical, has in fact advanced, when I have to add, in conclusion, that the mass of the planet Mars, discovered by this extremely delicate and elaborate process, was found to be practically coincident with the accurate value speedily and surely proved when once the satellites had become known.

A curious literary point was soon remarked in connection with the satellites of Mars. We should not naturally turn to "Gulliver's Travels" as an authentic manual of astronomy, yet, strange to say, in that remarkable work the astronomers, in the flying Island of Laputa are found to have already anticipated Professor Hall. These people, we are assured, "are very bad reasoners, and vehemently given to opposition, unless when they happen to be of the right opinion, which is seldom the case." Nevertheless, we learn that they have "discovered two lesser stars or satellites, which revolve about Mars, whereof the innermost is distant from the centre of the primary planet exactly three of his diameters, and the outermost five. The former revolves in the space of ten hours, and the latter in twenty-one and a half." This was certainly a marvellous anticipation of the actual facts of the case. The astonishing feature is that the periodic time attributed by Swift to the interior planet, should have been so near correct.

CHAPTER XIII.

THE GREATEST PLANET.

MARS is, as we have seen, much smaller than the earth. We now turn to a planet which is very much greater—which is, in fact, the greatest of all planets—the majestic globe of Jupiter. This superb world far exceeds in bulk any other body in our system, the sun alone excepted. Nay, if all the other planets could be welded into one, their united mass would fall short both in bulk and in weight of the stupendous mass of Jupiter. Our earth has a diameter not one-tenth part that of Jupiter, and the diameter of Jupiter is more than twenty times as great as the diameter of Mars. The path in which the giant planet pursues his stately course is shown in Figure 16, while the inner of the two circles is the orbit of the earth, both drawn to scale. The actual diameter of Jupiter's orbit is about five times that of the earth. It should, however, be noticed that though these orbits are nearly circular, and though I often find it convenient to speak of them as actual circles, yet that when very careful measures are made, they are found to be ellipses instead of circles. Thus, if we take the earth's distance from the sun as 100, the distance of Jupiter from the same centre would be

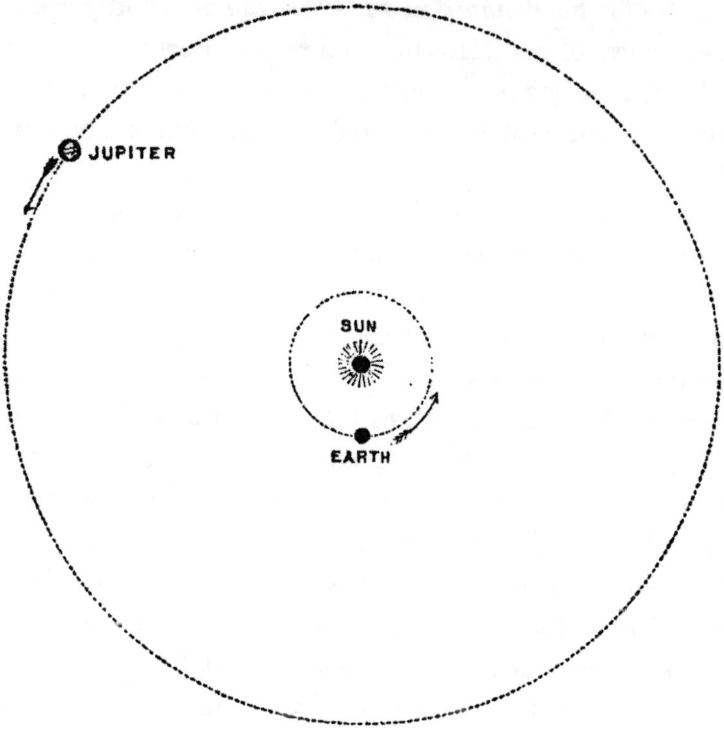

Fig. 16.—Orbits of Jupiter and the Earth.

sometimes as much as 545 and sometimes as low as 495. Under the most favourable combination of circumstances we are still left at an inconveniently great distance from Jupiter when we wish to study his surface. He will still be about four times as far from us as we are from the sun. Hence it follows that in our telescopic scrutiny of the great planet it is only objects of colossal proportions on his globe that can be at all visible. In this respect we are placed much more disadvantageously with regard to Jupiter than with regard to Mars, though, on the other hand, the much greater size of Jupiter more than compensates for his distance in so far as the size and general effectiveness of his telescopic picture is concerned.

A view showing the relative dimensions of the chief planets in our system compared with the sun is given in Fig. 17.

Jupiter is obviously flattened at the poles and protuberant at the equator. Our earth is also shaped in a similar fashion, but the extent of the protuberance on the earth is much less than that on Jupiter. Nor is it difficult to explain the reason of this peculiarity of shape, and of the excessive degree in which Jupiter is affected by it. We have already seen that Mars revolves on its axis, as does our earth, and we might probably assert that rotation of this kind was a universal attribute of celestial bodies—at all events, Jupiter possesses it in a very marked degree. Though our little globe—for little it must be regarded beside Jupiter—takes 24 hours to go round, yet Jupiter accomplishes his complete spin in less than half as much—in fact, in 9 hrs. 55½ mins.

Owing to the rapidity of Jupiter's rotation and to the immense size of the planet, the actual speed of the surface of the body must be enormously great. A point on the equator of Jupiter moves about twenty-seven times as fast as a point on our equator. The protuberance at the equator of the great planet is to be ascribed to this fact. As the body is revolving so rapidly, the yielding materials of which it is made accommodate themselves to the shape which nature demands, and the characteristic aspect of the planet is the result.

We have seen that Mars is a body, in some respects, at all events, resembling or analogous to our earth. In fact, as Herschel wrote years ago, the resemblance between the earth and Mars appeared to be the most striking analogy in the whole solar system. But a very brief examination of Jupiter shows that we have here a body which, while still a planet, is quite unlike our earth, and still more

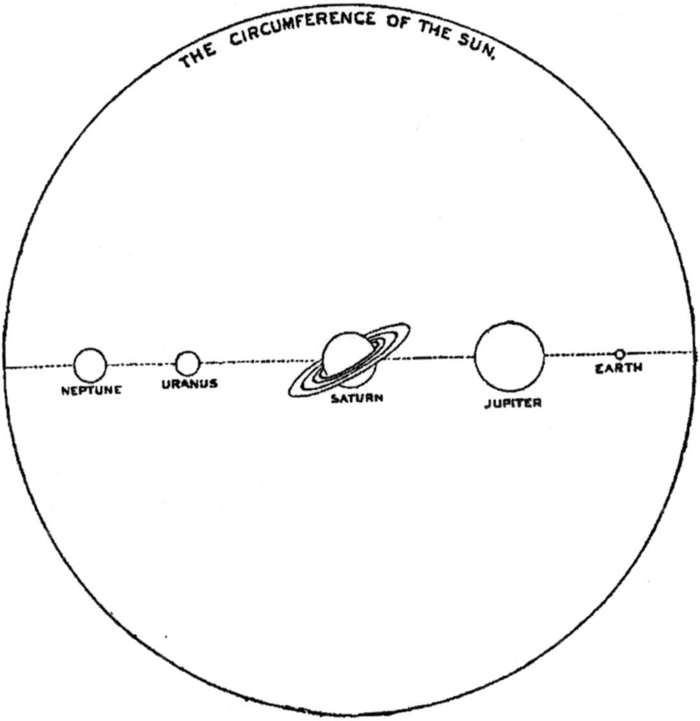

Fig. 17.—Comparative Sizes of the Sun and the Planets

unlike Mars. It becomes, therefore, of special interest to study Jupiter, as it affords an instructive chapter in planetary history.

The general aspect of the great planet is fortunately within the compass of moderate telescopic power. It has been scrutinized with unintermitting zeal since first instruments have been directed to the sky. Of recent years the powers of great instruments have been devoted to the study of Jupiter, and consequently we have at our disposal an ample body of facts and an extensive collection of drawings and measurements.

The appearance of the planet in a telescope of any reasonable pretensions generally shows several markings on his surface (see Fig. 18). Especially noticeable under ordinary circumstances are a pair of belts parallel to the planet's equator, one to the north and the other to the south. These features are well represented in the cut, which delineates a series of telescopic appearances of the planet. As we watch the globe from hour to hour, various changes in its appearance force themselves on our notice. No doubt these are partly to be accounted for by the rotation of the planet on its axis. Certain features gradually pass away into invisibility on one side, while new features come in on the other. Even the actual appearance of them at the centre of the disc is more or less affected by the varying degrees of foreshortening under which they are exposed. But after all allowance has been made for such mere apparent changes, it is speedily seen by the attentive observer that the actual marks themselves are not permanent, that they are waxing and waning, now entirely disappearing, while ever and anon fresh features break forth. Even the two belts themselves are not constant; the uniformity of the belts is often interrupted, while their margins undergo considerable changes. Sometimes, indeed, the belts are not to be discerned at all, and sometimes, instead of merely a pair of belts, the globe reveals several. The longer the surface of Jupiter becomes studied, the more confident will the observer become that he is not looking at any solid objects—he is looking at a vast mass of clouds by which the entire globe of Jupiter is surrounded. He will see that these clouds are so thick and so dense that even his greatest telescope is never able

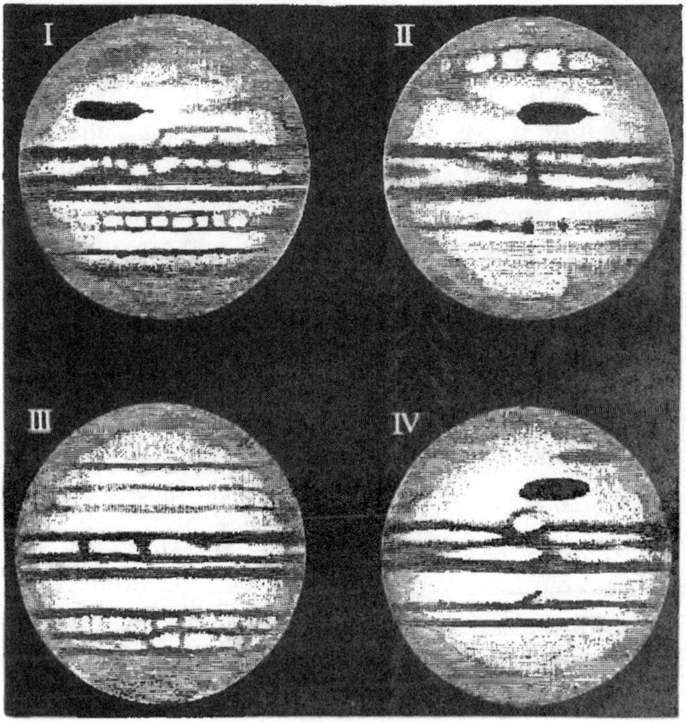

Fig. 18.—Views of Jupiter.

to pierce down through them and obtain a glimpse of the solid interior of the globe. Indeed, it seems very doubtful whether the words "solid interior" can be rightly used with regard to this planet.

Although we do not seem to see anything which can be regarded as solid on Jupiter, yet we can hardly draw the inference that it possesses nothing of a permanent character on its surface. It is true that we search in vain on the great planet for anything so definite as the Kaiser Sea, or one or two other objects that might be mentioned on Mars. But there is at least one mark on Jupiter which has been continuously observed for several years, and is known as the great red spot on Jupiter. In 1879 it had attained remarkable distinctness and such permanence that, though it has undergone no infrequent changes in brightness and appearance, it is a feature on the planet at the present time. A remarkable phenomenon in connection with the proof of the absence of anything like rigidity on the surface of Jupiter is strikingly brought out by the behaviour of the red spot and of a white spot in its vicinity. The rotation of the red spot, as computed in the *Observatory* for 1886, was accomplished in 9 hrs. 55 mins. 39 secs., while that of the white spot was 9 hrs. 50 mins. 10 secs. Thus it follows that the red spot took 5½ minutes longer to complete its circuit of the planet than was required for the white one. If the globe of Jupiter were really rigid, and if the spots were permanent objects on that globe, then, of course, the period of rotation concluded from either spot must be the same as that concluded from the other, and both must be equal to that of the rotation of the planet on its axis. In fact, to suppose that there could be any difference would be similar to saying that the day which is twenty-four hours long in London was five minutes less than twenty-four hours in Paris. It is obvious, therefore, when we find the objects on Jupiter differing by five minutes in the periods they give for the rotation, that one or both of these objects must have some proper motion on its own account, and can in no case be structurally a part of the rigid globe of the planet. In the "Companion to the Observatory" for 1886 tables will be found which show the times at which both the red spot and the white spot were to be expected during that year on the central meridian of Jupiter. Considering that these objects are of such an unstable material, we can hardly be surprised at the editor's complaint that the motion of the white spot has appeared of late to be irregular.

It has sometimes been thought that the great red spot may be a protuberance from the partially solid interior of the planet, which has been forced up through the overlying stratum of clouds, and thus brought into visibility. So long as it lasts it will provide us with a tolerably definite point on Jupiter from which longitudes can be measured, and thus take the place which Dawes' forked bay provides for us on Mars.

There is another instructive line of reasoning by which we can demonstrate that the Jupiter which we see is certainly not to be regarded as a solid or rigid body. Its bulk is so enormous that it is fully 1,200 times as big as our earth. So much for the *measurement* of the giant planet; now as to its *weight*. We have already explained in connection with the satellites of Mars how it is feasible, by observations of the satellites, to discover the mass of the planet to which those satellites are appended. In the application of this method to the determination of the mass of Jupiter we have a choice of no fewer than four fine satellites from which to make the observations. The mass of Jupiter can also be obtained by other methods of inquiry, so that it can be regarded as one of the most accurately known elements of our solar system. To express the result in the form best adapted for our present line of reasoning we may say that the mass of Jupiter is 310 times as great as the mass of the earth.

Truly Jupiter is a noble globe. If we imagine a stupendous pair of weighing scales constructed, and that Jupiter was placed in one pan, we should find that it would require 310 globes, each as ponderous as our earth, to be placed in the other pan before the beam began to turn. Yet while we are impressed with the gigantic mass of Jupiter, we recall the fact that the planet is 1,200 times as large, and then we are driven to inquire why it is that though Jupiter is 1,200 times as big as our earth it is only 310 times as heavy.

It is quite obvious that Jupiter must be a world of a kind very different indeed from that on which we stand. Our world is made up of rocks and minerals, largely also of iron, and all these materials together produce a globe of very high density, between five and six times the weight of a globe of water of equal dimensions. But the case with respect to Jupiter is widely different. If we take the earth as a standard of comparison, we see that as Jupiter exceeds us in bulk 1,200-fold, he should also be about 1,200 times as heavy, if the materials of his constitution were similar to and in the same state as those on the earth. But he only weighs about a quarter as much as this hypothesis would require. It therefore follows that Jupiter cannot be organized on anything like the same plan as our globe. His average density is only one-fourth as much as ours. Jupiter only weighs about once and a quarter as much as a globe of water the same size. This is quite incompatible with the supposition that his bulk is largely made up of materials at all resembling in density the solid substances on the earth. The true explanation must no doubt be that the mighty planet is, on his exterior at all events, largely composed of great oceans of clouds and vapours of density and thickness; that these vast clouds weigh but little in comparison with their bulk; and that thus the apparent size of Jupiter is swollen to dimensions greatly exceeding those to which he would retire if the materials now in vapour were condensed into more liquid or solid forms.

When we ponder on the inflated size of Jupiter, and when we apply to his globe the laws of heat, of gases, and of vapours, which we have learned from experiments, we are conducted to a very important discovery. There is only one method of accounting for this stupendous mass of impenetrable clouds which so persistently envelop the planet. Clouds cannot exist except there be heat to produce the requisite vapours. If the heat be absent, the clouds will resume the liquid state. We are therefore forced to the conclusion that the vast mass of clouds enveloping the great planet can only be sustained by the supposition that there must be some great source of heat available on Jupiter. It is natural to inquire whence this heat can be derived. Let us first compare or contrast the condition of Jupiter with that of our own earth.

We have no doubt a liberal supply of clouds supported in our atmosphere. But our clouds are neither so copious nor so continuously impenetrable as those on Jupiter. An astronomer on the latter planet, who gazed at us through a telescope of sufficient power, would no doubt generally find a large part of our globe obscured by suspended masses of vapour. He would also certainly see some traces of those belts of cloud, parallel to the equator, which mark the trade wind zones. And he would be struck with the instability and fickle character of the cloudy screen which in the course of a few hours would reveal or obscure whole kingdoms or oceans. The observations of the clouds alone would make the telescopic scrutiny of our world from some distant world a singularly interesting and instructive research. There are perhaps some regions on the globe which would be almost continuously quite free from cloud, and these the Jovian astronomer could draw without any special choice of opportunities. But to trace the majority of the outlines of the continents and the oceans would be an arduous, if even a possible, task; at the least it would require the patient astronomer to wait until openings in the clouds enabled the outlines of the coasts to be clearly apprehended. But on Jupiter the clouds are so massive, that no amount of patience ever enables us to see through them; the chance is never given to us. We are therefore compelled to suppose that the heat by which the vapours to form clouds are manufactured, must be much more abundant and intense than it is on our globe. The heat that provides moisture for our atmosphere is obtained from the sun. The warm rays beating down on our vast oceans create great volumes of water vapour, which ascend thousands of feet, and are then borne by winds to other less genial climes, where chills reduce the transparent water vapour to that opaque material of visible steam or cloud. For an explanation of all terrestrial clouds, we require no other heat than that which the sun dispenses so liberally and unceasingly.

In endeavouring to understand the clouds of Jupiter, the first attempt which we naturally make is to explain their origin in a manner similar to that of the clouds on the earth. Jupiter revolves around the sun as this world does, and like this world Jupiter is also illuminated by the sun and warmed by him. Can it not therefore be that the sunbeams on Jupiter generate the vast cloudy covering just as they do here?

This is a point on which a simple calculation will throw much light. The average distance of the great planet from the sun is $5\frac{1}{5}$ times as great as the distance of the earth. It can easily be shown that the intensity of the heat received from any source decreases as the distance of the source increases. The rate of decrease is indeed a rapid one. If the distance be doubled, the supply of heat is not alone halved, it is reduced to one-fourth of its original intensity. In fact, we may express the law generally in that form in which nature loves to work, that the intensity of the heat received from a source varies as the inverse square of the distance. It therefore follows that to compare the sun heat received on Jupiter with the sun heat received on the earth, we must square the number $5\frac{1}{5}$; that is, multiply it by itself. The result is very close to 27, and hence we learn the significant fact that the intensity of sun heat on Jupiter is only one twenty-seventh part of that which is received on the earth.

We cannot believe that the sun's rays, enfeebled to a twenty-seventh part of the intensity in which we know them, can possibly be adequate to evaporate enough fluid on Jupiter to give rise to that vast mass of clouds which surrounds him. More clouds require for their explanation a larger supply of heat than that on the earth. Yet the sun only conveys to the great planet less than four per cent. of the heat on the same area that he sends to us. There is only one interpretation to be put on these facts. We must admit that the sun's heat is utterly inadequate to the accomplishment of the work in progress on Jupiter, and hence we must look to the presence of some other source of heat.

Whence can Jupiter derive heat if not from the sun? Assuredly there is no other body in the universe which can radiate even the millionth part of what he gets from the sun. The stars are no doubt hot enough, but they are so enormously distant that the influence of their heat is evanescent, and need not for a moment be considered. The other planets and their satellites can of course render no assistance. Like Jupiter himself, they are recipients of heat from the sun in varying degrees, according to their distance. The only heat they can dispense will be of the very feeblest, and be quite imperceptible. It is certainly true that Jupiter cannot receive heat from any external body to any appreciable extent, except from the sun, and yet the utmost that the sun can do is quite inadequate to account for the warmth of the great planet.

At first it might be thought that we had arrived at a paradox, but this is not really so. There is a most rational explanation of the phenomenon entirely consistent with all the facts.

There are many reasons for knowing that the different

bodies of our solar system were originally much hotter than they are at present; they have all been steadily cooling, and the process has been going on for uncounted ages. The small bodies have cooled more rapidly than the large ones. Thus the moon, which is one of the smallest of the bodies in our system, appears to have parted with almost all its heat. The sun, at the other extreme, on account of his gigantic dimensions, amounting as they do to more than a thousand times the size of Jupiter, which is itself larger than all the rest of our system together, is large enough to have retained so much heat that he still glows with excessive fervour.

Between the sun and the moon as the extreme limits of size, may be ranked the other bodies of the system. We find that many of the different bodies show more heat or less heat, according to their size. Thus, our earth being so much larger than the moon, and so much smaller than the sun, might be expected to have still retained some of its heat, though the glowing stage in the progress of cooling has long since been passed; and this is what we do actually find. Our globe shows many indications of a high interior temperature. We have the well-known phenomena of volcanoes, and of hot springs, to show us that there are stores of heat beneath our feet, and our belief in internal heat is confirmed by the gradual increase of temperature that is found in every mine, the deeper it penetrates into the earth.

Jupiter, being 1,200 times as big as the earth, has not yet cooled to the same extent. It still retains vast stores of internal heat, which are sufficient to preserve in the vaporous form the oceans that shall one day roll upon its surface. No longer need the dense clouds of the giant planet be a mystery; they are merely an indication of a certain stage in the process of cooling, through which Jupiter, like every other globe in our system, has to pass. They are of interest and instruction to us. In the present appearance of Jupiter, we may see what our earth was once in those early days ere it had cooled to such an extent that the oceans passed from the vaporous to the fluid form in which we now find them.

Such studies convey to our minds an imposing idea of the magnificence of the universe. We have only been speaking of a few of the bodies belonging to our own system, and such systems are spread in countless myriads through space. They raise in us a majestic conception of the extent and splendour of that universe we see, which must itself be only an inconceivably small fraction of the entire extent of the universe, of which the greater part lies for ever beyond our view.

CHAPTER XIV

THE NAMES OF THE PLANETS.

I PROPOSE in this chapter to discuss some points which seem specially interesting with respect to the names of the celestial bodies. The study of the heavens in bygone days possessed an importance of a wholly different kind from that which we now attribute to it. It was not then supposed that among the stars there could be worlds comparable in importance with our globe. In the belief of the ancients our earth was the central body of the universe. The sun, moon, and stars were merely regarded as objects placed in the heavens for the purpose of ministering to human wants. The relations of the sun and moon to the inhabitants of the earth were, of course, obvious, but the other bodies also had their terrestrial influences which were to be discovered by occult science. Accordingly a system of astrology was created for the purpose of interpreting the movement of the stars.

It is, perhaps, hardly necessary to say that we now only regard these notions of the old astrologers as curiosities. We remember that our earth occupies but an insignificant portion of space, and that the stars and planets are generally globes far greater than that on which we dwell. The movements of the heavenly bodies are no longer believed to contain indications of human affairs. We do not cast the horoscope, nor do we now think that the career of a man is decided by the configuration of the planets at the moment he happened to be born. It is, however, interesting to note the different ways in which traces of the old astrological beliefs still survive among us. In former days, when any great undertaking was in contemplation, the stars were consulted to know if the auspices were favourable. Though we do not at the present day think this necessary, yet we do at least admit that we ought carefully to consider the prospects of the enterprise. Astrology has provided us with the word, for *consider* is derived from the Latin word *sidus*, a star, and signifies literally that we consult the stars. Should the undertaking not turn out fortunately, we often describe it as *ill-starred;* and here we recognise that a good star has not favoured our efforts, but that they have been under the malign influence of an evil one. When a serious misfortune occurs we may sometimes speak of it as a *disaster*. This is a word derived from the Greek, and signifies that our star has been unfavourable. Need I add that it is the same Greek root that gives us the first half of the word astronomy?

Remembering the importance of the stars to the ancient astrologers, it is not unnatural that they watched them with the closest attention. They observed that the sun and the moon changed their places on the heavens, so that these bodies were fitly described as "wanderers." It seems to have been known from the remotest antiquity that there were also some starlike objects which moved about. Of these the earliest to be observed was, doubtless, the planet Venus. Its brilliancy, as the evening star or the morning star, seems to have attracted attention from all intelligent nations of which we have any record. As Venus continually changed its place, and so far resembled the sun and the moon, the astrologers credited this planet with a significant intervention in terrestrial matters. But there were other planets also to be discerned by those who carefully watched the sky. Three bright objects, Jupiter, Saturn, and Mars, showed by their movements that they were bodies wholly different from ordinary stars. The list of planets known to the ancients was completed by the discovery of Mercury. It is impossible to reflect on this achievement without admiring the acuteness of observation which disclosed the nature of this rarely seen object, and identified its successive appearances. Mercury seems to have been discovered independently by two or three nations at dates antecedent to those of exact history. It will thus be seen that there were in all five planets, namely, Jupiter, Saturn, Venus, Mars, and Mercury. If to these we add the sun and the moon we have the total seven "wanderers" with which the astrologers used to conduct their mystic operations.

There is no doubt that the ancient significance of the number seven is attributable to the fact that there were believed to be neither more nor less than seven of these bodies. The most striking illustration that we can give of the survival of astrological notions is found in the connection between the names of the seven days of the week and the names of the seven wanderers. In fact, it appears that the use of a week of seven days has been confined to those races who had recognised these seven planets. The Incas of Peru seem to have detected no other planet than Venus, and their week had nine days, to accord, apparently, with one-third of the duration of the moon's revolution around the earth. The Aztecs of Mexico, who were also in ignorance of the planets, Venus alone excepted, employed a week of thirteen days.

Among the ancient nations of the old world, not only the number of the days in the week, but the names of those days, were associated with the names of the seven wanderers to which they respectively corresponded. The ancient astronomers, though ignorant of the true relations of the celestial bodies, had yet been enabled to arrange the wanderers in their true order of distance from the earth, at least in so far as it is possible to place bodies in such an order when their distances are incessantly changing. The dimness of Saturn and the slowness of his movements justified them in regarding him as the most remote of the seven. Next came Jupiter, and then came Mars. It is to be remembered that, according to the ancients, the sun was classified as a wanderer with the bodies we now speak of as planets. His distance was less than that of Mars and greater than that of Venus. Mercury was nearer to us than Venus, while the moon was the nearest body of all to the earth. We thus write the seven wanderers, in order of their distances, as follows—Saturn, Jupiter, Mars, Sun, Venus, Mercury, Moon. This is not, however, the order in which these planets stand when they represent the seven days of the week. The succession of the week days is arrived at in the way we shall now mention.

In ancient times the day and night together were divided, as at present, into twenty-four hours. Each one of these hours was consecrated to one of the planets. The order in which the hours were appropriated to the different wanderers was simply the order of their distances, and each day bore the name of the wanderer to which its first hour was devoted. As a beginning the first hour is consecrated to the most distant object, Saturn, and accordingly the corresponding day is Saturn-day, or Saturday; the second hour belongs to Jupiter, the third to Mars, the fourth to the Sun, the fifth to Venus, the sixth to Mercury, and the seventh to the Moon. Then the eighth hour begins with Saturn again, the ninth with Jupiter, and so on until after twenty-one hours the list of the wanderers has been repeated three times over. The twenty-second hour begins, of course, with Saturn again, the twenty-third belongs to Jupiter, the twenty-fourth to Mars, and thus the whole twenty-four hours of Saturday are complete. The twenty-fifth hour, which is the first hour of the next day, falls to the wanderer next to Mars, that is to the Sun. The first hour of the day next after Saturday is accordingly consecrated to the Sun, and as the name of each day is derived from that of the planet presiding over its first hour it follows that the name of the day following Saturday is to be the Day of the Sun, that is, of course, Sunday. You may follow the same calculation throughout.

The following is an equivalent but shorter process. Write around a circle the names of the seven wanderers in the order of their distances, and then read them by beginning with Saturn, and skipping two each time. They will come into the following order:—Saturn, Sun, Moon, Mars, Mercury, Jupiter, Venus, and then Saturn again. Now we have reached the precise order of the days in the week. The meaning of Saturday and Sunday we have already explained, Monday is Moonday, and the French Lundi means also the Day of the Moon. Tuesday is connected with Mars; in fact, the French word Mardi, meaning Tuesday, is obviously Mars' Day. Wednesday, or Mercredi in French, is Mercury Day. Thursday is derived from Thor, a deity analogous to Jupiter. Friday is shown to be the day of Venus. Thus not only the seven days of the week, but the very names of the days themselves are directly related to the names of the seven planets.

It is a question of much interest as to why the names of the heathen deities should have been assigned to the planets. How comes it, for instance, that the God Jupiter should have given a name to the great planet? The question is not without some difficulty, but the origin of it appears to be as follows. There are at the present day—and doubtless ever have been—races who worshipped the sun as a deity. Considering that the sun was only one of the seven wanderers, it was not unnatural that devotional homage should also have been rendered to the other similar bodies. This was all the more natural because the movements of these bodies were believed to be intimately associated with human affairs. That globe which we now style the planet Jupiter was itself regarded as a deity, and as such was worshipped. A more refined creed afterwards separated the intangible deity from the actual globe, which thus came to be regarded merely as a symbol. The name, however, by which the planet was designated was borne both by the material body and by the deity of which that body was an emblem.

In modern days the naming of planets is quite a familiar operation. Every now and then a new planet is discovered, and it is the privilege of the discoverer to assign to the new object a name which other astronomers shall recognise. At least this is generally the case, but not invariably; for when William Herschel immortalized himself by discovering the planet now called Uranus, he proposed to name it the Georgium Sidus in honour of King George the Third. As this was the first planet ever found in addition to the five bodies of this kind which had been known from all antiquity, a wonderful interest was aroused among astronomers all over the world; but the old planets had borne the old classical names, and it was thought, especially by Continental astronomers, that it would be a little incongruous to bring the name of George the Third into the same category as the heathen divinities. Accordingly they set aside the wishes of the discoverer, and established the precedent which has since been generally followed, of choosing names for the newly discovered planets from classical mythology. Though the number of the planets is now more than 300, the resources of ancient literature seem not yet to give signs of exhaustion. Let Hebe and Hecuba, Diana and Sappho, which I select at random from the list of minor planets, serve as modern examples of how the heavenly bodies are named.

CHAPTER XV.

A FALLING STAR.

Every one who has occasionally taken a nocturnal walk in the open country will probably have seen what is called "a shooting star." Perhaps I might rather say that unless the observer be very inattentive he will have noticed dozens, or scores, or hundreds of these objects, either bright or faint, with long streaks or with short.

For the due exhibition of a shooting star, that part of the sky where it is displayed should, of course, be free from cloud, and the silvery streak will seem all the more vivid if the moon be absent. No telescope is needed. This is, indeed, the one branch of astronomical observation in which the unaided eye can advantageously dispense with optical assistance.

Our present knowledge as to the natural history of the shooting stars has been mainly acquired during the last hundred years. The first important step in the comprehension of these bodies was to recognise that the brilliant flash of light was caused by some object which came from without and plunged into our air. This was known at the end of the last century, largely by the labours of the philosopher Chladni in 1794. But even his sagacity did not prevent him from making some serious mistakes about the nature of shooting stars. It has been reserved for the present generation to organize a multitude of facts into a connected whole, and thus contribute a very interesting chapter to modern astronomy.

Could an ordinary shooting star tell us its actual history, the narrative would run somewhat as follows :—

"I was a small bit of material, chiefly, if not entirely, composed of substances which are formed from the same chemical elements as those you find on the earth. Not improbably I may have had some iron in my constitution, and also sodium and carbon, to mention only a few of the most familiar elements. I only weighed an ounce or two, perhaps more, perhaps less—but you could probably have held me in your closed hand, or put me into your waistcoat pocket. You would have described me as a sort of small stone, yet I think you would have added that I was very unlike the ordinary stones with which you were familiar. I have led a life of the most extraordinary activity; I have never known what it was to stay still; I have been ever on the move. Through the solitudes of space I have dashed along with a speed which you can hardly conceive. Compare my ordinary motion with your most rapid railway trains, place me in London beside the Scotch express to race to Edinburgh; my journey will be done ere the best locomotive ever built could have drawn the train out of the station. Pit me against your rifle bullets, against the shots from your one hundred-ton guns; before the missile from the mightiest piece of ordnance ever fired shall have gone ten yards I have gone 1,000 yards. I do not assert that my speed has been invariable—sometimes it has been faster, sometimes it has been slower; but I have generally done my million miles a day at the very least. Such has been my career, not for hours or days, but for years and for centuries, probably for untold ages. And the grand catastrophe in which I vanished has been befitting to a life of such transcendent excitement and activity; I have perished instantly, and in a streak of splendour. In the course of my immemorial wanderings I have occasionally passed near some of the great bodies in the heavens; I have also not improbably in former years hurried by that globe on which you live. On those occasions you never saw me, you never could have seen me, not even if you had used the mightiest telescope that has ever been directed to the heavens. But too close an approach to your globe was at last the occasion of my fall. You must remember that you live on the earth buried beneath a great ocean of air. Viewed from outside space your earth is seen to be a great ball, everywhere swathed with this thick coating of air. Beyond the appreciable limits of the air stretches the open space, and there it is that my prodigious journeys have been performed. Out there we have a freedom to move of which you who live in a dense atmosphere have no conception. Whenever you attempt to produce rapid motion on the earth, the resistance of your air largely detracts from the velocity that would be otherwise attainable. Your quick trains are impeded by air, your artillery ranges are shortened by it. Movements like mine would be impossible in air like yours.

"And this air it is which has ultimately compassed my destruction. So long as I merely passed near your earth, but kept clear of that deadly net which you have spread, in the shape of your atmosphere, to entrap the shooting stars, all went well with me. I felt the ponderous mass of the earth, and I swerved a little in compliance with its attraction; but my supreme velocity preserved me, and I hurried past unscathed. I had many narrow escapes from capture during the lapse of those countless ages in which I have been wandering through space. But at last I approached once too often to the earth. On this fatal occasion my course led me to graze your globe so closely that I could not get by without traversing the higher parts of the atmosphere. Accordingly, a frightful catastrophe immediately occurred. Not to you; it did you no harm; indeed, quite the contrary. My dissolution gave you a pleasing and instructive exhibition. It was then, for the first time, that you were permitted to see me, and you called me a shooting star or a meteor.

"You are quite familiar with the disasters associated with the word collision. Some of the most awful accidents you have ever heard of arose from the collision of two railway trains on land or of two ships in the ocean. You are thus able to realise the frightful consequences of a collision between two heavy bodies. But in the collision which annihilated me I did not impinge against any other heavy body. I only struck the upper and extremely rare layers of your atmosphere. I was, however, moving with a speed so terrific that the impulse to which I was exposed when I passed from empty space even into thin air was sufficient for my total disruption.

"Had the speed with which I entered your atmosphere been more moderate—had it been, for instance, not greater than that of a rifle bullet, or even only four or five times as fast, this plunge would not have been fatal to me. I could have pierced through with comparative safety, and then have tumbled down in my original form on the ground. Indeed, on rare occasions something of this kind does actually happen. Perhaps it is fortunate for you dwellers on the earth that we shooting stars do generally become dissipated in the upper air. Were it not so, the many thousands of us which would be daily pelting down on your earth would introduce a new source of anxiety into your lives. Fortunately for you, we dart in at a speed of some twenty miles or more a second. Unfortunately for us, we learn that it is the 'pace which kills.'

"When from the freedom of open space I darted into the atmosphere, I rubbed past every particle of air which I touched in my impetuous flight, and in doing so I experienced the usual consequence of friction—I was warmed by the operation. If you rub a button on a board it will become warm. If you rub two pieces of wood together you can warm them, and you could even produce fire if you possessed the cunning skill of some people whom you are accustomed to speak of as savages. Nor need you be surprised to find that I was warmed by merely rubbing against air. If you visit a rifle range and pick up a fragment of a bullet which has just struck the target you will find it warm; you will even find it so hot that you will generally drop it. Now whence came this heat? The bullet was certainly cold ere the trigger was pulled.

No doubt there is some heat developed by the combustion of the gunpowder, but the bullet cannot be much warmed thereby; it is, indeed, protected from the immediate effect of the heat of the powder by the wad. The bullet is partly warmed by the friction of rubbing against the barrel of the rifle, but doubtless it also receives some heat by the friction of the air and some from the consequence of its percussion against the target. You need not, then, wonder how it is that when I am checked by your atmosphere I, too, am heated.

"Remember that I move a hundred times as swiftly as your rifle bullet, and that the heat developed in the checking of the motion of a body increases enormously when the velocity of the body increases. Your mathematicians can calculate how much. They tell you that the amount of heat potentially contained in a moving body varies as the square of the velocity. To give an illustration of what this means, suppose that two rifles were fired at a target, and that the sizes of the bullets and the ranges were the same, but that the charge in one of the rifles was such that its bullet had twice the initial velocity of the other. Then the mathematician will say that the heat developed during the flight of the rapid bullet might be not alone twice but even four times as great as that developed in the slower bullet. If we could fire two bullets one of which had three times the speed of the other, then, under similar circumstances, the heat generated ere the two bullets were brought to rest would be nine times greater for the more rapidly flying bullet than for the other one. Now you can readily comprehend the immense quantity of heat that will have been produced ere friction could deprive me of a speed of twenty miles a second. That heat not merely warmed me, but I rapidly became red-hot, white-hot, then I melted, even though composed of materials of a most refractory kind. Still friction had much more to do, and it actually drove me off into vapour, and I vanished. You, standing on your earth many miles below, never saw me—never could have seen me—until this supreme moment, when, glowing with an instantaneous fervour, I for a brief second became visible. You shouted, 'Oh! there is a shooting star.'

"Nature knows no annihilation, and though I had been driven off into vapour and the trial by fire had scattered and dispersed me, yet in the lofty heights of the atmosphere those vapours cooled and condensed. They did not, they never could again reunite and reproduce my pristine structure. Here and there in wide diffusion I repassed from the vaporous to the solid form, and in this state I wore the appearance of a streak of minute granules distributed all along the highway I had followed. These granules gradually subsided through the air to the earth. On Alpine snows, far removed from the haunts of men and from the contamination of chimneys, minute particles have been gathered, many of which have unquestionably been derived from the scattered remains of shooting stars. Into the sea similar particles are for ever falling, and they have been subsequently dredged up from profound depths, having subsided through an ocean of water after sinking through an ocean of air.

"The motes by which a sunbeam through a chink in a

closed shutter is rendered visible, are no doubt mainly of organic origin, but they must also frequently comprise the meteoric granules. These motes gradually subside upon the tops of your bookcases or into other congenial retreats to form that dust of which good housekeepers have such a horror. It is certain that the great majority of the particles of which ordinary dust is constituted have purely terrestrial sources which it would be impossible to endow with any romantic interest. It is equally certain that in a loathed dust-heap are many atoms which, considering their celestial origin and their transcendent voyages, would have merited a more honoured resting-place."

The discovery of the height at which the streaks of shooting stars are produced is an important element in obtaining any precise knowledge of these bodies. To determine it requires the joint action of at least two observers situated at stations widely distant. It will thus be seen that the occasions on which such observations can be obtained are mainly fortuitous. We cannot foretell the occurrence of conspicuous shooting stars so as to enable the two observers to arrange a combined system of observations. We can no doubt in certain cases predict the advent of a shower of shooting stars, but then the very profusion in which the meteors appear tends to baffle any preconcerted agreement, because it is so difficult to insure that identical streaks shall be observed at the two stations. It does, however, sometimes happen that a shooting star observed in one place can by a time comparison be proved to be identical with a shooting star observed in another place. If the two observers have each possessed the skill and taken the pains to note accurately the spot of the heavens where the object appeared, or rather the point either of the beginning or of the termination of its track, then the discovery of its distance is rendered practicable.

It is an interesting application of some few propositions in Euclid to determine the meteor's height from these observations. We shall, however, here be content with describing two special cases, in the first of which the general problem has been somewhat simplified. I shall suppose that an observer at London sees a shooting star, and notices that the luminous streak commences at the point of the heavens exactly over his head. It also happens that an observer who resides at Bristol sees a shooting star, and notices that it lies to the east, and that the point where the streak commences is at an elevation of forty-five degrees, that is half-way from the horizon to the zenith. On subsequent comparison these observers find that their observations were made at the same moment; and as neither of them saw any other shooting star about the same time it is obvious that they must have both observed the same object. We have now to consider a triangle of which the three corners are respectively London, Bristol, and the shooting star (or rather the point at the commencement of its track). It is plain that this triangle has a right angle and equal sides, and that consequently the distance from London to the shooting star must be the same as from London to Bristol. Thus the height of a shooting star has been found. Of course the observer at London will not usually be so fortunate as to see the object directly over his head, and the observer at Bristol will not often find the angle of elevation to be half a right angle. The calculation therefore will usually be not quite so simple as in the case we have supposed, but it presents no real difficulty.

In addition to this somewhat imaginary illustration I shall mention an actual instance, and I naturally take a recent meteor that suits my purpose. It is one which has been fully described by the well-known astronomer, Mr. W. F. Denning, who was himself one of the observers, and who afterwards calculated the position of the meteor's track. From his account I gather the following particulars.

A careful observer of these bodies, who resides at Leeds, Mr. D. Booth, was keeping watch on the evening of January 2nd, 1888, when at 10h. 58m. P.M. a splendid meteor, which appeared to him to be as bright as Jupiter, travelled across the heavens, through the constellation Aries, towards the south. On the same evening Mr. Denning, who was on the look out at Bristol, saw the same bright meteor in the northern part of the sky, in the constellation Draco. That the object seen at Leeds and the object seen at Bristol were the same is obvious from the fact that the times noted by the two observers were identical. Nor was there any other bright meteor recorded at either place which would admit of the possibility of confusion. No doubt the parts of the sky in which each observer located the meteor were utterly different. From Leeds it appeared high up in the south-western quarter of the heavens, from Bristol it was seen in the north, almost under the Pole. But the different situations do not imply that there were two distinct objects; they are merely aspects of the same object obtained from widely different points of view. It is, in fact, the very difference between these positions which renders it possible to discover the true situation of the luminous streak.

The point at which the meteor appeared to vanish from Bristol was at an elevation of nearly 30°, a little to the west of north. Lay, therefore, a map of England on the table, fasten with a pin a piece of thread at Bristol, and then stretch the thread up towards the north at an inclination of one-third of a right angle above the surface of the map. The observation at Bristol then assures us that the vanishing point of the meteor was *somewhere* along that line. The observation at Leeds tells us that the vanishing point of the meteor was towards the south-west. A little study of the map shows us that the line of sight from Bristol to the meteor passes nearly over Chester, and that Chester is south-west from Leeds. Hence we see that the vanishing point must have been directly over Chester, and the slope of the incline from Bristol indicates that the height of the meteor must there have been about sixty miles. If any inhabitant of Chester were fortunate enough to have noticed that bright meteor he would apparently have seen it terminate at a point exactly over his head.

The terminal point of the meteor is usually much better observed than the initial point. Nor is this a matter for surprise. The attention of an observer is often directed towards the object by a bright light, while he may be looking in quite another direction. He turns round and, of course, follows the glorious object to its close at a point the situation of which he can note accurately. It seems in this case that the meteor was observed at a much earlier part of its flight at Bristol than at Leeds. We may, however, conclude, from a study of both observations, that the body commenced its brilliant career at a point ninety-eight miles high above a spot to the west of Appleby.

We have thus the means of determining the actual path which the meteor has traversed, and I would suggest to the reader that he should construct, for his own information, a little model, which will give him a clear picture of the career of this curious visitor. Put a map of England on a board and stick through it and into the board two straight wires (knitting needles will do admirably), one near Appleby and the other at Chester. A string is then to be stretched from one of these needles to the other, but the height at which its two ends are to be fastened to the needles will of course depend upon the scale of the map. The little model that is now before me is made with the map from Bradshaw's Railway Guide. On the scale of that map ninety-eight miles will be nearly $4\frac{3}{4}$ inches. Accordingly I have fastened one end of the string to the knitting needle through Appleby at the height of $4\frac{3}{4}$ inches. Similarly sixty miles correspond on this map to about 3 inches, and therefore the other extremity of the string is to be secured 3 inches over Chester, and an instructive model is complete. We can at once learn from it the actual length of the meteor's path. The distance between the two extremities of the string is a little over 5 inches, and consequently we see from the scale of the map that the length of flight is over 100 miles. Mr. Denning, from his accurate methods of calculation, states it at 109 miles.

A glance at the model will also explain what might

otherwise appear to be paradoxical, and that is the assertion by Mr. Booth at Leeds that the meteor was rather swift, while Mr. Denning from Bristol assures us that the motion was very slow. The apparent discrepancy vanishes when we see how the course of the meteor actually lies. The observer from Leeds sees the celestial rocket moving squarely across his line of sight from right to left. He could hardly have observed it under more favourable circumstances so far as the direction of the motion is concerned. But to the observer at Bristol the aspect of the meteor's path was wholly different. The object was moving towards him. In fact, if we continue the line of flight sufficiently far, we find it sloping downwards to the Bristol Channel, and finally touching earth in Devonshire. From Bristol therefore the track was extremely foreshortened; and consequently during its whole flight the meteor appeared from Bristol to traverse but a comparatively small part of the heavens: to an observer there this motion would seem very slow when compared with such a view of the object as was presented from Leeds. It will also be noted that at the centre of its journey the meteor must have been about 200 miles distant from Bristol, and the greatness ot this distance is another reason why it should appear to move slowly.

The spectacle was witnessed by Mr. Backhouse at Sunderland; he describes the meteor to have been as bright as the star Sirius, and it appeared near the constellation of Orion. It would lead me too far to pursue this matter, so I shall dismiss it with the remark that these facts can be shown to tally with the path ascertained by the observations at Leeds and at Bristol.

The track of this meteor may be taken as fairly representative of the course pursued by those more splendid shooting stars which are often called fire-balls. They move, however, in every direction. They come from the east, and from the west, from the north, and from the south. There is no hour of the night at which they have not occasionally been seen. Even in daylight it has happened not once or twice, but on several occasions, that a brilliant meteor has forced itself upon our astonished notice. They generally first make their appearance at a height which is between 50 and 100 miles above the ground. They hurry down their inclined path, but generally become extinguished while still at least 20 miles aloft. In their more ambitious flights meteors have been known to span a kingdom. Nor are even greater strides unrecorded. The length of a continent may be compared with the track of that terrific meteor of 5th September, 1868, which broke into visibility at a great height above the Black Sea, and had not expended its stupendous energy until it passed over the smiling vineyards of France.

CHAPTER XVI.

FIRE-BALLS.

GREAT fire-balls are much more numerous than any one would suppose who had not paid attention to the subject. Nor need this be a matter for surprise if it be remembered that when a fire-ball does arrive it is only by a favourable combination of circumstances that any particular individual is privileged to witness the exhibition. Let us examine the conditions that are necessary. In the first place, the observer who desires to look out for meteors will naturally choose some station which commands the most uninterrupted view of the sky on all sides. The deck of a ship on the open sea, or, better still, the summit of a lofty mountain, will represent ideal sites for the purpose. But only a very small fraction of the entire atmosphere of our globe is within the sphere of observation from one locality. If a fire-ball plunges into the air it may perhaps be seen if in any part of its track it is above the horizon. With sufficient precision we may assert that the proportion of the total atmosphere which is above the horizon at any one place is $\frac{1}{500}$th of the whole, and that anything which may occur in the remaining 499 parts is of course occluded from view. Even were the sky so perfectly clear as to permit an unintermitting watch being maintained from one year's end to the other, we could not expect from any single station to see more than a mere fraction of the total number of fire-balls that had actually descended. It must also be remembered that the fire-balls which do travel above the horizon will have many chances of escaping notice, for an observer cannot be always on the look out. He will be indeed a diligent astronomer and situated in a favoured clime who should spend a thousand hours in the year on the watch for shooting stars. Even this will, however, only amount to one hour out of every eight. We may reasonably suppose that meteors and fire-balls will be as likely to arrive in any one of the seven hours during which an observer is not on the watch as in the single hour during which he is present.

This will explain why it is that though fire-balls are really so very abundant, yet that the opportunities enjoyed by any individual for seeing them are comparatively infrequent. As a random example of the yearly crop of fire-balls, I take from the middle of 1877 to the middle of 1878. A list of the fire-balls noticed during this period will be found in that storehouse of valuable information, the Reports of the British Association. In the year referred to I see that eighty-six great fire-balls have been recorded. They have appeared in various localities, both in the old hemisphere and in the new. The most arduous observer may think himself fortunate if he had even seen one of them.

As to the brilliant light from some of these great fire-balls, there are numerous statements. We are not infrequently told that even the beams of the full moon are ineffectual in comparison with the blaze of the meteor; and we find a high authority asserting that one of these bodies displayed a flash as "blinding as the sun." But our knowledge of the actual illuminating power of meteors is almost unavoidably of rather an inaccurate description. We could measure the light, no doubt, with all practical precision if we knew when and where to expect it, for then we could bring a suitable photometric apparatus to bear at the critical moment. In the absence of any precise information, we are forced to make the most of such occasional comparisons as may be available. On the 29th July, 1878, a fire-ball was seen which created so splendid an illumination that "the smallest objects were visible at Manchester." An eye-witness states that when at its best the fire-ball had the lustre of a powerful electric light seen from a distance of thirty or forty yards, though at the moment the fire-ball must certainly have been forty-five miles away. We can make a comparative estimate of the intrinsic intensity of a light which, when received from a distance of forty-five miles, has a brilliancy equal to that of a known source thirty-five yards away. It is thus shown that the fire-ball must have emitted more light than five million electric lamps.

Fortunate indeed would the astronomer have been who, guided by some miraculous prescience, had gone to the ancient city of York on the evening of the 23rd of February, 1879, and on the tower of the glorious minster spent the night in observation of the heavens. It would have been his privilege to witness a majestic meteor under circumstances of almost unique magnificence.

Unhappily, there was no expectant astronomer at once ready to observe and competent to record the great event on the morning of the 24th. The time of its occurrence was also the most unpropitious, so far as the attention of casual observers was concerned. Did a nocturnal fire-ball desire that its splendours should be witnessed by as few persons as possible, it could choose no hour so favourable as about three o'clock in the morning. Those who sit up latest have at last got to sleep ; those who rise the earliest have not yet awakened. It was at seven minutes before three that such few stragglers as the streets of York still contained saw a pear-shaped ball of fire travelling across the sky. It drenched the ancient city with a flood of light. The superb front of the minster never before glowed with a more romantic illumination. The unwonted brilliancy streamed through every aperture in every window in the city; every wakeful eye was instantly on the alert; every light sleeper started up suddenly to know what was the matter. Even those whom the blaze of midnight light had failed to awaken were only permitted to protract their slumbers for another minute and a half—only until an awful crash, like a mighty peal of thunder, burst over the town, shaking the doors, the windows, and even the houses themselves. The whole city was thus alarmed. Every one started at the noise. But that noise was not a clap of thunder. Nor was it produced by an earthquake. It was merely the explosion of the fire-ball which flung itself against the atmosphere after its immeasurable voyage through space.

Let us imagine a wayfarer in the streets of Newcastle on the same morning. He is struggling on his way in dense darkness, and through a raging storm of snow. An instantaneous transformation scene takes place. Suddenly there is light above and around which renders the white mantle of the city as bright as a summer day. The observer at once sees that this illumination is not lightning. A flash of lightning lasts for an inconceivably small fraction of a second. But while a man could count fifty the town glows with this strange illumination. And strange it is, for the source of the light is not visible. As the snowstorm would have hidden the sun itself at mid-day, so in the dead of night it hides the great meteor. An exquisite phase of the phenomenon was presented by the changes in the hue of the light, which passed from a brilliant white to a beautiful blue ere it disappeared.

Perhaps the most remarkable instance of the *explosion* of a meteor is recorded in the case of the great fire-ball so widely observed in America on the 21st December, 1876. The movements of this superb object have been carefully studied by Professor H. A. Newton and Professor D Kirkwood. For the prodigious span of a thousand miles this meteor tore over the American continent with a speed of some ten or fifteen miles a second. It first appeared over Kansas at a height of seventy-five miles. Thence it glided over the Mississippi, over the Missouri; it passed to the south of Lake Michigan; it made a short voyage over Lake Erie, and it cannot have been very far from the Falls of Niagara, when by becoming invisible all further traces of its movements were lost. While passing a point midway between Chicago and St. Louis a violent explosion shivered the meteor into a cluster of brilliant balls of fire, which seemed to chase each other across the sky. This cluster must have been about forty miles long and five miles wide. The detonation by which the explosion was accompanied was a specially notable incident of this meteor. It was not only heard with terrific intensity in the neighbourhood, but the volume of sound was borne to great distances. Bloomington, in Indiana, is one hundred and eighty-five miles from the actual point in the sky where the meteor was rent in pieces, yet about the neighbourhood of Bloomington not only was the sound of a frightful explosion heard, but the shock of the concussion was actually felt to such a degree that some of those who experienced it thought an earthquake must have happened.

The tremendous volume of sound that must have been emitted is forcibly presented to us when we consider the interval of time that elapsed between the moment when the inhabitants of Bloomington saw the gorgeous procession of fire-balls streaming over the heavens, and the moment when the appalling crash burst on their ears. Every one is familiar with the fact that the flash of a gun is seen ere the report is heard, and the greater the distance of the gun the longer is the interval by which the light and the noise are separated. Sound takes five seconds to travel a mile; light travels so quickly that the time necessary to traverse a mile, or a hundred miles, or a thousand miles, is utterly inappreciable by ordinary measurement.

The celestial spectacle had excited the utmost astonishment; doubtless it had been discussed and notes had been compared by those whose good fortune had permitted them to see it. But the immediate excitement was over, friends had parted for the night; some of them had entered their houses; others had renewed their walk homewards, and had travelled nearly a mile on their journey; vehicles had driven a couple of miles; trains had run half-a-dozen miles; columns of newspapers had been read. Many who had seen the meteor had already forgotten it, when their ears were deafened by the arrival of the awful crash. The waves of sound had to travel a distance as great as from London to Liverpool, and even at the rate of a mile every five seconds this cannot be done in less than a quarter of an hour. Probably many of those who both heard the noise and saw the light found it hard to believe in their connection. We are indebted to the care of one observer at Bloomington, who by looking at his clock when the fire-balls were seen, and again when the explosion was heard, has added an important particular to our knowledge of this great meteor.

Nor need we feel much astonishment at the stupendous phenomena, both of light and of sound, which accompany the advent of a splendid and detonating fire-ball. I must here give a few figures which will show how great is the store of energy possessed by a meteor in virtue of the amazing velocity with which it is animated. I shall suppose that the material element of the meteor consists of a small mass of stone or of some more or less metallic material which weighs one pound. We shall examine the circumstances under which we must endeavour by mechanical agents to project this small body with the meteoric speed of, let us say, twenty-five miles a second. Our utmost attempts with a cannon could hardly produce a speed of one-hundredth part of the required amount, and even for this a charge of gunpowder, certainly not less than a quarter of a pound, would be consumed. If a cannon of amazing strength and of ideal efficiency could be conceived, in which all the energy of the exploding powder should be usefully concentrated upon communicating velocity to the projectile, we should find that to double the speed the charge must be quadrupled. To treble the speed we should have to increase the charge ninefold. If the speed were to be increased ten times, we must put one hundred times as much powder into the cannon. Finally, if we could procure a piece of ordnance strong enough and gunpowder rapid enough to impart meteoric velocity to the missile, a charge would be necessary which is ten thousand times as great as the quarter of a pound that is sufficient under the conditions of ordinary artillery. This argument shows us that the energy of an entire ton weight of gunpowder would be required to impart to a stone one pound in weight the velocity of an ordinary fire-ball.

Whatever may have been the original source whence the meteor acquired its energy (and this is a point on which I do not at present make any remark), that energy will be retained so long as the meteor retains its velocity. Even if the meteor moved through empty space for a million years, it would still be able to restore, if its motion were arrested, the precise quantity of energy which it had originally received. Hence, when the supreme moment has arrived, the meteor expends in the throes of its dissolution all the energy it contains. Everything that the energy liberated by the explosion of a ton of gunpowder can do that meteor weighing only a pound is competent to accomplish. If the weight of the missile were greater than one pound, the velocity remaining the same, the available energy would be increased in the same proportion. For example, if the meteor weighed ten pounds, one hundred pounds, or one thousand pounds, it would discharge as much energy as could be awakened by the detonation of ten tons, of one hundred tons, or of one thousand tons of gunpowder. Need we wonder, then, that gorgeous lights and that majestic thunders have occasionally accompanied the annihilation of large meteors?

There is another instructive method for obtaining a due estimate of the potency of a meteor to produce tremendous effects notwithstanding its comparatively small size. In our present illustration we shall employ that great source of energy which is familiar in the steam-engine. Let us think of a powerful steamship, the engines of which have, let us say, 8,200 horse-power. Let us conceive such appropriate mechanism as would permit the Titanic power of these engines to be concentrated on the single duty of imparting velocity to a small piece of matter one pound in weight. It can then be shown that the piece of matter would, after the lapse of sixty seconds, have acquired a meteoric speed. So long as the meteor retained that speed it would retain the energy the engine had given to it, nor could the meteor surrender its rapid motion except the energy were transformed into some other form. If then the meteor lost its speed by piercing its way for a minute through our atmosphere it would reproduce all the energy that 8,200 horse-power can exert in the same time.

Suppose that in the elevated regions of our atmosphere

in the dead of night all the vigour of a set of engines, whose collective strength was equal to that of forty thousand horses, was concentrated on the production of an electric light; suppose, further, that the dazzling glare thus created was accompanied by the music from an orchestra of fog-horns blown by another forty thousand horses, surely a scare would be produced which the most pretentious fire-ball might be content to emulate. Yet the figures we have already given will prove that a meteor only ten pounds in weight, which a child could carry, bears in the mere swiftness of its flight a capacity adequate to such a display.

The glory of a meteor is often so evanescent that we just get a glimpse and it is gone. The sky resumes its ordinary aspect; the familiar stars are there, and even the very situation of the brilliant streak has become unrecognisable. But this is not always so; it sometimes happens that the brief career of the meteor leaves a notable trace behind it, so that for seconds and for minutes the sky is diversified by an unwonted spectacle. The path of the meteor leaves a stain of pearly light on the sky to mark the highway pursued by our celestial visitor.

In its fearful career the meteor is often rent to fragments, reduced to dust, dissolved into vapour. The glowing atoms of the wreck lie strewn along the path, just as the ghastly remnants of Napoleon's mighty army limned out the awful retreat from Moscow.

A pencil-shaped cloud of meteoric debris, perhaps eighty or a hundred miles in length, and four or five miles in diameter, thus hangs poised in air. It is at night. The sun has sunk so far below the horizon that there is no trace of the feeblest twilight glow. An ordinary cloud would, of course, be invisible except as concealing the stars; no beams of light fall upon it; there is nothing to render it luminous. So, too, the meteoric streak will often pass instantly into invisibility, but, as I have said, this is not always the case. There is a well-authenticated instance in which the trail of a superb meteor remained visible for nearly an hour. I have endeavoured up to the present to explain the various phenomena presented to us in the fall of a meteor, but here, for the first time, we have to note a circumstance for which it is not easy to account. We can explain why it is that the long meteoric cloud should be there, but we cannot so easily explain why we should be able to see it. Whence comes this beautiful pearly luminosity? It seems that the meteoric dust must glow with some intrinsic luminosity. I have only heard one attempt to offer a rational explanation of the true character of this interesting phenomenon. It is as follows.

There are certain substances which are called *phosphorescent*, because they possess the power of actually absorbing and retaining the light to which they have been exposed, and then gradually dispensing it afterwards. Phosphorescent materials have some useful applications as ingredients in the so-called "luminous paint." A gate covered with this preparation will absorb the sunlight during the day, and during the night will radiate forth its store in a feeble glow. Clock faces have been similarly illuminated, and match-boxes are made so that the hand shall be guided to them in the dark by a radiance more ghostlike than beautiful. The persistent streak of a meteor can be explained by the supposition that some particles of these phosphorescent substances have been present in the meteoric mass. These particles have been ignited to brilliance during the progress of the meteor, and they still continue to glow until their store of luminous energy shall have become exhausted.

The meteoric streak is subjected to the same influences as those which affect an aqueous cloud in the lofty regions of the atmosphere. It must be dissipated by air currents, and accordingly we observe that the trail, which was at first so nearly straight, becomes bent and curved, sometimes even serpentine, ere its outlines have gradually softened out and all visible traces of the meteor have vanished.

CHAPTER XVII.

SHOWERS OF SHOOTING STARS.

I HAVE thought it convenient to illustrate the leading phenomena of meteors by reference to some of the more imposing of these bodies, but it must not be supposed that the smaller meteors, and even the tiniest of shooting stars, are unworthy of our close attention. Indeed, the smaller shooting stars, by their greater frequency, have taught us much more about meteors than we could have ever learned from the great fire-balls. Even regarded from the merely spectacular point of view, the splendours of the latter are sometimes eclipsed by the gorgeous showers of comparatively small meteors, to which we shall presently have to refer.

We have spoken of dazzling fire-balls which generate for a brief moment a light which eye-witnesses, with possibly a pardonable exaggeration, have ventured to compare with the beams of the sun himself. Other meteors are described as being as bright as the full moon. Descending still lower in the scale of splendour, we read of fire-balls as bright as Venus or Jupiter, as bright as Sirius, or as a star of the first magnitude. With each step downwards in brilliancy we find the meteors to increase in numerical abundance. Shooting stars as bright as the stars of the second or third magnitude are comparatively frequent; they are still more numerous of the fourth and fifth magnitudes. Every night brings its tale of shooting stars whose brightness is just sufficient to impress the unaided eye. Nor do the shooting stars which even the most attentive eye can detect represent a fraction of their entire number. As there are telescopic stars which the unaided eye cannot see, so it might fairly be conjectured that, as we can trace meteors of successive stages of brightness down to the limit of unaided eye visibility, so there may be meteors still and still smaller which would be detected could we only direct a telescope towards them. If it be impossible to turn a telescope with sufficient dexterity to scan a visible shooting star, how, it may well be asked, can we use the telescope to discover shooting stars which the unaided eye cannot see?

We must here depend entirely, or almost entirely, on the chapter of accidents. The observer who really sought to discover telescopic shooting stars would generally find that many hours of watching were rewarded with but very meagre results. No doubt if, at properly appointed times, he directed his telescope to certain particular constellations, he would have more prospect of success than if he merely pointed his telescope at random. But though the experience of actually looking out for telescopic shooting stars has not led to much, yet every astronomer who is in the habit of making nightly observations with a good telescope, in almost any branch of astronomical work, will frequently find a bright streak of light flash across his field. This is a meteor, and a comparison with any stars which may happen to be in the field of view will probably show him that the object was far too small to have been seen with the naked eye. We must remember that the field of view of a large telescope is but an extremely small fraction of the entire extent of the heavens. It would be easy to show, by the doctrine of chances, that if a telescopic shooting star were to dive to extinction into the air, the chance against its being seen by any particular telescope at that moment directed to the sky would be at least fifty thousand to one; but every astronomer knows that the perception of a telescopic shooting star is a common incident in the observatory. If, therefore, we reflect that for every one that is seen there must be thousands which dart in unseen, we obtain an imposing idea of the myriads of shooting stars that daily rain in upon our globe.

The world is thus pelted on all sides day and night, year after year, century after century, by troops and battalions of shooting stars of every size, from objects not much larger than grains of sand up to mighty masses which can only be expressed in tons. In the lapse of ages our globe must thus be gradually growing by the everlasting deposit of meteoric debris. Looking back through the vistas of time past, it becomes impossible to estimate how much of the solid earth may not owe its origin to this celestial source.

It will greatly promote our comprehension of these bodies if we group them into classes so as to discover some of the laws by which their movements are guided.

The first and most important truth with regard to the recurrence of the meteors is their occasional appearance in what are known as "meteoric showers." During such displays it sometimes happens that shooting stars in shoals break forth simultaneously, so as to produce a spectacle which we now regard as of the utmost beauty and interest, but which in earlier times has often been the source of the direst terror and dismay.

Let me, for the sake of illustration, give some account of one of these great showers of shooting stars. It occurred on the 13th November, 1866. Doubtless many of those who read these lines will remember that event. It dwells in my memory along with one or two other superb astronomical spectacles that it has been my privilege to witness. I have never seen a total eclipse of the sun under favourable circumstances. This is, I apprehend, about the most sublime of all the occasional phenomena which the heavens present to us. I have, however, seen the great comet of 1858, the shower of shooting stars in 1866, and the transit of Venus in 1882. The last was of interest rather from its rarity and its delicacy than from its actual appearance regarded as a spectacle. Of the phenomena in the heavens which I have seen, I must give the first place to the wonderful shower of shooting stars in November, 1866. Although I have previously had occasion to describe my experience as an eye-witness of this event, yet I think it will bear telling again.

In the year 1866 I occupied the position of astronomer to the late Earl of Rosse, who is specially known to fame as having been the builder of the greatest telescope the world has ever seen. This grand instrument at the time

I was in charge of it was devoted to the observation of the nebulæ, a branch of astronomical work for which the vast size of the great reflector made it eminently suited. In clear weather it was my duty, and I may truly add, my delight, to scan the heavens during the long winter nights, for the purpose of sketching and of measuring those dim, faint nebulæ which seem to lie on the confines of the visible universe. The giant telescope is in the open air; it swings between two walls of castellated masonry, and by ladders and galleries of ingenious construction the observer is enabled to reach the mouth of the telescope in all its positions. I say mouth of the telescope, for a reflector of this description is not employed like the ordinary telescope, *through* which we look. In the reflector we must get access to the top and gaze down on the reflections of the stars in the great mirror below. As the telescope is sixty feet long it thus follows that the observers are sometimes sixty feet high in the air, and as the telescope is placed in a very open situation in Lord Rosse's beautiful demesne at Parsonstown, the position for observing the shooting star shower was an exceptionally favourable one. Beside the observer an attendant stands, whose duty it is to move the gallery backwards and forwards, so as to keep the observer conveniently placed near the eye-piece of the telescope.

The memorable night between November 13th and 14th, 1866, was a very fine one; the moon was absent, a very important consideration in regard to the effectiveness of the display. The stars shone out clearly, and I was diligently examining some faint nebulæ in the eye-piece of the great telescope when a sudden exclamation from the attendant caused me to look up from the eye-piece just in time to catch a glimpse of a fine shooting star, which, like a great sky-rocket, but without its accompanying noise, shot across the sky over our heads. About this time I was joined at the telescope by Lord Oxmantown, as he then was, but who is now the present distinguished Earl of Rosse, and we resumed our observations of the nebulæ, but a grander spectacle soon diverted our attention from these faint objects. The great shooting star which had already appeared was merely the herald announcing the advent of a mighty host. At first the meteors came singly, and then, as the hours wore on, they arrived in twos and in threes, in dozens, in scores, in hundreds. Our work at the telescope was forsaken; we went to the top of the castellated walls of the great telescope and abandoned ourselves to the enjoyment of the gorgeous spectacle.

To number the meteors baffled all our arithmetic; while we strove to count on the one side many of them hurried by on the other. The vivid brilliance of the meteors was sharply contrasted with the silence of their flight. We heard on that marvellous night no sounds save those with which we were familiar. The flights of the celestial rockets were attended with no noises that we could hear. The meteors were no doubt somewhat various as to size, but the characteristic feature of this shower, as contrasted with another great shower I have also seen, was the remarkable brilliance of the shooting stars. It was their exceptional splendour even more than their innumerable profusion that gave to the shower its peculiarity. As to the actual brilliancy of the meteors

I am enabled to give the accurate estimate made by Mr. Baxendell at Manchester, where the shower was well seen. Out of every hundred of these meteors ten were brighter than a first magnitude star, and two or three of them were brighter than Sirius. Fifteen out of each hundred were between the first and second magnitudes, and twenty-five were between the second and third magnitudes, while the remainder were smaller. These results may be placed in a somewhat more simple aspect in a different way. Think of the brightness of the seven stars in that most familiar of all the constellations, the Great Bear; about half of the meteors noticed during the continuance of the shower were as bright as, or brighter than, the stars of the Great Bear. The remaining half of the visible meteors must be compared with stars of a fainter description.

I have described how that great November shower of stars began, but I have not asserted that the display came upon us entirely by surprise. I certainly was surprised at its magnificence, but we confidently anticipated that a shooting star shower of some notable kind would occur on that very night. How, it may well be asked, could we know that such a spectacle might be expected? The story is a wonderful romance in modern science.

We expect that the sun will rise to-morrow morning. Now why do we so expect it? Without entering into any profound disquisition on the subject, we may say that the practical grounds of this expectation depend upon the fact that we have always found that the sun does rise, and that as this operation has continued with unfailing regularity for untold ages, we have reason to anticipate a repetition of the phenomenon to-morrow as well as on the following mornings. It was on similar grounds that we were able to predict the occurrence of that great November shower.

Just thirty-three years previously, in the year 1833, a splendid shower of shooting stars had been witnessed in the same month of November and on the same day of the month. That two great showers should both have occurred, at the same epoch of the year, after an interval of thirty-three years, was in itself a circumstance not a little remarkable. But this might have been regarded as merely a coincidence, if we had only been acquainted with these two showers, and if we did not know their true relations. Researches into history have, however, brought to light the interesting fact that these two showers were not mere isolated events, but that they were only the two latest members of a long and connected series of great November showers of meteors. As we look back through the records of the past we find occasional mention of what can only have been great displays of shooting stars. Within the last century or two such gorgeous phenomena were witnessed in an age when scientific knowledge enabled the spectacle to be in some degree appreciated, but as we peer back still earlier and earlier we find the records of these great events assume a different complexion. Many centuries ago the advent of a great shooting-star shower was viewed with terror by a superstitious and ignorant people. Such reords of the event as have been preserved are tinged with such credulity, and so devoid of accurate description, that all we can elicit are the facts that on the dates specified certain celestial phenomena were witnessed which we now know to have been showers of shooting stars.

The earliest of the records is nearly a thousand years old, and from that period down to the present the earth has probably been the scene of about thirty or more superb showers belonging to the system we are now considering. Whether all these displays were actually witnessed we do not know. Thick and cloudy weather would be sufficient to have obscured even the most splendid of these showers. Bright moonlight would have greatly impaired the effectiveness of others. Even those which were seen may not have been all recorded. Even all that have been recorded may not yet have disclosed themselves to the diligent search of Professor H. Newton and the other astronomers who have laboured at this interesting subject. The records which have been found are not always easy to interpret. In the days when astrologers taught, and when the people believed, that the configurations of the stars were designed to shadow forth the vicissitudes of human affairs, it was not likely that any very lucid interpretation would be given to such an event as a shower of shooting stars. Such phenomena have been regarded as miraculous, and they were often thought to be portents conveying and threatening divine wrath. They were occasionally interpreted as gracious manifestations of divine approval.

Some important facts with regard to ancient shooting-star showers have, however, survived the thousand and one casualties to which historical records are exposed. A careful discussion of those which are sufficiently accurate to be intelligible discloses to us the remarkable law of a thirty-three year period in the occasional recurrence of grand shooting-star showers. The chief qualifications of this statement would be twofold. In the first place, the interval has been occasionally thirty-four years. In the second place, it sometimes happens that at the return of the thirty-three year period the passage of the meteors makes no visible display, two consecutive years are rendered memorable by great showers. At present this particular shower occurs about the 15th November; but in earlier ages we find the date to shift slowly towards the commencement of the year. Thus the display which took place in A.D. 1698 was on the 9th of November; while, looking back still farther to one of the very earliest records, viz., that of the year 934, we find the date has receded to October 14th. This change of the day on which the shower occurs is of profound theoretical importance in connection with the discovery of the orbit which these meteors pursue. The advance of the date is, however, so slow that for the past few generations as well as for the next, we may sufficiently define this particular shower by the meteors which enliven the skies between the 14th and the 16th of November. In fact, the poetaster has parodied the well-known lines for the days of the month by a similar effort, which will serve to remind us also of another periodic shower of shooting stars which occurs in August. He writes:—

"If you November's stars would see,
About the fifteenth watching be.
In August too stars shine from heaven,
On nights between nine and eleven."

These lines are intended to imply that the day named will usually bring, in every November, a few meteors at all events belonging to the grand shower. These are stragglers, as it were, from the mighty host which visits us from time to time.

Astronomers have a special name for this group of November meteors. They are called the "Leonids." To explain why this name has been given, and why it is appropriate, we must dwell on an important part of the phenomena of the shower, to which we have not yet alluded; and this we shall now do.

Among the constellations there is a fine sickle-shaped group, forming a part of Leo, one of the signs of the Zodiac. That part of the sky defined by Lee is curiously related to the meteors of the 12th to the 14th of November. Every shooting star truly belonging to that great shower pursued a track across the heavens, the direction of which, if carried back far enough, was always found to pierce through the sickle of Leo. Indeed, the paths of all the meteors formed a set of rays spreading away from that one point in the constellation. An invariable characteristic of this particular shower is its connection with the constellation of Leo, hence the appropriateness of the name of Leonids.

And now for the explanation—and it is a remarkable one—which astronomers have been able to give of the annual appearance to some extent of the Leonids, and of their occasional majestic displays.

Picture to yourself a mighty host of small particles out in space. They are organized into a great shoal, but they are so sparsely distributed that each particle is perhaps a dozen miles away from its neighbours on each side. How large each of these particles is we cannot indeed say. No doubt they vary in size, but they are probably not larger than the pebbles on an ordinary gravel walk, and possibly much less. The shape in which this host is marshalled is remarkable. It is a long column, of which the width is small in comparison with the length. The dimension of this celestial host is indeed portentous. We sometimes judge of the length of a procession of carriages by stating how long they take to pass a certain point. We can express the length of this great procession of meteors by saying that, if we were to stand still and watch them file past, not less than a year must elapse before the mighty host would have passed by. This is, of course, an imperfect conception until we realise the velocity with which the meteoric procession is moving. Their speed is certainly short of that which flashes through the electric wire, but none the less does it utterly transcend any speed which we can produce mechanically. The velocity of the Leonids sometimes exceeds twenty-six miles a second, a pace which is more than fifteen hundred times swifter than the swiftest express train.

The width of this column as it passes along is prodigious when measured by ordinary standards. A cord that would go four times round our earth would barely suffice to stretch across the meteoric current, which is 100,000 miles from side to side. But this dimension shrinks into insignificance when compared with the length. To realise the true shape of the mighty host, we may use Mr. Stoney's admirable illustration. He says, take a piece of the finest sewing silk, about a foot and a half long. Then imagine the silk to be magnified, while still preserving its proportions, until its width is about one hundred thousand miles and its length about fifteen thousand times as great. Such is the shape of the mighty shoal which has, for the past thousand years, given us perennial displays of Leonids. It is at this moment and at every moment pursuing a mighty path through space.

The matter is so important that I venture to repeat here an illustration which I have already given in "Star Land." Think of a racecourse which is oval-shaped, or elliptical, as it should be more properly called. Think of a number of men who started together on that course to run a race. Let us further suppose that the number of competitors is a large one, and that they have to complete a considerable number of rounds ere the winning tape will be stretched across the track. We should then find that the shape of the group of athletes was continually being extended. We should also find that some few exceptionally good runners were able to draw ahead in advance of the main body. No doubt a large field would also contain some tardy runners who would inevitably be left far behind, so that as the successive rounds were completed we should see that the first were actually overtaking the last, and thus gaining an entire circuit. After a time a condition of the field would be reached in which the main body of average runners was in a stream occupying a small fraction of the entire course, while the rest of the track would be dotted here and there with those competitors who were either exceptionally swift or exceptionally slow.

Submit this illustration to an imaginary species of transformation and of enlargement. Instead of the small course a fraction of a mile in circumference, let us think of a course still oval in shape, but many hundreds of millions of miles round. Let the competitors be replaced by the small objects which are suitable for the manufacture of shooting stars. Let the number of these be magnified until they attain to untold billions. Thus we obtain a notion of the mighty celestial racecourse on which the Leonids have for a thousand years at least been hurrying along in a race, which is still in a comparatively early stage of its progress. Many circuits have no doubt been accomplished, the original host which started has been drawn out into the long thin line which we have already compared to a piece of silk. This contains the great mass of the Leonids, but there are many of the meteors which have been endowed with the gift of exceptional fleetness. On the other hand, there are some which seem not to have been able to keep up with the tremendous speed of the main body. Thus it happens that all around the mighty racecourse there are stragglers to be found, each of which pursues its journey in its own fashion.

If I have succeeded in giving you a picture of the condition of the Leonids, of enabling you to realise how the greater portion of the meteors form a comparatively dense shoal, while around the rest of the course the meteors are few and far between, it will then be easy to understand the laws of recurrence of the November showers.

It must be borne in mind that we can never see the meteors until the fatal moment when they dive into our atmosphere. We could, indeed, at any time point our telescope to the spot in the heavens where we know the great shoal must certainly be located. But the mightiest telescope in the world does not disclose the shoal to us. In fact we would never have seen these Leonids at all, we would never have become conscious that such a shoal of meteors existed, had it not been for a certain circumstance, which, for want of a better expression, I must speak of as accidental.

Our globe pursues a certain definite track around the sun. Year after year, with undeviating regularity, the earth performs the stages of its journey. If it reaches certain points on the 1st of January and the 12th of October in one year, then it reaches the same points on the 1st of January and the 12th of October respectively on next year, or any other year. The same may be asserted with regard to any other dates, so that when a date is given the station at which the earth will then have arrived is at once indicated.

The Leonids and the earth have each a certain track. It might of course have happened that one of these tracks lay quite outside or quite inside the other. It might also have been the case that one of these tracks passed through the other, so that the two orbits were related in the manner of a pair of consecutive links of a chain. Had any of these conditions prevailed, the two tracks would have been quite independent, and the meteors could never have become known to us. It might, however, have happened that the two tracks did actually intersect, and had therefore the point of crossing common to both orbits. This would, generally speaking, be an unlikely circumstance, but it is an indispensable condition if the meteors are to be visible from the earth. In the case of the Leonids, it has chanced that their orbit does intersect the orbit of the earth, and to this circumstance we are indebted for the glorious displays every thirty-three years.

We shall now be able to explain the chief features exhibited by the famous showers. In the first place a shower can only occur in that precise locality where the earth in its path crosses the path of the meteors. This junction is of course at a definite part of the earth's path. We may conveniently mark such a point in the path by the date at which the earth is to be found there in the progress of its annual voyage. This particular point, or rather region, of crossing happens to be in the place through which the earth passes each year between the 14th and the 16th of November. Hence it follows that if we are to see any Leonids at all it can only be at these dates, and thus we at once explain that peculiar feature of the shower, which is expressed in the fact that it can only recur on certain special days.

Scattered along the great meteoric highway run those irregular meteors that have forsaken the main host, either by rushing on too fast or by delaying too much. As the earth swoops across the highway it will be very likely, indeed it will be certain, to capture some of these stragglers. They will appear to us who stand on the surface far below to dart in from the constellation of Leo. Thus it is from the 14th to the 16th November we often witness some of the shooting stars belonging to this particular system. As these stragglers are but few in number, we shall not usually be gratified by any striking spectacle. A diligent observer may note on such an occasion a dozen or twenty Leonids, or sometimes even more, but they are neither brilliant enough nor numerous enough to attract special notice.

Sometimes, however, it will happen that the earth

arrives at the critical point of its path on the 15th of November, during the time the mighty procession of the long meteor stream is filing past. At once our globe plunges into the current, and for a few hours must forge its way across the stream, while all the time it is exposed to a perfect hurricane of meteors. In their untold myriads the little missiles dash themselves with unutterable pace into the comparatively stagnant air-case in which this world is enclosed. Destruction swift and complete is the doom of every one of the meteors that has the misfortune to graze our atmosphere. We on the earth's surface, unmindful of the rapid voyage of our globe, only become apprised of the singular cosmical event that is in progress by seeing a beautiful shower of shooting stars.

For a few hours the grand display lasts, that is, until the earth has traversed the stream and once more resumed its way through space comparatively void. Nor can any more Leonids be seen until the following 15th of November, when again in its annual course the earth reaches the locality of the last display.

It will generally have happened that the whole of the great shoal will have completely passed by the critical point during the lapse of a twelvemonth, so that the earth will at the next return only capture a few of the stragglers. Sometimes, however, it is found that the long shoal has not had time, even in a year, to completely hurry past the critical point. Accordingly the earth must take another rush across the stream, and will again encounter a meteoric tempest. We shall thus have two grand displays of shooting stars in two consecutive years. By the time the earth has once again fulfilled its course, and now for a third time approaches the spot so specially pertaining to this shower, the great shoal must certainly have passed, and only a few of the occasional Leonids will this time enter the net. Many years must elapse before we can again encounter the great host. They pursue without interruption their appointed journey. For sixteen or seventeen years they gradually retreat farther and farther away from the neighbourhood of this world, then they begin to turn round, and after the lapse of sixteen or seventeen years more they regain our vicinity, when great showers of Leonids are again to be anticipated. Now we see how the great showers sometimes appear at intervals of about thirty-three years. This is the period which the swarm of little bodies require for the one circuit. They did not appear in 1899.

There are many other periodic showers of shooting stars besides those notable Leonids on which we have dwelt so long. None of the other showers, however, possess the same importance as the Leonids, nor do they ever manifest celestial splendour comparable with that of those of the 13th of November. The Perseids, for example, which appear from the 9th to the 11th of August, are tolerably constant in their appearance, but have little spectacular interest. There is also another shower called the Andromedes, which occurs on the 27th of November. It has produced certain displays, one of the most remarkable of which took place in 1872. The meteors were excessively numerous on that occasion, but they were so short in their paths, and so insignificant as to brilliance, that the spectacle, though of great scientific interest, could not be compared as to splendour with that of the Leonids in 1866.

There are also several other showers which appear with greater or less regularity. Each of these possesses two distinct characteristics by which its meteors can be identified. One of these characters is the date on which the shower appears. The other is the constellation or point on the heavens from which all the meteors appear to radiate. Thus when we speak of the Andromedes on the 27th of November, we express that the shower on the 27th November comes from the part of the heavens marked by the constellation of Andromeda.

A striking discovery has been made which points to a curious connection between comets and shooting stars. We have seen how a shoal of meteors pursues a definite orbit through space. It has been found that the track followed by a great shower of meteors is often identical with the track pursued by a comet. It is wholly beyond the province of mere chance that an orbit such as that of the Leonids should, both as to its size and its position in space, be likewise that of a comet, unless the comet and the meteor swarm were objects related to each other.

In drawing this chapter to its close, I would remind my readers that though we have been occupied in treating of bodies which are often quite insignificent as to dimensions, yet we have been really following one of the most interesting and instructive branches of modern astronomical research.

The great sun guides our world through its long annual journey. The mighty mass of the earth yields compliance to the potent sway of the ruler of our system. But the sun does not merely exercise a control over the vast planets which circulate around him. The supreme law of gravitation constrains the veriest mote that ever floated in a sunbeam, with the same unremitting care that it does the mightiest of planets. Thus it is that each little meteor is guided in its journeys for untold ages. Each of these little objects hurries along, deflected at every moment, to follow its beautifully curved path by the incessant attraction of the sun. At last, however, the fatal plunge is taken. The long wanderings of the meteor have come to an end and it vanishes in a streak of splendour.

CHAPTER XVIII

THE NUMBER OF THE STARS.

Of all the discoveries that have ever been made in science there are two which especially baffle our powers of comprehension. They lie at the opposite extremes of nature. One relates to objects which are infinitely small, the other relates to objects which are almost infinitely great. The microscope teaches us that there are animals so minute that if a thousand of them were ranged abreast they would easily swim without being thrown out of line through the eye of the finest cambric needle. Each of those minute creatures is a highly organized number of particles, capable of moving about, of finding and devouring its food, and of behaving in all other respects as becomes an animal as distinguished from an unorganized piece of matter. The mind is incapable of realising the structure of these little creatures, and of fully appreciating their marvellous adaptation to the life they are destined to lead. If these animals excite our astonishment by reason of their extreme minuteness, there is an appeal made to conceptions of an entirely different character when we learn the lessons which the telescope teaches. As the microscope reveals the excessively minute so does the telescope disclose the sublimely great. In each case myriads of objects are submitted to our astonished view, but while the microscope brings before us creatures of which countless millions could swim about freely in a thimbleful of water, the telescope conducts our vision to uncounted legions of stars, many of them millions of times larger than the earth.

The grandest truth in the whole of nature is conveyed in that first lesson in astronomy which answers the question—What are the stars? This is a question that a child will ask, and I have heard of a child's pretty idea that the stars were little holes in the sky to let the glory of Heaven shine through. The philosopher will replace this explanation by another hardly less poetical, which will enable us to form some more adequate notion of the real magnificence of the universe. Each star that we see is, it is true, only a glittering little point of light, but that is merely because we are a long way from it. An electric light which will dazzle your eye when quite close will be reduced to an agreeable illumination if it is at a little distance, will become a faint light a mile away, and at no great distance will become altogether invisible. We must remember that out in space there is plenty of room—there are no bounds; and therefore when we see light glistening in the far distant depths we cannot at once conclude that the light is a faint one because it appears to us to be faint. It may be that the light is only faint because it comes from such a tremendous distance. In fact the brightest light conceivable could be reduced to the insignificance of a small star if only it were removed sufficiently far.

The most intense light we know of comes, of course, from the light which rules by day, from our sun himself. The sun pours his unrivalled beams around us in all directions with prodigal abundance, notwithstanding his enormous distance of ninety-three millions of miles. Let me describe an experiment with respect to our sun, an experiment, it is needless to say, which could never be performed, but the results to which it leads us are none the less certain. Astronomers have demonstrated them in many other ways.

Suppose that the sun were gradually to be moved away farther and farther into space; suppose that by this time to-morrow the great luminary should be twice as far as it is now, and the next day should be three times as far, and the day after that four times, and so on until in a year's time we should find that the sun was 365 times the distance from us that it is at present. Let us now trace the changes which we should see in the brilliancy of our orb of day. When he had reached double his distance from us we should find that the light had decreased to a quarter of its present amount, and the heat which we derived from his beams would have decreased in the same proportion. In ten days we should find that the light had become so feeble as to be only one-hundredth part of that which we enjoy now. The apparent size of the sun would also be steadily decreasing, for as the distance of a body increases its apparent dimensions diminish. Sometimes the diminution of apparent size with distance is well illustrated on a clock tower. You would hardly believe that the hands and face of a clock like that at Westminster were so large until you happen to see a man cleaning or repairing it, when he appears a mere pigmy in comparison with the mighty dial which points out the hours. In a similar way with every increase of distance, the apparent size of the sun would decline, and in the lapse of a year the sunlight would be reduced to a feeble twilight. The sun itself would remain visible for many years, even if it were steadily moving away, though its lustre would continually decline, and its size would continually diminish, until at last it would have shrunk to the insignificance of a small point of light, still visible as a glittering object, but too minute to enable any definite form to be perceived. Further still, the sun might recede until it passed beyond the reach of vision of the unaided eye; the telescope would, however, be able to pursue the retreating luminary until at last it sank into the depths of space beyond the reach of any instrument whatever.

This little argument will prepare us for an explanation of the stars. They merely appear to us to be points of light of varying degrees of brightness, but we have seen that our own sun might be reduced in lustre to that of the very dimmest of the stars if only it were removed sufficiently far. If, therefore, the stars are at a great enough distance from our system, it may indeed be that they also are suns, possibly equalling, or possibly even surpassing, our own sun in magnificence.

Here is indeed an imposing suggestion. Can it be that the host of stars which adorn our midnight sky are actually suns themselves of an importance comparable with that of our own? This is a great thought, and we desire to test it by every means in our power. You will see from the reasoning I have given that the whole question turns simply on one point, and that is: How far off are the stars? The tiniest point of light that is just seen as a glimmer in the mightiest of telescopes may be indeed a sun as great, or indeed a million times greater, than our sun, if only that star be sufficiently far off. To find the distance of a star is a problem which taxes the utmost powers of the painstaking astronomer; every refinement of skill in making his measurements and of care in the calculation of his observations has to be lavished on the operation. Alas! it but too often happens that the astronomer's labours prove to be futile. The surveying navigator often has to mark on his chart that no bottom could be found in the depths of the sea. His appliances would not work, or work reliably in those ocean abysses; so too, the astronomer, when he tries to sound the depths of space to the distances of the stars, has also to mark, generally speaking, "no bottom here," as the result of most of his investigations. When this is the case we know for certain that the star on which his calculations have been made must be a gorgeous sun, because we are assured of the greatness of its distance, even though we have not been able to find out what that distance was. There are, however, some few places through the sky where the astronomer's sounding line can, so to speak, touch bottom; there are a few stars of which we do know the distance, and the result is not a little significant. Were our sun to be withdrawn from us to a distance so great as that of the very nearest of the stars, our magnificent ruler and benefactor would certainly have lost all his splendour; he would, in fact, have shrunk to the similitude of a little star not nearly so bright as many of those which we see over our heads every night. Imagine the sun's light subdivided into two hundred thousand parts, each of which would give us only a feeble illumination, and then imagine that each of these parts was again divided into two hundred thousand parts more, and it is one of these last fragments that would represent the miserable lustre which the sun would then display.

From these considerations we can enunciate the magnificent truth which astronomy discloses to us. I do not think that in the whole range of nature there is any thought so magnificent or so imposing as that which teaches us to regard every star of every constellation as a sun. We cannot indeed assert that they are all so great as our sun, but we can affirm with certainty that many of them are far greater and far more splendid. Considering that our sun presides over a system of worlds of which the earth is one, that it gives light and heat to those worlds, and guides them in their movements, it would greatly enlarge our conceptions of the universe if we were assured that there was even one more sun as large and as splendidly attended as is our own. But now we find that not only is there one additional sun, but that they teem in uncounted thousands through space. Look, for example, on the next fine night at the Great Bear, the best known of all our northern constellations, and there you see seven stars forming the well-known feature. Figure in your mind's eye each one of those stars in the likeness of a majestic sun as big, warm, and bright as our sun, and look at other parts of the sky and repeat the process with the other constellations, and your conception of the magnificence of the starry system will begin to assume proper proportions. But this is only the first step, you must next look at the smaller stars, and reflect that they, too, are also suns, only much farther off, as a general rule, than the brighter stars, though this is by no means invariably the case. Thus your estimate of the number of suns in the universe will rise to thousands, but you will not stop there, you will get a telescope to help you, and to your extreme delight and wonder you will find that there are hosts of stars—too faint to be visible to the eye, but which the telescope will immediately disclose. You will get a more powerful instrument, and then you will perceive that the stars are to be numbered by tens of thousands, and even by millions, and with every fresh accession of power in your telescope fresh troops and myriads of suns are revealed. Suns in clusters, suns strewn thickly here and sparsely there, so as to give us the notion that the only limit to the number we can see is the power of the telescopes we are using. Attempts at actual numeration are futile, for who can tell the number of the stars?

We can, however, form an estimate, and by taking samples, so to speak, of the sky here and other samples there, we have been enabled to learn the overwhelming fact that our universe does contain at the very least one hundred millions of suns.

CHAPTER XIX.

THE EXTENT OF THE SIDEREAL HEAVENS.

In discussing the extent of the visible universe, it must always be borne in mind that the farther a source of light is from us the fainter is the illumination which we receive from it. Suppose that a star which just lies on the limits of naked-eye visibility were somehow to be transported to a distance which is twice as great, then the lustre of that star would be diminished to one-fourth of its original amount. It would, therefore, be of course invisible to the unaided eye, but could still be easily perceived by a telescope. Indeed, the very word *telescope* means an instrument for looking at objects a long way off, and the effect of the telescope is to reduce the apparent distance of the object. Thus the binocular glass that the mariner uses at sea has the seeming effect of reducing distances to about one-third of their amount, so that if a star were carried off to three times its actual distance from us it would still be shown as clearly in a binocular as it would be seen by the unaided eye when placed at its original distance. A star just on the verge of naked-eye visibility would still remain within the grasp of such an instrument even were it three times as far away. The instrument the astronomer uses must, however, be much more powerful than that which suffices for the mariner. A telescope small enough to be held in the hands would be competent to retain a star within its ken even though the star were removed to a distance ten times as great as when it was just visible with the unaided eye. The larger instruments would be sufficiently powerful to follow a star even though it were removed to a distance one hundred times as great as that at which it could be just glimpsed by the naked eye, while the greatest instruments of which our observatories can boast would still hold every lucid star in the heavens within view even were those stars wafted off one thousand times as far as they are at present.

These facts give us some notion of the extraordinary extent to which great telescopes increase the range of our vision. We are permitted by their aid to sound to a depth in space one thousand times as great as that to which the unaided eye would enable us to penetrate. Above and on each side, and around us in every direction the range of our vision is increased a thousand-fold. At first it might appear that the extent of space accessible to our telescopes would also be increased to one thousand times the extent of naked-eye vision. This would, however, give a very inadequate conception of the truth. With our unaided eyes we are able to see all the objects around us which lie within a certain mighty globe of which our earth is the centre. When we employ great telescopes we can explore a globe of which the radius has been enlarged one thousand-fold, therefore the quantity of space that we can examine in the two cases must be represented by two globes, one of which has a diameter a thousand times as great as the other. The volumes of two such spheres have a ratio so great that perhaps we do not readily comprehend it. The point I now wish to illustrate is one which very frequently arises in the consideration of problems in astronomy, and, indeed, in other subjects as well.

Let us take a very simple example. Suppose a cow is tethered by chain in a field; she will, of course, be only able to graze over the grass which grows within the circle to which her movements are confined. If we desire to give the cow double as much grass as she had before, would that end be accomplished by doubling the length of the chain? It would be more than accomplished; in fact, she would then have four times as much pasture as she had before. The circle over which she can graze has double the diameter, no doubt, but then its area is four times as great. Thus we see that the area increases in a far more rapid ratio than that in which the radius increases. Think next of two bird cages. We may suppose them to be both shaped like globes, the diameter of the larger being double that of the smaller. What will be the freedom enjoyed by the bird in the larger cage as compared with that of the less fortunate bird in the other? The volume of space over which the bird in the big globe can fly is not twice nor even four times as great as that allotted to the other bird; it is no less than eight times as great.

The bulk of a grain of sand as compared with the bulk of a football may illustrate the space accessible to our eyes when compared with the space accessible to one of the great telescopes. The larger of these spaces has a thousand times the diameter of the others; therefore, the relative quantities of these spaces are to be obtained by multiplying 1,000 by 1,000 and by 1,000 again. Thus we finally learn that the amplitude of our vision is augmented to one thousand million times its original extent by the use of our greatest telescopes. It need, therefore, be no matter for surprise that the number of stars visible through our great telescopes or recorded on the sensitive films of photographic plates should number scores of millions. In fact, it would sometimes seem surprising that the number of telescopic stars is not even greater than it actually appears to be. If we are able to explore one thousand million times as much space we might expect that the number of objects disclosed would be also increased about a thousand million fold, but this is certainly not the case. The truth seems to be that our sun is but one star of a mighty cluster of stars; we happen to lie near the middle of the cluster, and the rest of the stars belonging to it form what we know as the Milky Way. There are, of course, other clusters scattered through the heavens, some of them, perhaps, as great as that body of stars which forms the Milky Way. Owing to our residence in this cluster we see the neighbouring suns in multitudes, and thus we receive the impression that the solar system lies in an exceptionally rich part of the universe in as far as the distribution of stars is concerned.

On the outskirts of the universe lie those faintest and dimmest of objects which we can just perceive through our greatest telescopes. We know that many of the stars around us would still remain visible in great instruments, even though they were removed a thousand times as far off. Among the myriads of faint stars which we see from our observatories there may be many, indeed there must be many, which are fully a thousand times as distant as the bright stars which twinkle in our comparative neighbourhood. We thus obtain some conception of the stupendous distance at which the outskirts of the universe are situated. There are different ways of illustrating this point, but I think the simplest, as well as the most striking, is that which is founded on the velocity of light. It is a remarkable fact that the beautiful star known as Vega has a distance from us so tremendous that its light must have taken somewhere about eighteen years to travel hither from thence. Notwithstanding that the light dashes along with such inconceivable speed that it will cover 185,000 miles in every second, notwithstanding that a journey at this pace will complete the entire circuit of this globe seven or eight times between two successive ticks of a clock, the light will, nevertheless, take eighteen years to reach our eye from the time it leaves Vega. We do not, therefore, see the star as it is at present; we see it as it was eighteen years ago. For the light which this evening enters our eyes has been all that time on its journey. Indeed, if Vega were actually to be blotted out from existence it would still continue to shine out as vividly as ever for eighteen years before all the light on its way had reached us.

We have been led to the belief that among the more distant stars in the universe there must be many which are fully a thousand times as far from us as is Vega, hence we arrive at the startling conception that the light they emit has been on its journey for 18,000 years before it reached us. When we look at those lights to-night we are actually viewing them as they were 18,000 years ago. In fact, those stars might have totally vanished 17,000 years ago, though we and our descendants may still see them glittering for yet another thousand years.

We shall realise a little more fully what this reasoning involves if we suppose that astronomers dwelt on such a star, and that they had eyes and telescopes sufficiently keen not only to discern our little earth, but even to scrutinise its surface with attention. Let us suppose that the stellar astronomers looked at England: do you think they would see a network of railways joining mighty and populous cities, furnished with immense manufactories and with countless institutions. Such would be the England of to-day. But from the distance at which these astronomers are situated light takes 18,000 years for its journey, and, therefore, what they would see would be England as it was 18,000 years ago. To them England would even now appear as a country mainly covered with forests inhabited by bears and wolves, and totally void of any trace of civilisation. This illustration will at all events serve to convey some conception of the distance at which the outskirts of our visible universe are plunged in the depths of space.

CHAPTER XX.

THE MOVEMENTS OF THE STARS.*

I SHALL follow the precedent set by my illustrious predecessors in this chair, and endeavour to lay before you some of the recent acquisitions of knowledge in those branches of science with which I am myself most particularly connected.

It has been my privilege on not a few occasions to discourse to the members of the Midland Institute on various astronomical matters, but our science is ever growing, it has shown quite unexpected vitality within the last year or two, and consequently I find myself in possession of abundant material. Discoveries are just now being made with ever increasing volume; results we despaired of attaining yesterday are familiar to us to-day, while to-morrow will see the van of the army of research advancing into some wholly new territory. I could not attempt to give any comprehensive insight into the marvellous accumulations of facts that have recently been garnered by students of the heavens. I will rather endeavour to develop with fitting detail that particular line of

* Presidential address at the Midland Institute, Birmingham.

research which of all others seems to have yielded the most striking results. The subject which I chiefly propose to discuss is the application of the spectroscope to the study of the movements of the heavenly bodies, a subject with which the name of Huggins is primarily associated.

We have been long accustomed to receive with interest the tidings which the spectroscope conveys as to the constitution of the bodies throughout space. It was the primary function of that beautiful instrument to analyse the light which came from afar; and by decomposing the composite beam into its constituents, the spectroscope declared to us the actual materials present in the bodies from which the light emanated. It was astonishing to learn that thirty-five of the elements known on this earth were present on the sun. Somewhat similar announcements were made with respect to the stars and various other heavenly bodies. The information thus won was a most important accession to our knowledge of the material construction of the universe. Certain philosophers had even formulated the doctrine that to discover the elements present in the stars must necessarily lie beyond the province of man's powers. The events, however, entirely disconcerted these rash assertions. We have learned much as to the elementary bodies present in various celestial orbs, and quite recently we have come to believe not only that the elements in the sun have much in common with those in the earth, but that the two bodies are so similar in constitution that, in the striking words of Sir William Huggins in his address to the British Association (1891), it almost seems that, if the earth were heated to the same temperature as the sun, it would emit a spectrum of the same character. To have demonstrated the material unity of the universe is indeed a notable achievement for that little instrument, the spectroscope. But it seems possible that the services of the prism to science are now taking a direction in which the results to be achieved will outshine in importance and interest even that grand discovery of material unity, to which we have referred. Within the last year or two the spectroscope has made revelations with regard to the movements of certain of the heavenly bodies of a character which have startled the scientific world quite as much as did the fundamental discovery made some thirty years ago of terrestrial elements in the sun. Let me unfold the matter.

Look at a star such as Sirius or Aldebaran. Bring to bear upon it the meridian circle of the observatory, with all its refinements for exact measurement, and we can determine the exact place of the star in the heavens. We can do so with an accuracy which makes the fixed star a landmark of the universe. Years roll on, and by a repetition of the observations, the place of that star is again determined, and the two places do not agree. They are purged from every source of error, but still a discrepancy remains, the place of the star as now observed is not the same as its place was years ago; it has what we call a proper motion.

Tested in this way almost all the stars will probably be found to be in motion. We talk of these objects often as fixed, but the word must be used in a relative sense. To our ephemeral glance the stars seem fixed; but what is indeed fixed when sufficient time is allowed? The cloud that now caps a mountain summit is obviously unstable;

in an hour it may have dissolved into the transparent vapour from which it had been originally condensed. We are apt to contrast the evanescent cloud with the great mountain by which it was gathered. The mountain itself seems the ideal of stability. For thousands of years it has lasted, for thousands of years it seems destined to endure; but when sufficient time is allowed, the mountain is no more permanent than the cloud. The avalanche that thunders down its side is only a somewhat vigorous indication of the agencies that are incessantly tending to bear down the mighty mass. The Matterhorn of to-day will assuredly vanish in time just as many other mighty mountains have done in the course of geological history.

Indeed it may be remarked that nature on a grand scale exhibits no qualities of permanence. The Alps may last longer than the ruins of Palmyra, but everything that we know of geology teaches us that the sea has rolled where Mount Blanc now rears its head, and that for anything we can tell it may do so again. For permanence in nature we must look not to great planets; we find it, if at all, only in the atoms of matter. The little pulsating molecule, too small to be visible in the most powerful microscope, even if the object were a thousand times larger than it is, seems to possess attributes qualifying it for indefinite duration.

The constellations are no doubt so far fixed that in the course of a lifetime, or even in the lifetime of a nation, they undergo but little change. The Orion at which Job looked was almost the Orion of our skies to-night. I say almost, because when close examination is made it will be found that the stars in the constellations are gradually changing. We sometimes think that those groups of stars to which from all antiquity certain names have been assigned have bonds of affinity, and that their proximity on the heavens is not to be attributed to a mere casual arrangement, but is to be taken as indicating a community of origin. In some cases there can be no doubt that this is so. In the great group of Orion, for instance, to which I have already referred, modern researches demonstrate that the several stars of that grand constellation possess a structure which may be described as peculiar to themselves, inasmuch as a similar structure has only been observed in one other star in the sky except those of Orion. In this case we have the evidence not only of juxtaposition in the heavens, but also of an allied material composition. Under these circumstances it seems almost impossible to doubt that the glorious assemblage of stars forming the constellation of Orion does really represent portions of a mighty system. If any further corroboration of this view be required, it may be obtained from recent discoveries with respect to the peerless nebula by which Orion is most familiar to astronomers (p. 126). The beautiful photographs which have been obtained by Common and other astronomers have tended to disclose ever widening boundaries to the great nebula when sufficiently long exposure has been given. We thus see that the glowing gas encroaches on the surrounding space to an extent much wider than mere eye observation would have indicated. Several of the bright stars are already seen to be invested with whatever glory residence in the interior of a glowing nebula may confer. Adding this circumstance to those we have already mentioned of juxtaposition and of material congruity, it seems impossible to doubt that Orion, the finest constellation in the heavens, is not a mere fortuitous concourse of stars, but is a system possessing indications of a common origin.

In a similar way we are entitled to infer that many other remarkable groups of stars give evidence of a certain physical connection which corroborates the presumption obtained from the fact that the stars happen to be close neighbours. I do not suppose that anyone ever could have doubted that so striking a group as the Pleiades had some natural connection. But if there were such doubts they must be dispelled when the photographs of the Messrs. Henry and of Mr. Roberts show the seven stars of the Pleiades to be immersed in a single nebula, invisible to the eye, and perceptible only to the delicacy of the photographic plate. In other famous groups also there are indications of relationship drawn from their common movements. If seven fish were seen near together in the sea there would be a certain presumption that they formed a related group, and this presumption would be greatly strengthened if it should appear that all the fish were swimming in parallel directions. We can sometimes apply a similar principle to the study of a constellation. If seven bright stars lie comparatively near each other in the sky, and if it be found that they participate in a common motion so far as direction is concerned, we may not unnaturally conclude that those stars belong to an organized system, and that they are not merely a number of discrete objects scattered promiscuously on the sky.

Picture this vast firmament of stars, some in associated groups, some more sporadic and isolated, and all more or less in motion. For centuries, for untold thousands of years, these stars have been moving, fresh stars have come in from the abyss of space, and have gradually sunk away again to invisibility. There is no permanence in the heavens. Even in the lapse of geological time the heavens must have worn a succession of aspects, each wholly different from the other. The sky as we see it to-night presents us with an arrangement of stars different from the stars which were visible to the eye of the first man that trod this earth, and the stars which the first man saw must have been widely different from those on which in far earlier times the ichthyosaurus may have looked, while these again must have been totally different from the stars which spangled the sky in those excessively remote times when life began to dawn on the earth.

In our attempt to understand the nature of things celestial there is nothing of more importance than a clear comprehension of the mode in which the universe of stars is gradually transforming itself. We want to learn how each star is moving, and whither it is moving; and when we have obtained such knowledge, we are in a position to learn more truly the disposition of that vast array in which our sun is only one of the units. Astronomers had well-nigh despaired of attaining any comprehensive knowledge on this subject within the lifetime of the present generation. Centuries must elapse before the majority of the stars have advanced by proper motion to a sufficient distance from their present places to render the change conspicuous. We want some readier way of determining the pace at which a star is going—we want an instrument which shall tell us at once the speed of the body without having to deduce that speed from a tardy comparison between the places of the stars obtained after the lapse of a sufficient interval between them. This the spectroscope supplies, it tells us while we are looking at the star the speed at which it is winging its flight.

To determine the rate at which a star is moving towards or from us requires no nice comparison and discussion of observations made after an interval of a century by different observers using different methods and obtaining determinations which are entitled to very different degrees of confidence. The modern spectroscopic observer takes his seat at his instrument, adjusts his spectroscope on the star. He fixes his attention on a certain line in the spectrum, a line, for instance, known to belong to the element hydrogen; he sees it shifted to the right or to the left of a standard hydrogen line, introduced for the purpose of comparison. If the shift be one way, the star is urging its course towards us, if the shift be the other way the star is retreating from us, while by measuring the amount of the shift the actual velocity of the motion is determined. There is a certain indicator sometimes put on a locomotive engine which shows by a dial the speed at which the engine is running. By a glance at this dial the engine-driver learns at once the pace he is making. The spectroscope is like this little indicator; it shows at once the pace of the body to or from the observer without the necessity for awaiting the time necessary to pass over a certain interval. Thus the spectroscope offers to us a means of obtaining promptly valuable information with regard to the proper motions of the stars.

I must, however, be careful to explain that though I have thus drawn an antithesis between the spectroscopic method of observing proper motions and the telescopic method, yet that from another point of view the two methods are to be regarded rather as complementary to each other. Each purports to tell us something which the other is wholly incompetent to tell. This will be plain if we endeavour to realise the character that the motion of a star will usually present. Let us suppose that the only movement possessed by the star was directly towards the observer, or directly from him, that there was, in fact, no movement across the line of vision. In this case the star would never appear to change its place with respect to the stars in its neighbourhood; in fact, the only conceivable alteration in the telescopic appearance of the star would be, that in the course of time it would become brighter if approaching or fainter if receding. But any change of this kind would be so insignificant that we can afford to disregard it. On the other hand, it might happen that the movement of the star was such as to lie entirely across the celestial sphere, so that it was neither approaching to nor receding from the observer. In this case the entire proper motion would disclose itself by the displacement of the star relatively to the other stars in the heavens, and these are precisely the circumstances in which the old telescopic method is available. In fact, the spectroscope will only show motion directed along the line of sight, while the telescope only shows the motion which is perpendicular to the line of sight. Thus each of the methods exhibits that particular movement which the other is incompetent to perceive. Of course it will not often happen that the movement of a star is so adjusted as to be either entirely in the line of sight or entirely perpendicular to the line of sight. The movement will generally be of such a character that, to use the well-known language of mechanics, it will have one component along the line of vision and another perpendicular thereto. For the complete determination of the movement of the star it is necessary for us to know both these components, and it will be plain in what sense the spectroscopic method and the telescopic method are complementary; the latter determines the movement perpendicular to the line of vision, and the former gives us the movement along the line of vision. Each method just gives what the other is unable to give; there remains, however, the important difference, that the spectroscope indicates instantly, if I may so speak, the velocity of the body along the line of sight, while the telescope only indicates the portion of the velocity perpendicular to the line of sight by a comparison of observations separated by a long interval of time.

There is another essential distinction to be noticed between the information conveyed by the spectroscope and that yielded by the older method of observing proper motions. It is a distinct advantage of the spectroscopic method that, so far as its indications are concerned, the distance of the body from the observer is immaterial; the shift of the line which is observed has a magnitude which depends solely on the relative speed with which the body emitting the light is approaching to or receding from the observer. A star which shows a certain shift of spectral lines due to its velocity would exhibit precisely the same shift were its distance ten times or a hundred times that which it actually happens to be, but the matter is quite otherwise when proper motions are being measured by the ordinary telescopic method. The displacement which the telescope observes depends partly on the velocity with which the body is moving and partly upon the distance at which it is situated. If two stars had equal velocities perpendicular to the line of sight, but if one of those stars was ten times as far as the other, then the apparent movement of the more distant star, as measured by its displacement on the heavens, would only seem to be one-tenth part that of the nearer star. In the case of bodies which are extremely distant from us, the circumstance that I have just mentioned causes the determination of its movement on the heavens to be impossible, owing to its minuteness. A star might be so far off that even if it moved as quickly as the most rapidly moving body that we know of, still its apparent displacement on the heavens might be quite inappreciable after the lapse of a year or many years, and consequently we could hardly obtain any information as to its movements across the face of the heavens. On the other hand, the excessive distance of the star would be no bar to the application of the spectroscopic method, so long as the spectrum was bright enough to enable the lines to be seen. The form, too, in which the spectroscope offers to us its results is especially satisfactory; it announces definitely that the star is moving towards us or moving from us, and it determines the velocity of that motion. The telescopic method merely indicates that the star traverses so many seconds of arc, or often mere fractions of a second, in the course of a twelvemonth. We cannot express the result in speed of miles per second unless we happen to know the distance of the star from the earth, and with this important element we are, in the majority of cases, quite unacquainted.

Quite otherwise is it in the spectroscopic method of measuring proper motions along the line of vision; what we now obtain is not a measurement of arc on the sky, it is the velocity in miles per second that is given to us, and this, be it observed, not after the lapse of a long period of time between the first observation and the last, but directly, so that by turning the spectroscope on one star we may, for example, say that it is approaching at the rate of ten miles a second, while the same method applied to another star may show a recession at the rate of ten, fifteen, or any other number of miles per second. To obtain a complete knowledge of the movement of the stars we require both the spectroscopic method and the old-fashioned telescopic method. By the union of the two classes of measurement a complete knowledge is obtained of the way in which each star is moving.

Let me now elucidate with sufficient detail the principle of the very beautiful process on which the spectroscopic method of determining movements on the line of sight is based. Light is known to be caused by waves in that mysterious fluid, the ether. The ether fills all space, at least, so far as space contains objects visible to us, and the light from a star is caused by ethereal waves which have trembled along an appalling distance of many billions of miles from their origin in the glowing star to the retina, where they set the nerves in vibration.

Everyone who has stood on a sea-beach and watched the sea rolling in can find no difficulty in comprehending what we mean by the wave length. We do not here refer to the length of the wave in the same sense as we could speak of the length of the beach: we simply mean the interval between one wave and the next, or, to speak more definitely, the number of feet between the crest of one wave and the crest of the wave following it; nor will there be any difficulty in understanding from the analogy of the beach the difference between long waves and short waves. It is true that in many respects the analogy of waves on the beach is defective when we would seek to understand the waves in the ether; we must rather think of the latter as a succession of throbs rapidly succeeding each other throughout this invisible and intangible fluid. If the throbs succeed each other at comparatively long intervals, then the light of which they convey the impression is red; the waves that are the shortest, so far as visual rays are concerned, correspond to light of a violet hue.

We thus assign a length to each wave, and we can regard that length as in direct correspondence with th colour of the light; this may be submitted to strict numerical expression, in fact, we know the wave lengths of the principal rays of light with an accuracy which is one of the most marvellous results of modern physical research. These waves are very minute; take the very longest we can see, which corresponds to extremely deep red at the very end of the spectrum, the wave length of the ray identified by the Fraunhofer line known as A is expressed as 7604·04 tenth-metres. Let me attempt to illustrate what this length really corresponds to; where are we to find an object small enough for the comparison? If we divide an inch into 1,000 equal parts, yet each of these would be 30 times as long as this tiny wave of light. At the other end of the visual spectrum is the extreme violet, the wave lengths are only about half as long, while in that ultra-violet region occupied by rays incompetent to excite any nerves possessed by our retina, but acutely perceptible by the peculiar sensibility of the photographic plate, the waves are shorter still.

Light travels across space with a tremendous speed of 185,000 miles per second. It gives us a wonderful impression of the subtlety of the ether to think that waves, of which tens of thousands are comprised within the length of a single inch, can oscillate with such astonishing rapidity that in a single second of time 185,000 miles shall be travelled, each mile having 1,760 yards, each yard having three feet, each foot twelve inches, and each inch some thirty or forty thousand wave lengths.

A remarkable circumstance must now be mentioned; it has been discovered that rays of every colour travel with the same speed. If a ray of blue and a ray of red be started at the same moment they will require precisely the same time to travel a million miles or any other distance. If in the depths of space a blue star and a red star simultaneously sprang into existence, we should become aware of the two creations at the same instant, provided the stars were equally distant from us. Hence we are able to conclude the time of vibration of a wave of any given colour. The vibrations of the ether as it conveys a red ray of light are not so rapid as those which convey a ray from the violet end of the spectrum; or, to speak a little more correctly, when certain nerves on the retina are tingling with so many vibrations a second, the brain is conscious of a red light, while vibrations of other numbers per second correspond to the orange and blue rays respectively. We must, therefore, understand that our sense of vision distinguishes between one colour and another solely by the different number of vibrations of the ether to which the rays correspond. On the correct apprehension of this principle depends the right understanding of the spectroscopic method for the detection of motion along the line of sight.

We have been hitherto supposing that the body from which the light emanates is at rest. Now let us suppose that it is in motion to or from the observer; we shall see that this would have the effect of modifying the interpretation which the brain puts on the sensations which it receives from the retina. The subject is one of some difficulty, but I hope by the help of a few illustrations to make it intelligible.

I remember some time ago hearing a question propounded something of this kind. Suppose that it takes a week for a steamer to cross from Liverpool to New York, and that one steamer starts from each end every day. Of course we may suppose that, on an average, one arrives every day, so that in the course of a week seven steamers reach Liverpool. But now let us suppose that the observer, instead of being stationed at Liverpool, takes his berth on one of the outgoing steamers. Then the question may be asked as to how many returning steamers he will pass in the course of his week's voyage to New York. One might hastily answer seven, that is the same number, no doubt, that would be counted in a week from the landing-stage at Liverpool, but the case is very different as far as the outward bound ship is concerned. When the observer started on his voyage there were already seven steamers at different situations in their homeward passage; all of these the outward-going steamer must pass, but during the week that he is on his voyage seven more steamers must have left New York, and these, too, must also be passed by the outward bound ship before she reaches harbour on the other side of the Atlantic. Thus you see that our passenger outward bound will, in the course of a week, pass fourteen vessels coming the other way. In fact, he will pass two vessels per day, whereas, if he remained at Liverpool, he would only find one per day arriving, on the supposition which we have made. Suppose that the sensations caused by the moving of the vessel were overlooked, so that, in fact, the observer was unconscious of the fact that he was in rapid motion; he would not unnaturally seek for an explanation of the phenomena he had observed in the movements of the other vessels. In other words, he would conclude that the vessels were leaving New York twice every day, the fact that he was himself in motion having had the effect of making the other vessels seem to arrive twice as often as they would otherwise have done.

Instead of ships crossing the Atlantic, let us now return to the conception of waves of light radiating from a star in the depth of space. If the star is voyaging towards the earth, then the number of waves that arrive every second will depend not alone on the light itself, but also on the relative velocity with which the bodies are approaching or receding. If the two bodies are approaching, then more waves will reach the eye in the same period. If, however, the two bodies are retreating, then fewer waves per second will enter the eye than in the former case. We have, however, already seen that the colour of the light depends on the number of undulations in a second which strike the retina; if this number be altered, then the colour of the light, at least as interpreted by our senses, will be altered also; this principle leads to some curious consequences, and in order to explain the matter fully it will be necessary for me to take a somewhat simpler case than any that actually occurs in nature.

Generally speaking, the light radiated from a star or from any other luminous source is of a highly composite character, consisting of a number of undulations of very varied wave lengths—in fact, of a multitude of hues blended together. Thus, in the case of the sun, as well as in most of the stars, the light received from them consists of hues of all the colours of the rainbow, as well as of many rays which are invisible, because they vibrate too quickly in regions beyond the violet, or because they vibrate too slowly for our eyes to recognise in regions beyond the red. Let us, however, for the moment assume that a star existed which dispensed rays of a perfectly uniform type, which it will be convenient to take at a central part of the spectrum, say in the position of the green. Let our supposed star shed forth a flood of undulations all of precisely similar wave length, and let us study the modifications that would be caused in the appearance of that star if it moved rapidly towards the earth.

According to the principle we have already explained, as the two bodies come together, more undulations would enter the eye in a second than would be the case if the two bodies were relatively stationary. But we have already seen that our senses have no means of interpreting the hue of any beam that enters the eye except by the number of undulations per second that it causes on the retina. It follows that in the case we have supposed, when the eye received more vibrations per second than was appropriate to that particular shade of green, the appearance presented to us would be that the star had a different hue from that which it actually possessed—it would, in fact, shine with a shade of colour nearer the blue end of the spectrum. Indeed, if the speed of approach were sufficiently great the star would cease to appear green at all, and would manifest a bluish hue—and if we allow sufficient scope to our imagination in the matter of velocity, we could conceive a star approaching so fast that its colour, though originally green, appeared to be indigo or even violet, while by a still farther stretch we might suppose that the star is dashing towards us with a pace even greater than that which would transform its original green to an apparent violet. The vibrations would then be poured into the eye with such rapidity that no nerves on the retina, constructed as it is, would be adapted to respond to them, and consequently the star would become actually invisible to us.

On the other hand, let us suppose that this green-coloured monochromatic star was dashing away from the earth with sufficient speed, or, what comes to the same thing, that we were dashing away from it—then a transformation in the apparent character of the light would take place in the opposite direction. The shift of the green colour would be, in this case, not towards the blue end of the spectrum but towards the red end. If the star retreated sufficiently fast, its green colour would assume a yellowish hue; were its motion faster still, the yellow would be transformed into a red, while if the speed be still further accelerated the red would continually deepen corresponding to the lessened number of waves that entered the eye in a second, until at last the vibrations would become so slow that invisibility would again result from the want of nerves on the retina competent to perceive the vibrations of the character thus presented.

It was once supposed that the colours actually observed in the stars might be, as a matter of fact, explained as consequences of their varied movements to us and from us; the suggestion was an attractive one, but it will not bear the light of examination. It must be particularly observed that in the case we have supposed the light of the star is strictly monochromatic, but this is a condition of things which certainly does not exist in any ordinary star. In fact, in this respect the radiation from the stars may be said to resemble the radiations from the sun. There is an immense variety of different coloured light blended together—not only all the hues of the visible spectrum, but abundance of ultra-violet rays and abundance of rays beyond the red. If, therefore, as in our first case, the star be so hurrying towards us that the green light from the central parts of the spectrum is carried on towards the blue, the place of the green is itself filled by other rays advancing from the red end. The rays initially red have their places taken by rays from the invisible ultra-red region, which, by a quickening in the number of vibrations perceived per second in consequence of the rapid approach, pass from the invisible into the visible region. Thus, the general character presented by the appearance of the star is not altered. No doubt there is a conceivable velocity of approach so great that all the rays except a few should be hurried into the ultra-violet, and then, of course, the star would only have a violet or bluish colour; and there is a conceivable velocity of retreat from the earth by which all the rays except a few should have their periods of vibrations so lengthened that the only appeal to the eye would be the glimmer of a ruddy object. The velocities, however, that would be required for the display of such phenomena, so enormously transcend those actually possessed by any known body in space, that we may at once dismiss the supposition that the observed colours of the stars are to be explained in this manner. In fact, we have evidence presented by the spectroscope itself, which shows that we must look for an explanation of the colours of the stars in quite a different direction. It was thus known that the ingenious supposition that some stars seemed red merely because they were hurrying away from us, and that some stars seemed blue merely because they were hurrying towards us, must be set aside.

But, though the notion of Doppler was, we now know, in a large measure incorrect, yet we are indebted to it for a suggestion which has already borne much fruit in modern astronomical research, and which bids fair to extend our knowledge of the heavens to an extent that never would have been dreamed of until the last few years. It is quite true that the celestial velocities are insufficient to cause any grand transmutation in the hues of celestial objects. We must not look for their effects on so coarse a canvas as that which suffices for our mere visual impressions of colour. When we study the refinements of spectroscopic analysis, the indications of celestial movement become visible enough, even though they are insufficient to turn a green into a blue, or a yellow into a red. The development of this subject is one of immense interest, but it also possesses some little difficulty; and I therefore entreat your most particular attention.

I shall revert again to the supposition of a green star, the radiation from which is monochromatic. If the light from such an object were examined through a spectroscope the appearance presented would not be that of a band of varied colours which form the glories of the ordinary spectrum; it would be rather a single line of vivid green light, and occupying a particular position in the spectrum as defined by its wave length. If the body were moving towards us the line would shift towards the blue end. If the body were moving from us the lines would shift towards the red end. Let us suppose that our spectroscope is furnished with a measuring apparatus by which we are enabled to determine the amount of the shift with the necessary accuracy. Suppose, in fact, that the wave lengths of the light, when the object is relatively at rest, be the 30,000th of an inch, but that when the object is moving towards us it is found that the vibrations are 30,003 in the inch; it then follows that the fact of this body's movement towards us has caused us to receive one ten-thousandth part more vibrations per second than when the body was at rest. It therefore follows that the velocity with which the body is dashing towards us must be a ten-thousandth part of the velocity of light—in other words, about eighteen miles a second. It is a velocity of a magnitude comparable with this that we generally meet in the celestial regions. It may perhaps be two or three times as great, or in some cases possibly as much as ten times as great—in any case, however, the velocities of approach or recession are very small in comparison with the velocity of light. Rarely, indeed, will the actual velocity of a celestial body be so much as a thousandth part of the velocity of light, and consequently no alterations in the apparent quality of a ray arising from movement can at the utmost do more than affect its wave length by one-thousandth part of its total amount.

It would be useful to obtain some concrete notion as to the nature of the magnitudes with which we have to deal when discussing the problem of celestial movements in the line of sight. Let us look therefore at that ever-beautiful object the solar spectrum, especially at the double line D, which is caused by the presence of the element sodium. The wave lengths of these lines expressed in ten-millionths of a millimetre are, according to Professor Rowland, 5896·08, 5890·12; the difference, amounting as it does to 5·96, is about one-thousandth part of the whole amount. We are thus able to form the general conception that the greatest possible shift that could be caused in the spectrum is not likely to exceed the length of the interval between the two lines of sodium. It should be observed that in this calculation I have taken an extreme value for the velocity, and many of the velocities met with in space will not be one-tenth as great. It therefore follows that we must be prepared to make very exact measurements when the phenomena with which we have to deal are of such a delicate character that they do not extend to a shift of the lines of the spectrum through more than a fractional part of the interval between the components of the sodium line.

To understand the method of procedure it is necessary to recall the appearance presented by the spectrum of a star. It gives us generally the red, orange, yellow, green, blue, indigo, violet, forming the spectrum band so familiar to every one who has ever looked through a prism. From one end of this band to the other transverse lines variously grouped—often double, sometimes exquisitely fine, sometimes more or less ill-defined—are to be seen. The interpretation of these lines is now well understood. They are due to the presence of metallic or other vapours in the atmosphere surrounding the star. Such is at least the general description of the origin of the majority of the lines. Some are, however, caused by the presence in the atmosphere of the star of other substances besides metals; there are, for example, numbers of stars of which the brilliant Sirius may be taken as the type, the characteristic feature of which is the presence of a number of lines due to the element hydrogen.

For our present purpose, however, it is especially essential to observe that the lines are caused by something pertaining to the star itself. We have to invoke their aid for the measurement of the movements of the body in the line of sight. For the purpose of description, I shall take the line known as F in the solar spectrum. This line is also found in a good many stars, and it is known to be an indication of the presence of the element hydrogen. The wave length of this line in air is represented by the number 4860·72, the unit being, as usual, the ten-millionth of a millimetre. Now if the star is coming towards us, the line F will be displaced, with the rest of the spectrum, towards the blue end, and we want to measure the amount of that displacement. For this purpose we require a comparison spectrum which shall show where the line ought to be, if the body were at rest, relatively to the earth. We obtain this by availing ourselves of the wonderful principle discovered a quarter of a century ago, by which the interpretation of the dark lines in the spectrum is obtained.

Suppose that the element hydrogen be heated to incandescence by the electric spark, or in any other way, it will of course radiate light, and when that light is viewed through the spectrum certain brilliant lines will be perceived; these lines are characteristic of that particular element; where these lines are found hydrogen is present, where they are absent, hydrogen is absent; provided the conditions as to incandescence have been attended to. But these are bright lines on a dark background, whereas the lines in the spectrum of a star are often black lines on a brilliant background; how then are the two to be connected together? It is the unveiling of this connection that constitutes the discovery to which I have referred. The brilliant lines, it is to be observed, are produced by highly heated hydrogen; the dark lines in the spectrum of a star are due, not to heated materials, but to comparatively cool materials. In the upper regions of the star's atmosphere, the actual glowing surface sheds forth in copious abundance rays of every hue, but before these gain the outer space they have to pierce through the comparatively cold atmosphere with which each star may be surrounded.

Now, though that atmosphere may be sensibly transparent, it nevertheless levies a certain toll on the light passing through it; in fact, it stops some of the light.

Let us suppose, for the sake of argument, that the atmosphere surrounding the star was solely composed of hydrogen gas. This gas would be almost perfectly transparent, so far as most of the rays are concerned. It is essential, in this point, to pay attention to the wave lengths; most rays will be permitted to fly through unimpeded, but the passage of certain particular rays will be opposed, if not altogether prohibited, by the action of the hydrogen. Take, for instance, the ray whose wave-length is 4860·72, that particular ray will be more or less stopped; if its wave length had been a few units greater, or were a few units less, it would have been allowed to pass, but being what it is, its passport is refused. The same may be said of certain other wave lengths. The wave length of 6562·1 units, also will be stopped; while most rays more refrangible or most rays less refrangible are allowed to make their outward journey without hindrance. Here is indeed a remarkable property possessed by a so-called transparent gas; it picks out here and there certain wave lengths, and refuses all passage to rays which radiate in these forbidden periods, while rays of all other wave lengths pursue their way uninterfered with. At first it might seem that the rays which were stopped were selected apparently by caprice. Hydrogen, for instance, of which we are now particularly speaking, stops certain rays in all parts of the spectrum. But now comes the important discovery to which we have referred—the discovery which in fact renders spectrum analysis so important to the astronomer.

We have already seen that when hydrogen gas is heated, it radiates forth light which the spectroscope resolves into a certain number of bright lines in various parts of the spectrum, each with one particular wave length. We have also seen that when a cold atmosphere of hydrogen surrounds a star, the obstruction to the passage of the light is not indiscriminate, but only operates on rays of certain particular wave lengths.

And now for the extraordinary fact which has provided us with a key to the interpretation of spectroscopic phenomena. It has been discovered that the particular wave lengths which cold hydrogen is capable of stopping are precisely those wave lengths which characterize the light that heated hydrogen is capable of emitting. This is a very singular fact, and to understand it fully we must go a little further into the mechanism of the subject. For this problem, like many another problem in nature, resolves itself as a matter of last analysis into a question of dynamics.

Hydrogen is an invisible gas, the lightest body in nature, and we know that a gas consists of a number of molecules darting about in all directions; these molecules are so small and so close together, that many billions of them would fit into a lady's thimble. When the gas is heated the activities of the molecules are increased, each molecule in fact consists of a number of portions which are themselves moving with almost inconceivable rapidity, and with a complexity which we can only very partially understand. Fixing our attention for the moment on one particular wave length, corresponding to the ray F emitted by hydrogen; let us suppose that the hydrogen is heated to incandescence. We are to suppose that one of the modes of vibration in the molecule of the gas is so timed, that the oscillations it imparts to the ether are those competent to produce light of the character indicated by F. Let us now suppose that a light is radiated through a mass of cold hydrogen. The majority of the wave lengths of the light are such that no mode of vibration in the molecule corresponds to them, and consequently they are allowed to pass. Those particular rays, however, which vibrate with the period belonging to F, find the molecules in tune with them, so to speak; the molecules accordingly commence to vibrate, and thus absorb the particular energy belonging to that particular wave length.

Let me illustrate the matter from other branches of science. There are many analogous phenomena in the theory of sound; open a piano for instance, each string corresponds to a particular note. Sound a note from some other instrument, such as the human voice close by, and the piano resounds, but this resounding is not an indiscriminate return of the sound like an echo, for each note in the piano remains silent unless it has been appealed to by a precisely similar note from the other instrument. Thus the vibrations caused by the other instrument pass without effect over those notes with which they are not in tune, while the energy that they possess is absorbed by the strings which resound to them.

We may pursue this illustration a little farther. Let us suppose a multitude of piano wires stretched from floor to ceiling of an apartment, all tuned to one particular note; now of course if all these strings were struck, and if suitable sounding boards could be provided, then a vast volume of sound in this particular note would be the result. In other words, this apparatus would radiate, if I may use the expression, a note of one particular wave length. But suppose that the sounding boards were removed, and that the forest of strings was placed between an auditor and an orchestra, all the music from the orchestra would have to come through the strings before the auditor could hear it; the great majority of notes would pass through and between the strings, no doubt with some loss, but without any special interference. All those notes, however, from whatever instrument in the orchestra they might have come, which harmonized with a particular note to which the strings resounded, would be specially affected in their transit; as the music breathed past the wires they would commence to vibrate, because certain notes were tuned with the vibration that the strings were able to perform. The energy of the performers in the orchestra, so far as it was expended on the production of music of this particular note, would be employed in setting the forest of strings into a quiver, and would thus lose its power to affect the ears of the auditors at the end of the room.

In this case the forest of strings would have really acted as a sort of filter applied to the music diffused from the orchestra; they would have stopped the passage of one particular note, while they would have permitted notes of every other description to pass almost unmolested. The forest of strings is in fact opaque to one note, if I may use the expression, and transparent to every other note. But now observe that when the sounding boards are restored to the forest of strings, and when the orchestra is absent and the strings are set in vibration by fiddle bows or otherwise, they shed forth a volume of sound all of that one particular note, which alone they are competent to produce. In other words, we see that when the strings are used as a radiating source of music, the character of the music they emit is absolutely identical with those particular notes which they refuse to allow to pass when they are interposed between the orchestra and auditorium. In other words, the particular notes which are absorbed in the one case are identically the notes which are radiated in the other.

This illustration from sound will facilitate our explanation of the dark lines in the solar spectrum. Hydrogen in the sun's atmosphere, being cold compared with the deeper seated portions of the great luminary, stops certain light on its way outwards from the heated regions, and the light which the hydrogen stops is exactly the same which that gas will itself give out if heated to incandescence. We might make the illustration a little more complete by supposing that the forest of strings comprised not merely a single note, but that two, three, or even more notes each have many strings belonging to it. In that case the filtration from the music produced by the orchestra would remove from it every note of music to which there was a group of strings corresponding; the auditors might therefore find not only one note, but perhaps two, three, or even more wanting in different parts. Now we come very close indeed to our explanation of a system of dark lines corresponding to any particular element in the solar spectrum. The molecules of hydrogen, for instance, respond not merely to the particular wave length of light corresponding to the line F, but they also respond to the line C, and to several other lines as well. As the solar light, therefore, streams through the mighty encompassing atmosphere of the sun, in which hydrogen is a very important ingredient, it has filtered from it those rays which are of the same kind, as incandescent hydrogen is itself competent to produce. Accordingly, the dark lines belonging to hydrogen in the solar spectrum occupy the same positions as do the series of bright lines, which are generated when hydrogen is rendered incandescent in a vacuum tube.

I am aware that the illustrations I have given only render a very imperfect account of a great scientific doctrine, but they may suffice, at all events, for my present object, which is to show the use of the dark lines when we are studying the movements of the body from which the light radiates. Let us take a star, surrounded with hydrogen, and therefore showing in its spectrum the F lines as well as the other lines characteristic of this gas. Let us further suppose that the star is hurrying towards us, then, as we have already seen, the effect of this movement is to impart to the vibrations of each ray from the star, as interpreted by the eye, a somewhat greater rapidity than they actually possess. The F line of hydrogen coming from the star will pour more vibrations into the eye in a second than would have been the case if the star had no relative movement.

By the aid of the electric spark we are able to produce an artificial spectrum of hydrogen, and by suitable appliances we can introduce into the spectroscope the actual glowing spectrum of hydrogen side by side with the dark line spectrum of the same gas as it has come to us from the star. Here comes in the important principle on which I have laid so much stress, that the dark line spectrum produced by the cold hydrogen would be identically situated line for line with the bright line spectrum generated in the incandescent gas. We arrange, in fact, that two spectra shall be produced by the same system of prisms, so as to give every facility for the comparison. If the star were at rest relatively to the earth, each delicately bright line should be strictly continuous with each delicate dark line. If, however, the star be in relative movement to or from the earth, then the system of lines which it radiates will exhibit a shift relative to the system of lines produced by the incandescent hydrogen which is at rest with respect to the apparatus. Here, then, we have the means of measuring the velocity of the star along the line of sight. Take any one of the lines, the F line, for instance, its displacement relatively to the adjacent bright line can be measured. It can be measured with accuracy too, when the apparatus has been constructed with a delicacy that optical skill has now rendered possible.

We are gradually learning the full significance of the word light. We are now aware that the undulations which we see are only a couple of octaves, so to speak, out of an immense volume of undulations, which we have no senses for perceiving. We are thus at last attaining some conception of the majesty of these words, "Let there be light."

CHAPTER XXI.

PHOTOGRAPHING THE STARS.

We have quite recently experienced one of the greatest revolutions which the art of practical astronomy has ever undergone. Professor Young, in an admirable article on the subject, which has appeared in the *Princeton Review*, has indeed regarded the impending metamorphosis as parallel in importance to that which followed from the invention of the telescope. Perhaps we should hardly speak of the new departure as impending: we might rather say that it has already been in some degree realised. We may fairly derive an illustration from the somewhat similar change that our methods of illumination seem likely to undergo. It will be generally admitted that the present state of electric lighting is still in the initial and tentative stages; yet the overwhelming advantages of electricity for many purposes is no longer disputed. Somewhat similar to the invasion of electricity on old-fashioned sources of light is the invasion of photography into the time-honoured methods of conducting astronomical observations. We cannot indeed assert that the application of the photographic camera to the telescope is exactly novel. Nor can we for that matter deny that the electric light was invented half a century ago. But just as a few brilliant inventions have transformed electrical lighting from a scientific curiosity into an eminently practical reality, so the recent improvements in photography have rendered that art an indispensable auxiliary in the observatory of the future.

The applications of photography to astronomy are of the most widely diverse kind. We may employ it, in the first place, as an auxiliary in the production of accurate pictorial representations of particular objects in the universe, or in obtaining views of groups of such bodies; we may also employ it to aid the process of exact measurement. There are still other and more delicate branches of practical astronomy where the photograph is not merely a rapid or a convenient means of doing what could otherwise not be done so conveniently. Photography is a process for actually observing phenomena in such cases as entirely elude ordinary vision, and are only perceptible by the peculiar sensibility of the salts of silver contained in the film.

We shall first say a few words with regard to the suitability of the new method for the purpose of recording the appearances of the different celestial bodies. In all the applications of this process to the heavens we must bear in mind how widely different are the conditions under which a celestial photograph is to be procured from those which are met with in the more familiar pursuit of the art. In taking a portrait with the camera, there is of course only a few feet between the plate and the sitter. In the application of photography to the representation of landscape the distance between the objects and the camera is greatly increased; but even here the length of air which the rays have to traverse is generally much less than in the case where we attempt the portrait of a heavenly body. The atmosphere extends above our heads to an altitude which is still very uncertain. We learn, however, from the phenomena of shooting stars that the summit of the air is at least a couple of hundred miles aloft, and perhaps much more. The upper regions are so highly rarefied that they are incapable of exercising much deleterious influence on the rays of light; it is in the lower and the denser portions that the atmosphere is chiefly inimical to the photographer. Now, though to the portrait-taker the atmosphere signifies but little, except in so far as questions of light are involved, yet it is well known that the state of the atmosphere is very significant in landscape-photography; while in the case of the celestial photographer the behaviour of the atmosphere is of paramount importance. Even if the object be immediately over his head, the rays would have to make their way through two hundred miles of air before they entered his apparatus; while if the body lay far away from his zenith, as of course it usually does, the air-journey of the rays of light would be considerably longer. Any imperfections which the atmosphere is capable of producing must therefore be felt much more keenly by the celestial photographer than by the brothers in the craft who confine their attention to mere terrestrial objects. The qualities which characterize a suitable sky are steadiness, though wind is not necessarily objectionable, and photographic transparency, which is a very different property from visual transparency. By steadiness is meant such a regularity in the variations of density that each ray of light is persistently refracted along the same course throughout the duration of the exposure. By transparency the celestial photographer will mean a state of the air which will permit the particular rays of light which he wants to pass through. It will often happen that two nights which to the unaided eye, or even in the ordinary telescope, seem equally clear, may be of widely different clearness in so far as the photographic light is concerned.

To illustrate the opacity of the atmosphere to photographic rays I may mention a fact told me by the Rev. H. Swanzy, who accompanied the Rev. W. Green on his recent exploration of the Selkirk range in British Columbia. The plates they used required an exposure of three seconds or more in the valleys, while similar plates exposed at a height of ten thousand feet were found to be destroyed if the exposure was more than a small fraction of a second.

In the application of photography to celestial portraiture, we naturally first allude to the photographs of the sun, by far the most exquisite of which are those taken by Janssen at Meudon. His photographs, obtained by an extremely short exposure of a fraction of a second, display in a marvellous manner the actual texture of the sun under the conditions of its surface at the moment. They prove that the luminous parts are brilliant granules or cloudlets, floating, so to speak, in a less bright medium which is visible in the interstices between the cloudlets. Occasionally the openings between the small luminous portions are large enough to form dark spots. The photographic examination of the sun certainly bears out the view that the luminous surface is far from being continuous, even setting aside the presence of large spots. I must, however, say, that in none of the photographs that I have seen are the cloudlets at all of the willow-leaf or the rice-grain structure: they do not seem characterized by any specially elongated shape, except round the sun spots.

Photography has also been applied with success to the representation of the phenomena seen during the occurrence of a total eclipse of the sun. The total eclipses of recent years have been most assiduously observed by parties of astronomers who have visited whatever parts of the globe offered exceptional opportunities for the purpose. Special attention has been directed to the corona, and large photographic apparatus has been constructed with the object of obtaining coronal pictures. The result has been to produce most beautiful pictures.

Numerous photographs of the moon in very various phases have been taken. Among the earliest of them may be mentioned that of Rutherford, on March 6th, 1865, which is excellent, though of course now surpassed. Admirable pictures of the moon have been obtained at the Lick Observatory, in California, one of which is represented in the frontispiece.

Though the lunar photographs are interesting, and make beautiful transparencies to show on the screen, yet it will, I think, be admitted that, so far as the representation of lunar details is concerned, they are disappointing. Even the best of them will not bear much magnifying without becoming blurred and indistinct. The view that a photograph presents of any lunar mountain or crater, cannot be compared either in beauty or in sharpness with the picture that a telescope of adequate power will give the eye. In fact we may certainly say that no material addition to our knowledge of lunar topography has been contributed by photography. We may, however, hope for better things; for, with the extremely sensitive plates now procurable, a picture of the moon obtained under favourable atmospheric conditions with an extremely short exposure might prove much more capable of being magnified than any of the photographs that have heretofore been taken.

In the delineation of the planets, photography has comparatively been little applied, though the attempts which have been made are full of interest. The pictures of Jupiter by Henry at Paris, as well as those from the Lick Observatory, are excellent. The bands and other markings on the planet come out distinctly, and the renowned red spot is a very conspicuous object. In a few photographs, taken at intervals of half an hour, the gradual shifting of the features shows in an interesting manner the rotation of the planet on its axis. This very rotation is, however, one of the difficulties which impede successful photography of the planet. In the course of a long exposure the gradual displacement of the features by the rotation precludes the possibility of a sharp and well-defined picture. Here, again, very brief exposures and highly sensitive plates become the desideratum of the astronomer.

I cannot but think that photography will have a

considerable share in our further study of this the most gigantic of our planets. The marks on Jupiter are so incessantly varying that the photograph seems obviously the true method for recording its ever-fleeting details. It will be noticed that the circumstances are here quite different from those which attend the application of photography to the moon. In the latter the features are permanent, and the efforts of the eye and of artistic sketching can be persistently accumulated, with the result of giving us a delineation of the lunar surface as faithful as the powers of our telescope will permit. But there is no permanency in Jupiter, and our only means of becoming acquainted with the marvellous meteorology of that planet must be derived from the bringing together of as many accurate pictures of its disc as can be obtained in its ever-varying moods. For this object photography seems most admirably adapted. There is, however, a point which should be mentioned, and it has been brought before us very strongly while examining the beautiful Jovian photographs taken by the Henrys. It is that the photographic Jupiter and the visual Jupiter are different pictures. This is no doubt largely due to the atmosphere of the planet, which exercises a different degree of absorption on the photograph rays from that to which the visual rays are exposed. Here again the difference between the problem of photographing the airless moon and photographing a planet becomes significant. In the case of the moon the visual picture and the photographic picture tend to coincidence in proportion as they both approach perfection.

Pleasing pictures have also been taken of Saturn, especially by the Messrs. Henry. Not only does the broad division of the ring, usually known as Cassini's line, appear very distinctly, but many of the more delicate features are also perceptible. But the point which has struck me very forcibly about this picture of Saturn is the remarkable amount of shading which it gives to the Saturnian globe. As is well known to every practical astronomer, this globe usually possesses no very striking varieties of shade or of colouration in the telescope, and the extraordinary darkness about the poles of Saturn in the photograph will arrest the curiosity of every one who is familiar with the ordinary telescopic spectacle. The cause of this phenomenon appears to lie not in the actual colouration of the planet's globe, but in the atmospheric shell within which it is contained. It would seem that the Saturnian atmosphere, whatever be its character in other respects, must at all events possess the power of largely absorbing the photographic rays of light.

At the present time the question of the application of photography to the stellar regions is especially engrossing attention, and for this purpose it would seem that the new process is destined to effect a revolution in the art of astronomical observation. We must therefore consider the question of sidereal photography in some detail.

When a telescope is directed towards a star, it brings all the rays of that star to a focus; and the more excellent the construction of the optical part of the telescope, the more accurately will the image of the star approximate to that of a mathematical point. In the ordinary use of a telescope for visual purposes, all the rays of light collected by the aperture of the telescope are condensed to a point on the retina, and if the image there produced be sufficiently intense the sense of vision is excited, and the star is seen. If, however, the star be not perceived at the first glance, there is but little object in prolonging the gaze. It is true that expert practical astronomers know that a star which they fail to see when directly looking at it can sometimes be "glimpsed" when the eye is moved slightly away; the explanation apparently being that some fresher and more sensitive part of the retina is by this act brought into use. But by merely steadily staring at a faint star which is not bright enough to be detected at the first glance, there is little success to be expected. The fact is that the retina can only retain an impression for a small time—perhaps about one-seventh of a second—consequently there is no cumulative effect of the luminous impression to be obtained by prolonged watching.

But the case is very different when we place in the focus of the telescope a highly sensitive photographic plate, and permit the instrument to depict thereon an image of the star. The vibrations of the rays of light throw themselves assiduously on the plate, and steadily apply themselves to the task of shaking asunder the molecules of silver salts in the gelatine film. Just as the waves of ocean by incessantly beating against a shore will gradually wear away the mightiest cliffs of the toughest rock, so the innumerable millions of waves of light persistently impinging upon a single point of the plate will at length effect the necessary decomposition, and so engrave the image of the star. It will be obvious that this process will be the more complete the longer the exposure which is permitted, and thus we see one of the reasons why photography forms such an admirable method for depicting the stars. We can give exposures of many minutes, or of one, two, three, or even four hours; and all the time the effect is being gradually accumulated. Hence it is that a star which is altogether too feeble to produce an impression upon the most acute eye fortified by a telescope of the utmost power may yet be competent, when a sufficient exposure has been allowed, to leave its record on the plate. Thus it is that photographs of the heavens disclose to us the existence of myriads of stars which could never have been detected except for this cumulative method of observation which photography is competent to give.

There is another peculiarity about the photographic methods of observation which gives them an importance from quite a distinct point of view. The radiation from a star consists of a number of rays of very varied hues all blended together. If they were separated out, we should find that they were divisible into two great groups—namely, the visible and the invisible. As to the former, they characterize the well-known hues of the rainbow: the red, the orange, and the yellow, the green, blue, indigo, and violet. It is to these rays in varying degrees of combination that we are indebted for *visibility* in the star, either to our unaided eye, or even to the eye aided by a telescope. But it is conceivable that a star might dispense a rich stream of rays, and yet be totally invisible from the fact that none of those rays belonged to the special group which can alone excite vision. These invisible rays may be of different types. Some of them might be rays of heat, for the greater part of the rays of heat are of the invisible type; though no doubt some of them are also visible, as the red portions of the spectrum. I must also add that within the last few months wondrous possibilities have been opened up as to the discovery of innumerable other rays of much greater length, which do not directly appeal to any senses that we have been provided with. But with such extraordinary rays as those which can pass through a stone wall, and be refracted by a prism of pitch, we have not at this moment to do; though they are of the most intense interest, and possibly will admit of remarkable astronomical applications. The rays with which photography is concerned are mainly or largely of the invisible type, but they are rays of high refrangibility: they lie out beyond the violet.

Thus it happens that the rays from the star which are competent to excite an impression on the plate are partly in the visual portion, but chiefly in the invisible part of the total radiation. Now we can see another reason why the photograph may, and indeed must, largely extend our conceptions of the extent of the universe. It will grasp and depict light which would be utterly wasted so far as vision is concerned, for even were these rays poured in torrents into our eyes they could excite no sense of vision; and consequently all stars whose radiation did not contain a sufficient admixture of visual rays, no matter how copiously they diffused these ultra-violet rays, would, to the eye, be invisible in the most powerful telescope, though capable of being recorded by a photograph. It will thus be manifest that the grounds which the new method furnishes of increased powers to the astronomer are twofold. There is first the advantage of prolonged exposure; there is secondly the possibility of utilising invisible rays.

The late Dr. Roberts, whose experience and marvellous success in celestial photography entitle him to speak with confidence on the matter, gives us striking evidence of the detection of faint stars by the action of photography. With an exposure of an hour he has shown on a plate of about four square degrees a number of stars that he estimates at more than sixteen thousand, of which the brightest is less than the fifth magnitude. The circumstances appear to have been very favourable, for other photographs have been obtained of the same region and with exposures of equal duration. To all appearances the nights on the three occasions were equally clear; but clearness for visual purposes and clearness for photographic purposes involve different conditions; and this is remarkably illustrated by the three photographs referred to. One of them, by Messrs. Henry, showed three thousand stars; the next, by Mr. Roberts, showed five thousand stars; while the third, by the same operator and on the same region of the sky, disclosed more than three times the number.

It is of interest to attempt to estimate the total number of stars visible to the photographic eye over the entire surface of the heavens, assuming that the plate we have just referred to may be taken as an average specimen of the stellar richness of the entire firmament. The number of square degrees in the heavens is about forty-one thousand four hundred, and as the plate occupies four square degrees, it will follow that upwards of ten thousand plates of this size would be required to cover completely the whole vault above the horizon and below. If, then, there be over sixteen thousand stars on one of these plates, it follows that the total number over the sky capable of being disclosed by photography cannot be less than one hundred and sixty millions. It will be instructive to compare these figures with the stellar statistics afforded by other methods.

If we take a position on the equator, from whence, of course, all the heavens can be completely seen in the lapse of six months, the number of stars that can be reckoned with the unaided eye will, according to Houzeau, amount to about six thousand. If we augment our unaided vision by a telescope of even small dimensions, such as three inches in diameter, the number of stars in the northern hemisphere alone is upwards of three hundred thousand. We may assume that the southern hemisphere has an equally numerous star-population, so that the entire multitude visible with this optical aid is about six hundred thousand. Thus we see that the use of a telescope small enough to be carried in the hands suffices to multiply the lucid stars one hundredfold. Great telescopes no doubt soon show us that the hundreds of thousands are only the brighter members of a host of millions, and now we receive the assurance of photography that the telescopic stars are only the more conspicuous members of that vast universe. Mr. Roberts indeed declares that the multitudes of stars on the photographic plate grow with each increase of exposure to such a degree that it would almost seem as if the plate would be a well-nigh continuous mass of stars if the operations could be sufficiently protracted.

The long exposures necessary for celestial photography have introduced a new class of requirements into the construction of astronomical instruments. The questions here involved are of much practical importance, and are exciting a good deal of discussion at present.

There are, as is well known, two different classes of astronomical instruments—namely, the reflectors and the refractors; and it is still a matter of debate as to which class of instrument is the more suitable for the purposes of celestial photography.

In the reflector the rays from the star fall on the brilliant surface of a mirror carefully wrought into a special form. Formerly mirrors were made of speculum metal, consisting of two parts of copper to one of tin. This material was difficult to cast and tedious to shape. Its great weight was also a drawback, while the reflecting power, though very considerable, was still short of that possessed by silver. At present most of the reflectors are made of glass, and, after being accurately ground and polished to the true form, are chemically coated with silver.

The mirror, when used for celestial photography, is at the lower end of a tube, and the rays falling upon it from the star travel again up the tube to a focus on the plate, which is exposed with its face towards the mirror at the upper end. The plate is supported by slight arms from the side of the tube, and it offers of course an impenetrable obstacle to some of the rays from the star, and so far diminishes the effective size of the mirror. As however the diameter of the plate will not be more than perhaps one-fifth that of the mirror, it follows that only about four per cent of light is lost by this cause. The chief recommendation of the reflecting telescope is found in the circumstance that the rays of light of every description are all brought to the same focus. Thus if the plate be placed at the correct point for visual purposes, it is also correctly placed for the photographic rays. There is here no troublesome question as to the difficulty of securing a confluence of all the rays at a single point where their united action shall be devoted to engraving a mark on the plate. On the other hand, it has been customary to believe that the support of the mirror, and the precautions necessary to prevent the distortion of its figure by flexure, went far to neutralize the advantage of the useful indiscriminateness with which all rays were conducted to the same focus. The remarkable achievements of Mr. Roberts and of Mr. Common have, however, been accomplished by reflectors, in a way which proves that the difficulties attendant on this form can be surmounted.

For most of the great photographic enterprises which are now proposed to be undertaken refractors are being erected, and here a difficulty of a peculiar kind is encountered. A glass lens of accurate figure, when it receives a parallel beam of any homogeneous light, will direct all the rays of the beam to concentration at a focal point. To this extent the action of the lens and the action of the reflector are identical. By homogeneous light we mean light which we may with sufficient accuracy describe as being one of the prismatic colours. Thus a beam of pure red falling in parallel rays on the lens are all brought to the same focus. So also are the rays of a blue beam; but the point to which the blue rays are brought by a single lens is different from that in which a beam of red would be concentrated. The blue focus is nearer to the lens than the red focus. There is here a radical difference between the action of the lens upon light and the action of the mirror. In the latter case, every hûe, of whatever colour, if in the visible part, or indeed whether the rays belong to the visible portion of the spectrum or not, is brought to coincidence at the same point. The glass lens, however, has a different focus for every different quality of light which can fall upon it. Hence, when a beam from the sun or from a star, or indeed from almost any celestial source, falls upon a lens of glass, the composite nature of the light gives rise to the difficulty that the reds, the yellows, and the blues are all brought to different foci. It is therefore impossible for this reason to obtain a distinct and definite image of any celestial object with a single glass lens; for if the lens be focussed truly for some of the rays it is necessarily out of focus for others.

This difficulty is well known, and was for a long time regarded as presenting an insuperable difficulty in the way of constructing efficient refracting telescopes with glass lenses. Indeed, it was the perception of this difficulty that led Newton to turn his attention to the construction of reflectors, the best known form of which still bears his name. By the admirable discovery that what a single lens could not do a pair of glasses could certainly accomplish, the refracting telescope was made the valuable instrument we now find. The achromatic objective is formed of a lens of crown glass and a lens of flint glass. A beam of composite light, on passing through a powerful convex lens of crown, tends towards different foci. But in contact with, or very close to, the crown lens is a concave lens of flint glass, which proceeds to undo the bending which the beam has received from the crown. It is possible by a combination of two lenses to produce a single objective which shall bring the foci for any two desired hues into coincidence. If, for example, we arrange the proportions of the lenses appropriately, the red rays and the blue rays will be conducted to a common focus, and all the other visual rays of the intermediate hues will be brought to foci so close to the main focus that the telescope will be practically perfect for optical purposes. Such is the modern achromatic object-glass.

When an objective is to be employed for photography a new class of considerations arises. The rays most specially potent in their action on the salts of silver are not visual rays. The focus to which they would be brought by a single lens is much nearer the glass than is the focus of the extreme violet. In the ordinary adjustment of the achromatic objective for visual purposes the photographic rays are, as the optician says, allowed to go wild, for there would be no object in leading them to the common focus, and the attempt to do so would seriously impair the visual performance of the telescope. Hence we see the important fact that an achromatic telescope, however perfect for the ordinary purposes of astronomy, would be unsuited for the photographer. If a plate be placed at the ordinary optical focus of such an instrument, the visible rays from a star are no doubt brought to a point on that plate, but the photographic rays, not having the same focus, will be spread over a little circle instead of a point, and the resulting photograph will be entirely wanting in delicacy Nor will a mere alteration of the place of the plate suffice to give precision to the image, for there are so many different shades of photographic light that an ordinary objective when focussed for one kind of invisible light will be out of focus for another.

For photographic purposes we must therefore entirely reject the familiar objective of the observatory, and construct a different one. All the reds and yellows may with safety be permitted to run wild, inasmuch as their photographic capacities are insensible. But the true chemical rays, beginning in the blues and the violets and extending far off into the invisible portion of the spectrum, must be carefully gathered into one point. A pair of flint and crown lenses must thus be so wrought that the two ends of the chemical parts of the spectrum shall be practically brought to a common focus, in which, of course, the photographic plate is to be placed.

We thus obtain an objective which is utterly unsuited for visual purposes, but which will give an exquisitely defined photographic image of a star. But now comes one of the practical difficulties of the optician. In forming the visual objective it is easy for him to test the successive approaches to the perfect form of the lenses, but how is he to test the performance of the photographic objective? Here the eye cannot directly appreciate the degree of success which has been obtained.

At the request of Signor Anguiano, the present writer has tested the large photographic objective constructed by Sir Howard Grubb for the Observatory of Tacubaya belonging to the Mexican Government. A description of the test employed will show the peculiarities of a photographic objective. The instrument was directed on an artificial star a couple of hundred feet distant. The star was merely a reflecting bead, illuminated by a spectrum obtained by passing a beam from a small incandescent electric light through a prism; any part of the spectrum could be cast upon the bead, and thus stars of varied hues could be observed in the telescope. Were the objective designed for visual purposes, the focus of a star near the extreme red should coincide with the focus of a blue star, while the foci of all the other stars would be in the immediate vicinity. For the photographic telescope, however, the essential point is that all the bluish stars shall be brought practically to the same focus, and this being so for the visible stars, the invisible foci of photographic light will be all sufficiently concentrated. It should, however, be understood that the only final test of an objective consists in the nature of the photographs it produces.

Supposing that the photographic telescope, either reflector or refractor, has been prepared, the practical conduct of the work demands a few words of explanation. It is of course essential that the telescope be presented to the same part of the sky throughout the entire duration of the exposure. This condition is complied with by a simultaneous observation of the heavens through a visual telescope rigidly attached to the photographic tube with the axes of the two instruments parallel. The clock motion of the equatorial must be of the highest order of excellence, but notwithstanding the exquisite refinement obtained by the electrical control of the driving clock, it is impossible to dispense with simultaneous watching through the guiding telescope. A star is chosen, and this star is brought on the intersection of a pair of spider webs in the guiding telescope. During the entire exposure this star must remain in the same position, and this the attending astronomer will secure by gently correcting the speed of the driving clock. When this fiducial star has been kept carefully on one point throughout the exposure, then, assuming that other obvious conditions are fulfilled, each star will have been constantly brought to a focus on the same point of the photographic plate. The condition is a somewhat trying one, when we remember that the image of the star is an extremely small point, and that the duration of the exposure is in some cases as long as four hours, or even more.

A combined effort has been made to secure a representation of the entire surface of the heavens by photography. A congress met in Paris, under the presidency of Admiral Mouchez, consisting of astronomers from all parts of the world, and the conditions under which this stupendous survey of the universe was to be undertaken were then decided on. The operations are divided among a number of observatories situated over the world, and each of them undertakes to photograph on plates of a uniform size a certain region of the heavens. The work has been entered upon with the heartiest enthusiasm, and ere many years have elapsed we may anticipate being in possession of what will practically be a photograph of the entire heavens. This great piece of work will provide us with the means of making a reasonably complete inventory of the entire contents of that small portion of the universe which lies within the reach of our instruments.

That all the stars which can be exhibited on long exposed plates shall ever be completely catalogued is a task as much beyond our power to complete as it would be to obtain a descriptive list of the several pebbles on a sea beach or of the several leaves in an ample forest. The more modest scheme has, however, been suggested of taking the two million brightest stars and forming a complete catalogue of them, in which their brightness and their absolute positions in the heavens shall be given with all attainable precision. Even this is a sufficiently magnificent undertaking, but it is within the practical limits of scientific enterprise, and it ought to be done—it must be done. Not alone is it our manifest duty to obtain a comprehensive survey of that universe around us, but there are many other special astronomical problems that will be largely forwarded by its accomplishment. There are some problems indeed which must remain unsolved so long as this task remains unfulfilled. To mention only a single one of the questions for which the great survey is imperatively demanded, I may refer to the interstellar motion of our solar system. It is well known that our sun, accompanied by the whole system of planets, is at present bound on a voyage through space. Astronomy presents no grander problem than the discovery of the circumstances of this voyage. Whence has our system come, whither is it bound, and with what speed? We can never learn such particulars as these without the information that the great survey would be capable of giving us. It is impossible to allude to the present favourable aspect of this great undertaking without mentioning the name of His Majesty's Astronomer at the Cape of Good Hope, Sir David

Gill, K.C.B., to whose zeal in the pursuit of his science we are so much indebted for the initiative of the great survey.

Dr. Roberts propounded and proved to astronomers the practicability of making and engraving a chart of the heavens on which many more stars shall be depicted. He has devised a very ingenious and accurate instrument, by which a copy of the stars on the photographic plate can be faithfully engraved on copper. I have had the privilege of seeing and using this apparatus, and hardly know whether to admire most the accuracy of the measurements that can be made by it, or the celerity with which the copper-plate facsimile of the heavens can be obtained. The measures of the distances between stars that can be made with this instrument, either on the photographic plate itself, or on the copper engraved plate, or almost on the impressions taken from that plate on paper, may favourably compare with the most exact and laborious measurements that can be obtained with the heliometer or the micrometer on the actual stars in the heavens. The taking of the photographs being a comparatively simple matter, since an hour with a single telescope will book many thousands of stars, the practicability of the completion of the entire chart of the sky depends on the rapidity with which the plates can be transferred to the copper. Dr. Roberts found that he could easily engrave fifty stars in an hour; so that if twenty engraving instruments were steadily employed for ten years of reasonable working hours a magnificent celestial chart could be completely engraved, consisting of twenty-three millions of stars. This superb undertaking is quite feasible, and every one interested in astronomy will recognise its utility. Here is a splendid opportunity for some wealthy Englishman to accomplish a work which could be worthily mentioned beside the magnificent Draper Memorial now being reared by Professor Pickering in America.

Hitherto I have spoken of photography merely as an appliance for the simple purpose of charting or of mapping the stars. It remains to mention some of the numerous other applications of which it is susceptible. One of the most delicate problems of celestial measurement is the determination of the distance of a fixed star. This is derived from a series of measures made at varying seasons of the year between the star under examination and some more distant star which happens to lie nearly in the same direction of vision. If, therefore, a series of photographs at different seasons be obtained, the measurements made on these photographs will disclose the star's distance, if it be sufficiently near to admit of the application of the process. The late Dr. Pritchard, who had been a diligent cultivator of the photographic methods, had already made several successful attempts of this description by measures on photographs which he had obtained in the University Observatory at Oxford.

The applications of photography to the stars which I have already mentioned are mainly improvements on methods formerly used, except indeed in so far as they disclose to us stars which are not visibly perceptible, but we have now to speak of the manner in which photography has laid open to us discoveries of the most remarkable character in a province peculiarly its own. I can only mention the two most remarkable instances.

The great nebula in Andromeda is a familiar telescopic

object. It is indeed a unique spectacle in many respects, one of which is that it alone of all the thousands of nebulæ is visible to the unaided eye. Many drawings of the nebula in Andromeda have been made, and since the era of powerful telescopes it was perceived that the spindle-shaped nebulosity was marked by two remarkable dark "lanes," parallel, or nearly so, to the length of the spindle. These lanes are well shown in the later drawings of the nebula, but they seemed devoid of significance till quite lately.

Dr. Isaac Roberts, on a favourable night, exposed to the nebula for four hours one of the highly sensitive plates that he uses; and on developing and enlarging, a picture was obtained which struck me at the time I saw it, and which still appears to me, to be perhaps the most instructive portrait of any celestial object I have ever beheld. At once the significance of the mysterious lanes becomes apparent, and the structure of the mighty nebula is for the first time disclosed. It is obviously a somewhat disc-shaped or rather lens-shaped mass, tilted nearly edgeways towards us. The central portion is especially brilliant and greatly condensed, and it is surrounded by two or three rings of nebulous material. The lanes are thus shown to be merely the better marked portions of the divisions between these rings. They can be traced nearly the whole way round in the photograph, though, owing to the foreshortening, and the want of outline which is characteristic of nebulæ, they become a little confused at the extremities. The two other well-known nebulæ in the neighbourhood are also shown: they are obviously parts of the same system.

This marvellous structure will naturally suggest that Laplace could have no more appropriate picture to illustrate his nebular theory than the photograph of the nebula in Andromeda. There seems no doubt, indeed, that this nebula is condensing down, but the magnitudes involved show us that the solar system bears but little resemblance to the gigantic rings of the vast nebula. Look at the facts of the case. It happens that we have in the case of Andromeda a partial hint as to its actual dimensions of which we are usually destitute in objects of this description. A few years ago a variable star broke out in Andromeda under circumstances which rendered it in the highest degree probable that the star was actually in the nebula, and not merely accidentally on the line of sight. The parallax of this star was sought for by astronomers—myself among the number—and we came to the unanimous conclusion that the star, and therefore presumably the nebula, was too remote for our methods of survey to be successful. The diameter of the earth's orbit cannot subtend an angle at the very most of more than a couple of seconds at the nebula, which is itself more than a couple of degrees in length. We are hence assured that the diameter of the system which is being evolved in Andromeda, whatever it may be, is at the very least three thousand six hundred times as great as that of the earth's orbit round the sun.

Another superb achievement in the exclusive department of photography is the discovery of the nebulæ which surround some of the stars in the Pleiades. We may look in vain for them with the ordinary telescope, but the exquisite pictures of Roberts demonstrate their existence, and show that the stars of the Pleiades seem to have resulted from the condensation of a mighty nebula, some portions of which are still in the vicinity of the group. It seems clear that the results obtained in the case of the nebula in Andromeda, and of the Pleiades, would be alone sufficient to justify all the expenditure of time and trouble made on behalf of celestial photography.

Several photographs of the great nebula in Orion have also been taken, those of the Lick and Yerkes Observatories being especially successful. It would seem, however, as if the bluish nebulæ, such as Orion and the Dumb-bell, did not admit of such good photographic portraits as the nebula in Andromeda which is of a whiter hue. The draw-back to all nebular photographs is that, to give sufficient exposure for the faint parts, the bright parts must be over-exposed, while the stars are of course burnt into dis-figuring blotches.

It does not enter into the scheme of this chapter to discuss with any detail the splendid applications of photography to the spectroscopic study of the heavens. Here, indeed, the pre-eminent utility of photography comes out most distinctly. I must, however, give a few concluding lines to the subject. In this department of celestial spectro-scopy Sir William Huggins, K.C.B., is the most renowned discoverer, and he has obtained exquisite photographs of the spectra of stars. The white stars, such as Sirius and Vega, show a truly marvellous spectrum; there are a few lines in the visible part, and a great number of lines in the photographic part, due to hydrogen. The spectra of comets and of nebulæ have also been obtained, and are replete with truly marvellous interest and instruction.

But perhaps the most comprehensive piece of astronomical spectroscopy which has yet been undertaken is the great Draper Memorial, at which Professor Pickering is labouring with such consummate skill at Harvard College, Massachusetts.

Mrs. Draper, in memory of her accomplished husband, provided the means by which Professor Pickering might carry on his work. The photographs of the stellar spectra which have been obtained present a magnificent display of lines. His operations have been conducted on such a comprehensive scale that a complete spectroscopic review of all the stars in the heavens to the ninth magnitude has been obtained. One who has not visited Professor Pickering's observatory, and so has not seen the vast astronomical research that is there carried on, can have hardly any idea of the magnificence of the great task. Many other observations, both in the old world and the new, are also daily adding to our knowledge, until in these later days we have learned how full of meaning are the words, "One star differeth from another star in glory."

CHAPTER XXII.

AN ASTRONOMER'S THOUGHTS ABOUT KRAKATOA.

AN event like the great eruption of Krakatoa can only be studied properly when placed in suitable perspective. Accordingly years have been required before sufficient data could be collected to enable us to take an adequate view of the several incidents of the explosion. The eruption of Krakatoa in August, 1883, was not only a mighty and appalling incident in the neighbourhood of the Straits of Sunda. It was there no doubt that the fatal aspects of the disaster were exclusively developed. It was along the shores of Sumatra and Java that the inundations took place in which 36,380 lives are said to have been lost. But the phenomena of Krakatoa, which give it a peculiar interest, are of an innocuous type, and have had a far wider range than those of a tragical character. The shock given to our globe was such that the influence of the explosion has extended in some degree to almost every part. To appreciate all that Krakatoa implies it is therefore not sufficient merely to gather the information which can be procured at the seat of the volcano itself; we must extend our inquiries much farther afield. We have to learn what observers within many hundreds of miles tell us. Ships' logs have to be examined. The records of barometers and of magnetic instruments all over the globe, even to the very antipodes of Krakatoa, have to be brought together. The descriptions of extraordinary optical phenomena, such as wonderful ruddy glows at sunset and sunrise, or strange hues in which the sun and the moon were occasionally decked, have to be collected and scrutinized from numerous places scattered over both hemispheres. Need it be said that such a task as this must be a protracted one, but it has been accomplished, and now those interested in the matter have the opportunity of studying a unique chapter in the history of the earth.

It is to the Royal Society that we are indebted for the inception and the carrying out of this laborious undertaking. They appointed a Krakatoa Committee, under the chairmanship of the late Mr. Symons. So multitudinous were the phenomena to be investigated that the committee was divided into sections. To examine the eruption itself and the volcanic phenomena generally, a geological section was necessary. To study the air-waves and the sounds, as well as the distribution of dust and pumice by wind and water, required the aid of meteorologists. On the border territory, between the sciences of meteorology and of astronomy, must be placed the investigation of the twilight effects and the strange coronas and weird colours of the sun and moon. The great sea-waves must clearly be studied by hydrographers, and there were also some groups of facts connected with terrestrial magnetism and electricity. Immense numbers of letters and reports from all parts of the globe had to be brought to a focus, and the extensive printed literature relating to Krakatoa had to be ransacked. At length, however, by the spring of 1887, the manuscript was completed, and, in the autumn of 1888, a superb quarto volume of nearly 500 pages, copiously illustrated both by artistic drawings and by charts and maps, was issued.

Midway between Sumatra and Java lies a group of small islands, which, prior to 1883, were beautified by the dense forests and glorious vegetation of the tropics. Of these islands Krakatoa was the chief, though even of it but little was known. Its appearance from the sea must, indeed, have been familiar to the crews of the many vessels that navigated the Straits of Sunda, but it was not regularly inhabited. Glowing with tropical verdure, such an island seemed an unlikely theatre for the display of an unparalleled effect of plutonic energy, but yet there were certain circumstances which may tend to lessen our surprise at the outbreak. In the first place, as Professor Judd has so clearly pointed out, not only is Krakatoa situated in a region famous, or perhaps infamous, for volcanoes and earthquakes, but it actually happens to lie at the intersection of two main lines, along which volcanic phenomena are, in some degree, perennial. In the second place, history records that there have been previous eruptions at Krakatoa. The last of these appears to have occurred in May, 1680, but unfortunately only imperfect accounts of it have been preserved. It seems, however, to have annihilated the forests on the island, and to have ejected vast quantities of pumice, which cumbered the seas around. Krakatoa then remained active for a year and a half, after which the mighty fires subsided. The irrepressible tropical vegetation again resumed possession. The desolated islet again became clothed with beauty, and for a couple of centuries reposed in peace.

A few significant warnings were given before the recent tremendous outbreak. Admonitory earthquakes began to be felt in the vicinity some years before, and for a period of three months Krakatoa was gradually preparing for the majestic performance with which the world was astounded on August 26-27. The inhabitants of those regions were so accustomed to be threatened by volcanic phenomena that the early stages of the outbreak, which began on May 20, do not seem to have created any alarm; quite the reverse, indeed, for a pleasant excursion was organized from Batavia, and a trip made to Krakatoa in a steamer, to see what was going on. The party landed on the island, and found a large basin-shaped crater, more than half a mile across at the top, and almost 150 feet deep. In the centre of this was an aperture 150 feet in diameter, from which a column of steam issued with a terrific noise. Even at this early stage of the eruption the volcanic dust was projected aloft in quantities sufficient to be wafted to the adjoining shores of Sumatra and Java.

For the next fortnight or three weeks the intensity of the eruptive phenomena seemed at first to decline, but about the end of June other craters began to open on the island, and the volcanic energy from that date increased until the mighty climax. The actual nature of that awful event can only be imperfectly known. The Straits of Sunda were no longer a pleasant place for a steamboat excursion They had become the theatre of an appalling catastrophe. For many hours the adjacent shores were wrapped in profound darkness, while the tremendous agitation of the volcano originated great sea waves which swept away entire towns and villages, and in a great measure destroyed their populations.

It was one o'clock in the afternoon of Sunday, August 26, 1883, when Krakatoa commenced a series of gigantic volcanic efforts. Detonations were heard which succeeded each other at intervals of about ten minutes. These were loud enough to penetrate as far as Batavia and Buitenzorg, distant 96 and 100 miles respectively from the volcano. A vast column of steam, smoke, and ashes ascended to a prodigious elevation. It was measured at 2 P.M. from a ship 76 miles away, and was then judged to be 17 miles high—that is, three times the height of the loftiest mountain in the world. As the Sunday afternoon wore on, the volcanic manifestations became ever fiercer. At 3 P.M. the sounds were loudly heard in a town 150 miles away. At 5 P.M. every ear in the island of Java was engaged in listening to volcanic explosions, which were considered to be of quite unusual intensity even in that part of the world. These phenomena were, however, only introductory. Krakatoa was gathering strength. Between 5 and 6 P.M. the British ship *Charles Bal*, commanded by Captain Watson, was about ten miles south of the volcano. The ship had to shorten sail in the darkness, and a rain of pumice, in large pieces and quite warm, fell upon her decks. At 7 P.M. the mighty column of smoke is described as having the shape of a pine-tree, and as being brilliantly illuminated by electric flashes. The sulphurous air is laden with fine dust, while the lead dropped from a ship in its anxious navigation astounds the leadsman by coming up hot from the bottom of the sea. From sunset on Sunday till midnight the tremendous detonations followed each other so quickly that a continuous roar may be said to have issued from the island. The full terrors of the eruption were now approaching. The distance of 96 miles between Krakatoa and Batavia was not sufficient to permit the inhabitants of the town to enjoy their night's sleep. All night long the thunders of the volcano sounded like the discharges of artillery at their very doors, while the windows rattled with aërial vibrations.

On Monday morning, August 27, the eruption culminated in four terrific explosions, of which the third, shortly after 10 A.M. Krakatoa time, was by far the most violent. The quantity of material ejected was now so great that darkness prevailed even as far as Batavia soon after 11 A.M., and there was a rain of dust until three in the afternoon. The explosions continued with more or less intensity all the afternoon of Monday and throughout Monday night. They finally ceased at about 2·30 A.M. on Tuesday, August 28. The entire series of grand phenomena thus occupied a little more than thirty-six hours.

We may imagine several different standards by which the significance of a volcanic outbreak is to be estimated. The most obvious standard of comparison is, of course, that of the quantity of materials which are extruded. Another would be the area covered by the clouds of volcanic dust and the duration of the darkness thus caused. Other standards would be sought in the incidental effects of the outbreak, such as the great waves which are thereby propagated in the sea, and the distances to which the sounds are carried. Other more subtle, but not less interesting, phenomena are the waves in the atmospheric ocean, which are neither seen nor heard, but of which the barometer gives no uncertain indications. Among the remaining effects of a volcanic explosion are the curious sunset glows and the strange optical phenomena which are sometimes witnessed. We have thus a number of distinct points of view from which the significance of a volcano can be estimated.

We had all heard so much about Krakatoa that at first it is a little disappointing to read the assurances of Professor Judd that, so far as the first two of these standards are concerned, Krakatoa has been surpassed by other volcanoes. He enumerates three distinct outbreaks—viz., that of Papandayang, in Java, in 1772; of Skaptar Jökull (Varmárdalr), in Iceland, in 1783; and of Tomboro, in Sumbawa, in 1815—in all of which the quantity of matter poured forth was considerably greater than that from Krakatoa. However, even in this respect the achievements of Krakatoa if second-rate are at least respectable. The estimates made are necessarily founded on precarious data, but it seems to be certain that if all the materials poured forth from Krakatoa during the critical period could be collected together, the mass they would form would be considerably over a cubic mile in volume. It is in the other standards of comparison that the importance of the explosion at Krakatoa is to be sought. The intensity of this outbreak in its last throes was such that mighty sounds were heard and mighty waves arose in the sea for which we can find no parallel. Every part of our globe's surface felt the pulse of the air-waves, and beautiful optical phenomena made the circuit of the globe even more than once or twice. In these last respects the eruption of Krakatoa is unique.

Professor Judd has satisfactorily accounted for the enormous manufacture of dust during the eruption. It appears to consist of comminuted pumice, and is produced by the attrition of the pumice masses, as in successive outbursts they are hurled aloft, and then tumble back again into the crater.

It appears to me that the most remarkable incident connected with the eruption of Krakatoa was the production of the great air-wave by that particular explosion that occurred at ten o'clock on the morning of Monday, August 27. The great air-wave was truly of cosmical importance, affecting as it did every particle of the atmosphere on our globe. This phenomenon alone extends the study of Krakatoa beyond the province of vulcanology, and gives to the subject a particular interest in physical science.

A pebble tossed into a pond of unruffled water gives rise to a beautiful series of circular waves that gradually expand and ultimately become evanescent. A very large body falling into the ocean would originate waves that might diverge for miles from the centre of disturbance ere they became inappreciable. Waves can originate in air as well as in water. We are not at this moment speaking of those familiar air-waves by which sounds are conveyed. The waves we now mean are inaudible and apparently much longer undulations than those of sound.

Imagine a great globe, which for simplicity we may think of as smooth all over. Let us suppose that this globe has the stupendous dimensions expressed by a diameter of 8,000 miles, and imagine it to be enclosed in a uniform shell of air. Now, suppose that all is quiet, till at some point, which for the moment we may speak of as the pole, a mighty disturbance is originated. Let us regard this disturbance as produced by a sudden but local pushing up of the atmosphere by a force directed from the earth's surface outwards, and let us trace the effect thereby produced on the atmosphere. Such a sudden impulse will at once initiate a series of circular atmospheric waves, which will speed away from the centre of disturbance just like the waves caused by the pebble in the pond. If the original atmospheric impulse be large enough we shall find the circle growing larger and larger, its radius increasing from hundreds of miles to thousands of miles, until at last the wave reaches the equator. What is to happen when the diverging waves have attained the equator, and are now confronted by the opposite hemisphere? This is one of those cases in which the mathematician can guide us where the experimentalist would be otherwise somewhat at fault. We know that as the wave entered the opposite hemisphere it would at once move through a similar series of changes to those through which it had already gone, but in the inverse order. The wave will thus, after leaving the equator, glide onwards into a parallel small circle, ever decreasing in diameter, and converging toward the anti-pole. Finally, just as the waves all radiated from the original pole, so will they all concentrate towards the opposite one. But what is now to happen? Here, again, the mathematician will inform us. He can follow the oscillations after their confluence, and he finds that from the anti-pole they will again commence to diverge. Again they will expand, again they will reach the equator, and again will they gradually draw into concentration at the original pole. Nor will the process even here end. From the second confluence there will be a new divergence, and thus the oscillations will be sent quivering from one pole of the globe to the other, until they gradually subside by friction.

This comprehensive series of phenomena wherein the atmosphere of the entire globe participates in an organized vibration has, so far as we know, only once been witnessed, and that was after the greatest outbreak at Krakatoa, at ten o'clock on the morning of August 27. But the ebb and the flow of these mighty undulations are not immediately appreciable to the senses. The great wave, for instance, passed and re-passed and passed again over London, and no inhabitant was conscious of the fact. But the automatic records of the barometer at Greenwich show that the vibration from Krakatoa to its antipodes, and from the antipodes back to Krakatoa, was distinctly perceptible over London, not less then six or seven times. The instruments at the Kew Observatory confirm those at Greenwich, and if further confirmation were required it can be had from the barograms at many other places in England. This is truly a memorable incident, and the scientific value of the labours of those who so diligently obtain automatic barometric records year after year would be amply demonstrated, if demonstration were required, by this single discovery of the great Krakatoa air-wave.

From all parts of Europe, from Berlin to Palermo, from St. Petersburg to Valencia, we obtain the same indications.

Fortunately self-recording barometric instruments are now to be found all over the world. Almost all the instruments show distinctly the first great wave from Krakatoa to its antipodes in Central America, and the return wave from the antipodes to Krakatoa. They also all show the second great wave which sped from Krakatoa, as well as the second great wave which returned from the antipodes. Thus, the first four of the oscillations are depicted on upwards of forty of the barograms. The fifth and sixth oscillations are also to be distinguished on several of the curves, and even the seventh is certainly established at some few places, of which Kew is one. Then the gradually increasing faintness of the indications renders them unrecognisable, from which we conclude that after seven pulsations our atmosphere had sensibly regained its former condition ere it was disturbed by Krakatoa.

Among the instruments which have yielded valuable information about the air-wave, we have, curiously enough, to mention the register of the recording gasometer-indicator at Batavia. This apparatus, designed and employed for a widely different purpose, shows that extraordinary fluctuations in the barometric pressure occurred at the time when the great wave passed over the town.

It is of particular interest, from a physical point of view, to study the numerical facts with reference to the speed at which this world-embracing wave was propagated. We shall for this purpose select the records taken at Greenwich. The phase of the wave found most convenient for measurement was the depression following the outbreak, and the moment at which this phase started from Krakatoa was 3 hrs. 32 mins. P.M. on August 17,

Greenwich mean time. This is probably correct within two or three minutes. Diverging from its source this wave reached Greenwich after an interval of a little more than ten hours. The interesting point is, however, the determination of the period of a complete oscillation, that is to say, the interval between the passage of the wave over Greenwich and the next passage of the wave in the same direction also over Greenwich. It has been found convenient to designate the successive waves as i., ii., iii., iv., &c., the odd numbers being those from Krakatoa to its antipodes, and the even numbers being the return waves from the antipodes to Krakatoa. At Greenwich, for example, we find the interval between i. and iii. to have been 36·47 hours, between iii. and v. 36·82 hours, and between v. and vii. 37·05 hours. For the return waves the intervals between ii. and iv. was 34·78 hours, and between iv. and vi. 35·25 hours. The similar values vary slightly when obtained at the several stations, but the average results indicate that for its first circuit of the earth the wave required 36 hrs. 24 mins., for the second 36 hrs. 30 mins., and for the third 36 hrs. 50 mins. The similar periods for the waves travelling in the reverse way were 34 hrs. 46 mins., and 35 hrs. 4 mins. respectively. The average of all is very nearly a day and a half.

Before leaving this part of the subject, I must refer to the approximate identity between the velocity of this äërial disturbance and the velocity of ordinary sound. This is well brought out by General Strachey. The speed of the wave varied from 674 to 726 miles per hour. The speed of sound propagation is 723 miles at zero Fahrenheit, and is 781 miles at 80° Fahrenheit. Considering that the waves had, of course, to cross the poles in their journeys, it would almost seem that within the limits of probable error the speed of the great wave and the speed of ordinary sound waves were identical. It would, I think, have been an improvement on the plates containing the barograms, if the scale had been given, so that it would have been possible to obtain some definite notion of the amplitudes of the oscillations at the different stations. The only pressure-diagram contained in the plates which does give any scale measures, is that of the gasholder at Batavia; from this it would appear that the barometric fluctuation produced by the great wave was about four-tenths of an inch of mercury at a distance of 100 miles from the source of disturbance.

While the chapter on the air-waves is the most novel scientific feature in the Report of the Krakatoa Committee, it will be admitted that the most amazing features of the same work are those contained in the section on "Sounds." Here we find a collection of statements so marvellous that they would be well-nigh incredible were it not for the ample body of excellent testimony by which they are substantiated. In the whole annals of noise there is nothing which can be compared to the records set forth in a table which occupies not less than eight pages of the volume. (See Fig. 19.) Let us select a few instances, almost at random.

Lloyd's agent at Batavia, 94 miles distant, says that on the morning of the 27th of August the reports and concussions were simply deafening. At Carimon, Java Island, reports were heard which led to the belief that some vessel offshore was making signals of distress, and boats were accordingly put out to render succour, but no vessel was found, as the reports were from Krakatoa, at a distance of 355 miles. At Macassar, in Celebes, explosions were heard all over the province. Two steamers were sent out to discover the cause, for the authorities did not then know that what they heard came from Krakatoa, 969 miles away. But mere hundreds of miles will not suffice to exemplify the range of this stupendous siren. In St. Lucia Bay, in Borneo, a number of natives, who had been guilty of murder, thought they heard the sounds of vengeance in the approach of an attacking force. They fled from their village, little fancying that what alarmed them really came from Krakatoa, 1116 miles distant. All over the island of Timor alarming sounds were heard, and so urgent did the situation appear that the Government was aroused, and sent off a steamer to ascertain the cause. The sounds had, however, come 1351 miles, all the way from Krakatoa. In the Victoria Plains of West Australia the inhabitants were startled by the discharge of artillery—an unwonted noise in that peaceful district—but the artillery was at Krakatoa, 1700 miles distant. The inhabitants of Daly Waters, in South Australia, were rudely awakened at midnight on Sunday, August 26, by an explosion resembling the blasting of a rock, which lasted for a few minutes. The time and other circumstances show that here again was Krakatoa heard this time at the monstrous distance of 2023 miles. But there is undoubted testimony that to distances even greater than 2023 miles the waves of sound conveyed tidings of the mighty convulsion. Diego Garcia, in the Chagos Islands, is 2267 miles from Krakatoa, but the thunders traversed even this distance, and created the belief that there must be some ship in distress, for which a diligent but necessarily ineffectual search was made. To pass at once to the most remarkable case of all, we have a report from Mr. James

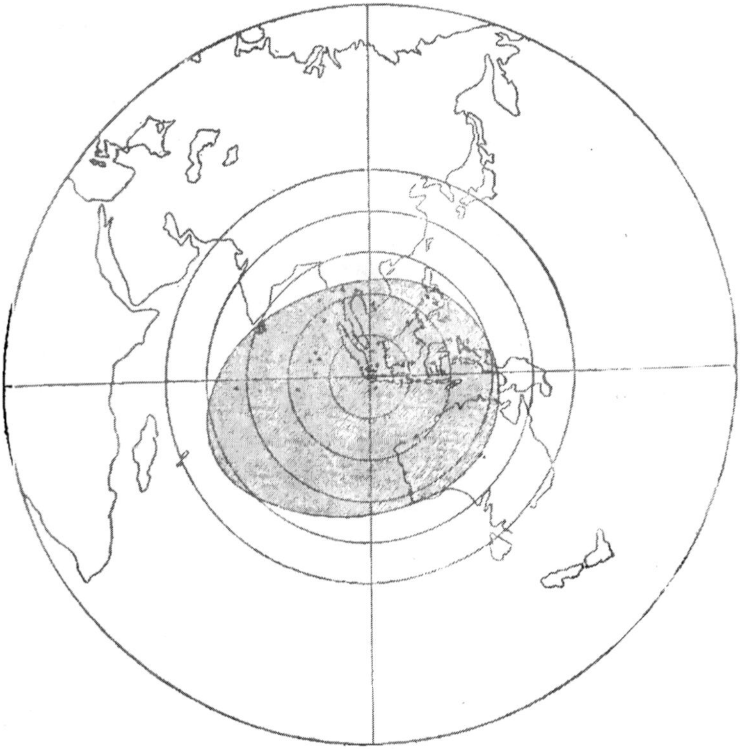

Fig. 19.—Krakatoa: Eruptions of August 26-27.

(The shaded portion indicates approximately the area over which the sounds were heard.)

Wallis, chief of police in Rodriguez, that "several times during the night of August 26-27, 1883, reports were heard coming from the eastward, like the distant roar of heavy guns. These reports continued at intervals of between three and four hours." Were it not for the continuous chain of evidence from places at gradually increasing distances from Krakatoa, we might well hesitate to believe that the noises Mr. Wallis heard were really from the great volcano, but a glance at the map, which shows the several stations where the great sounds were heard, leaves no room for doubt. We have thus the astounding fact that almost across the whole wide extent of the Indian Ocean, that is, to a distance of nearly 3000 miles (2968), the sound of the throes of Krakatoa was propagated.

We appreciate this result more strikingly if we reflect on the velocity of sound. Seconds or minutes may elapse between the appearance of a flash of lightning and the arrival of the thunder. But the volcanic sounds could not have been heard at Rodriguez until four hours after they had commenced to travel from Krakatoa. Were Vesuvius now to break out as Krakatoa has done, every inhabitant of Great Britain would apparently be quite near enough to hear the awful detonation.

I shall content myself with the mention of three facts in illustration of the great sea waves which accompanied the eruption of Krakatoa. Of these, probably the most unusual is the magnitude of the area over which the undulations were perceived. Thus, to mention but a single instance, and that not by any means an extreme one, we find that the tide gauge at Table Bay reveals waves which, notwithstanding that they have travelled 5100 miles from Krakatoa, have still a range of eighteen inches when they arrive at the southern coast of Africa. The second fact that I mention illustrates the magnitude of the seismic waves by the extraordinary inundations that they produced on the shores of the Straits of Sunda. Captain Wharton shows that the waves, as they deluged the land, must have been fifty feet, or, in one well-authenticated case, seventy-two feet high. It was, of course, these vast floods which caused the fearful loss of life. The third illustrative fact concerns the fate of a man-of-war, the *Berouw*. This unhappy vessel was borne from its normal element and left high and dry in Sumàtra, a mile and three-quarters inland, and thirty feet above the level of the sea.

Such incidents are not so unusual as the exquisite series of optical phenomena which has made most of the nations on the earth spectators in some degree of the wonders of Krakatoa. Resounding as were the crashes of the explosions, they still subsided thousands of miles to the east of Great Britain, and though the great aërial vibrations tingled to and fro through the air over every part of this globe, yet they were not perceptible to our unaided senses. But now we are to consider a splendid series of phenomena which scorned limitations of distance, and which obtruded their glories on our notice for weeks and even months together.

One of the most striking maps that the Report of the Royal Society contains is that which illustrates the progress of the main sky-phenomena from August 26 (evening) to September 9 1883. I doubt if the skies have ever presented to our vision, within atmospheric limits, a more singular series of phenomena than those which are most clearly depicted within the modest limits of this little map. (See Fig. 20.) Let me endeavour from the series of maps, of which this is one, as well as from the abundant body of matter so luminously set forth by the Hon. F. A. Rollo Russell and Mr. E. Douglas Archibald, to present a brief outline of this elaborately beautiful series of phenomena and their cause.

During the crisis on August 26-27, the volume of material blown into the air was sufficiently dense to obscure the coasts of Sumatra to such a degree that at

PROGRESS OF THE MAIN SKY PHENOMENA FROM AUG. 26 (EVENING) TO SEP. 9, 1883.

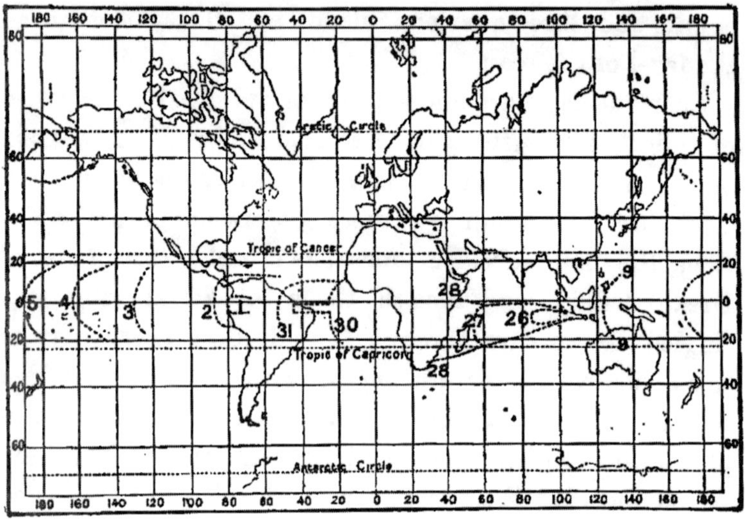

Fig. 20.

10 A.M. the darkness there is stated to have been more intense than it is even in the blackest of nights. The fire-dust ascended to an elevation which, as we have already mentioned, is estimated to have been as much as seventeen miles. Borne aloft into these higher regions of our atmosphere, the clouds of dust at once became the sport of the winds and the currents which may be found there. If we had not previously known the prevailing

tendency of the winds at these elevations and in these latitudes, the journey of the Krakatoa dust would have taught us. We shall confine our attention for the present to the chief phenomena, and we begin with the manifestation of these phenomena which were witnessed in the tropics.

It seems certain that, having attained their lofty elevation, the mighty clouds of dust were seized by easterly winds, and were swept along with a velocity which may not improbably be normal at a height of twenty miles above the earth's surface. It has been demonstrated by Dr. Vettin, at Berlin, that the upper cirrus clouds in winter at a height of only four or five miles have an average velocity of 44·5 miles an hour. The Rev. W. Clement Ley has shown that the velocities of the upper cirrus clouds often amount to 120 miles an hour. These facts enable us without hesitation to attribute velocities to the great clouds of Krakatoa dust which shall be quite sufficient to account for the various phenomena.

It appears that this cloud of dust started immediately from Krakatoa for a series of voyages round the world. The highway which it at first pursued may, for our present purpose, be sufficiently defined by the Tropic of Cancer and the Tropic of Capricorn, though it hardly approached these margins at first. Westward the dust of Krakatoa takes its way. In three days it had crossed the Indian Ocean and was rapidly flying over the heart of Equatorial Africa; for another couple of days it was making a transatlantic journey; and then it might be found, for still a couple of days more, over the forests of Brazil ere it commenced the great Pacific voyage, which brought it back to the East Indies. The dust of Krakatoa had put a girdle round the earth in thirteen days! The shape of the cloud appears to have been elongated, so that it took two or three days to complete the passage over any stated place.

When the dust-cloud had regained the Straits of Sunda the great eruption was over, but the winds were still the same as before, and again the comminuted pumice sped on its impetuous career. The density of the cloud had, however, lessened. Doubtless much of the material was subsiding, and the remainder was becoming diffused over a wider area. Accordingly, we find that the track of the stream during this second revolution is somewhat wider than it was on the first, though still mainly confined between the tropics. The speed with which the dust revolved was, however, unabated. Continents and oceans were again swept over with a velocity double that of an express train, and again the earth was surrounded within the fortnight. The dust-cloud had now further widened its limits, ut was still distinguishable, and with unlessened speed commenced for a third time to encircle the earth. The limits of the stream had spread themselves outside the tropics, though still falling short of Europe. There is no reason to think that there was any decline in the velocity of 76 miles per hour, but the gradual diffusion of the dust begins to obliterate the indications by which its movements could be perceived, so that during, and after, the third circuit the phenomena became so diffused that while their glory covered the earth, the distinction between the successive returns had vanished. In November the area which contained the Krakatoa dust had sufficiently expanded from its original tropical limits to include Europe and the greater part of North America. During the winter months the suspended material gradually subsided or, at all events, became evanescent, and in the following spring the earth regained its normal state in so far as the Straits of Sunda were concerned (Fig. 21).

It remains to give some brief account of the optical

APPROXIMATE NORTHERN LIMIT OF THE MAIN SKY PHENOMENA AT THE END OF NOVEMBER 1883.

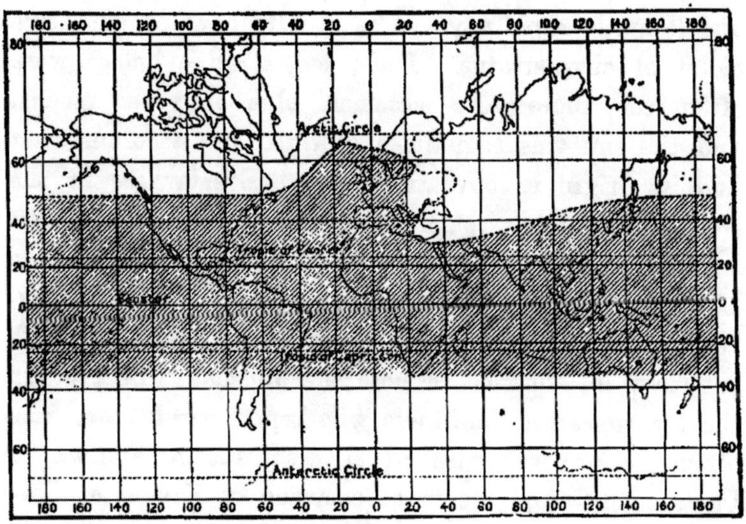

Fig. 21.

phenomena due to the presence of dust, unusual both in quantity and in character, in the upper atmosphere. The frontispiece of the volume shows some beautiful pictures of the twilight and after-glow effects as seen by Mr. W. Ascroft on the bank of the Thames a little west of London, on the evening of November 26, 1883. Analogous phenomena to those here depicted were seen almost universally during November and December in the same year.

Who is there that does not remember the wondrous loveliness of the twilights and the after-glows during that remarkable winter! These appearances at sunrise and sunset are only the more generally recognised of a whole system of strange optical phenomena. One of the most striking indications of the presence of the dust-stream in its first voyage round the earth was given by the strange blue hue it imparted to the sun. The dust-stream was also visible in its rapid voyages as a lofty haze or extensive cloud of cirro-stratus. Then, too, strange haloes were often seen, there were occasional blue or green moons, and the sun was sometimes glorified by a corona that had its origin in our atmosphere. Everywhere in the world there were remarkable features in the sky that winter: from Tierra del Fuego to Lake Superior; from China to the Gulf of Guinea; from Panama to Australia. Wherever on land there were inhabitants with sufficient intelligence to note the unusual, wherever on the sea there were mariners who kept a careful log, from all such observers we learn that in the autumn and winter months following the great eruption of Krakatoa, there were extraordinary manifestations witnessed in the heavens.

Just one point more in conclusion. We have recorded the great volcanic outbreak of Krakatoa, and we have recorded a wonderful series of optical phenomena. It remains to say a word as to the proof that the latter were indeed the consequence of the former. As the Committee have begun their book with pictures of sun-glows, and as they have occupied more than half of the work with descriptions of the purely optical effects, it seems as if they, at all events, entertained but little doubt that the dust of Krakatoa was responsible for the sunsets of Chelsea. Still I notice that some members of the Committee seem to shrink from deliberately committing themselves to this view. Indeed, the very title of their book exhibits a certain degree of caution on this point. They have called it "The Eruption of Krakatoa and *subsequent* Phenomena." The word I have italicized would not improbably have been *consequent* had it not been for the existence of some such reserve as that I have indicated. But the magnificent body of information which their labours have brought together will enable every one who will carefully study the volume to form his own opinion as to whether or not it was Krakatoa dust which painted our sunsets with those glorious hues. In attempting to decide this question we must first endeavour to conceive the kind of evidence which would be necessary and sufficient to establish the fact that the optical phenomena were consequent upon, as well as subsequent to, the great eruption.

First of all it would be natural to ask whether the existence of volcanic dust in the air could have produced the optical effects that have been observed. This must be answered in the affirmative. Then it would be proper to inquire whether other volcanic outbreaks in other parts of the world, and on other occasions, had been known to have been followed by similar results. Here, again, we have page after page of carefully stated and striking historical facts which answer this question also in the affirmative. Next it would be right to see whether the sequence in which the phenomena were produced at different places in the autumn of 1883 tallied with the supposition that they all diverged from Krakatoa. The instances that could be produced in support of the affirmative number many hundreds, though it must be admitted that there are some few cases about which there are difficulties. Surely we have here what is practically a demonstration. It is certain that these optical phenomena existed. No cause can be assigned for them except the presence, at that particular time, of vast volumes of dust in the air. What brought that dust into the air except the explosion of Krakatoa? Most people find themselves unable to share the scruples of those who think there can be a doubt on the matter. Would another eruption of Krakatoa, followed by a repetition of all the optical phenomena, convince them that in this case, at all events, *post hoc* was *propter hoc?* Perhaps not, if they have already failed to be convinced by the fact that, when Krakatoa exploded two centuries ago, blood-red skies appear to have been seen shortly afterwards even as far away as Denmark.

When we reflect that an explosion on an insignificant islet in the Straits of Sunda has sufficed to set the whole atmospheric covering of our globe trembling, when we remember that the dust then poured forth in a few days of volcanic activity was adequate to adorn the sunsets of every country in the earth, we are reminded once again of the old truth: "How small the world is after all!"

CHAPTER XXIII.

DARWINISM AND ITS RELATION TO OTHER BRANCHES OF SCIENCE.

In the year 1831 a naval expedition sailed from Devonport. That expedition consisted of a single vessel, His Majesty's ship *Beagle*, a ten-gun brig under the command of Captain Fitzroy, R.N. The *Beagle* was a stout old wooden ship, destined on this occasion for a most pacific enterprise. Her duty was to survey parts of the coast of South America and some islands in the Pacific, and to carry a chain of chronometrical measurements round the world. Five years later the *Beagle* returned from this cruise, and thus brought to a close one of the most remarkable voyages that can be found in the annals of the British navy. Now, why was the cruise of the *Beagle* of such unparalleled importance? There have been many other surveying expeditions quite as successful. No doubt the memorable voyage of the *Challenger* accomplished much more surveying than the voyage of the *Beagle*. But we are gradually learning that even such achievements as those of the *Challenger* must sink into insignificance when compared with the voyage of the *Beagle*. I would rather liken the voyage of the *Beagle* to the immortal voyage of Columbus. In each case a new world was discovered.

When the voyage of the *Beagle* was planned, the captain expressed a wish that some scientific observer should join the expedition. A young naturalist, eager to see the glories of the tropics, volunteered his services and was accepted. He sailed in the ship. For the whole five years he diligently sought every opportunity to gain a knowledge of nature. He pondered on that knowledge when he came home. He added to it by further observation and matured it by careful thought. After many years of labour and of thought the naturalist of the *Beagle* produced a book. The name of the book was the "Origin of Species," the name of the author was Charles Darwin.

The "Origin of Species" appeared when I was a student in college, and I can recall at this day the intense delight with which I read it. I was an instantaneous convert to the new doctrines, and I have felt their influence during all my subsequent life. And here let me hasten to anticipate an objection. It is in the domain of natural history that the great achievements of Darwin have been wrought. It might be urged that the discussion of such a subject lay within the province of biologists or of geologists, but could hardly be considered a legitimate enterprise for those whose studies led them in other directions. But this is a view from which I dissent. I cannot admit the "Origin of Species" to be the exclusive property of biologists. In a more extensive view of the subject it will be seen that the great doctrine of Evolution is of the very loftiest significance, and soars far above the distinction between one science and another to which we are accustomed.

It is interesting to note the wondrous change that is taking place, I might almost say that has taken place, in the popular estimate of the Darwinian theory. It has been well said that a new theory, if eventually proved true, has often to run through three different phases. In the first place, every one exclaims that the theory is not true; then it is urged that the theory is contrary to religion; and, lastly, that everybody knew it long ago. The great doctrine of natural selection promulgated by Darwin has run through these courses. At its first publication it was received with an outburst of incredulity among the unthinking part of the community. Every one recollects the denunciations it received and the ridicule which the new doctrine had to encounter. But the theory of Darwin has survived that stage. The truth inherent in the principles of Darwin has quietly brushed aside opposition, and now we hear but little of it. The funeral of Darwin at Westminster Abbey must be regarded as marking a momentous epoch in the history of thought. That the great doctrine would some day be accepted was a necessary truth, but I do not think that any one who recollects the publication of the "Origin of Species" could then have anticipated the enormous change in educated opinion which the next quarter of a century was to disclose. Still less likely would it have seemed that the whole nation would have so far acknowledged Darwin as, with one voice, to demand that his remains should be interred in the national mausoleum.

Darwin has worked out one of the most splendid details in the history of the universe. His methods and his theory have intimate connections with other branches of science, and some of these it is our object to consider in this chapter. In particular I propose to sketch the position which the Darwinian theory occupies with reference to a celebrated branch of astronomical speculation.

One hundred years ago the diameter of the sun was possibly four miles greater than it is at present. One thousand years ago the diameter of the sun was forty miles greater than it is at present. Ten thousand years ago the diameter of the sun was 400 miles greater than it is now. The advent of man upon the earth took place no doubt a long time ago, but in the history of the earth the advent of man is a comparatively recent phenomenon. Yet it seems certain that when man first trod our planet, the diameter of the sun must have been many hundreds, perhaps many thousands, of miles greater than it is at present. We must not, however, overestimate the significance of this statement. The diameter of the sun is at present 860,000 miles, so that a diminution of 10,000 miles would be little more than the hundredth part of its diameter. If the diameter of the sun were to shrink to-morrow to the extent of 10,000 miles, the change would not be appreciable to common observation, though even a much smaller change would not elude delicate astronomical measurement. The world on which the primitive man trod was certainly illuminated by a larger sun than that which now shines upon us. It does not necessarily follow that the climates must have been much hotter then than now. The question of warmth, as we have seen in a previous chapter

(p. 32), depends upon other matters besides sunbeams, so that we must be cautious in any inferences drawn in this way, nor are any such inferences needed for our present purpose.

But we must not stop in our retrospect at the epoch even of primeval man. We must go back earlier and earlier through the long ages of the geologists, and back still further to the earliest epochs, when life first began to dawn on the earth. Still we find no reason to suppose that the law of the sun's decreasing heat is not still maintained, and thus, as far as our present knowledge goes, we are bound to suppose that the sun must have been larger and larger the further our retrospect extends. I do not say that the rate at which the sun changes its diameter was then the same as the four miles per century which is an approximation to its present rate. It is sufficient for our purpose that the sun is larger and larger the further we peer back into the remote abyss of the past.

There was a time when the sun must have been twice as large as it is at present; it must once have been three times as large; it must once have been ten times as large. How long ago that was no one can venture to say; it would be rash to attempt any estimate. But we cannot stop at the stage when the sun was even ten times as large as it is at present; the arguments we have used will still apply with equal, if not greater, force. And, looking back earlier yet, there was a time when the sun was once swollen to such an extent that the mighty orbit of Neptune itself would be merely a girdle around the stupendous globe. At that time the sun must have been a gaseous mass of almost inconceivable tenuity. We are not to suppose that the earth and the other planets were solid bodies deeply buried in the vast bulk of the sun. It seems evident that the planets were gaseous masses in those ancient days and undistinguishable from the sun, which gave them birth.

We are now able to make an attempt to trace the history of the solar system, and to indicate the share which Darwin has had in the solution of the noble problem. We do not inquire how the original nebula came into being; our history must commence with the actual existence of this nebula. There is, let it be confessed, a great deal of obscurity still clinging to the subject. Though we may be sure that the great nebula once existed, we cannot with much confidence trace out the method by which the planets were actually formed. It seems to be generally thought that the nebula must have been originally endowed with a certain rotation. This may be regarded as certain; indeed, it would be infinitely improbable that the nebula should not have had some rotation. As the nebula began to radiate heat, so it must have begun to contract; and as it began to contract, it began to rotate more rapidly. This is only the consequence of a well-known dynamical principle. But as the nebula spins more and more rapidly, the cohesion of its parts is lessened by centrifugal force. The moment at length arrives when the centrifugal force detaches a fragment of the nebula. The process of condensation still continues both in the fragment and in the central mass; the fragment changes from the gaseous state to the liquid, perhaps even from the liquid to the solid, and thus becomes a planet. Still the central mass condenses, and spins more and more rapidly, until a rupture again takes place and a second planet is produced.

Again, and still again, the same process is repeated, until at length we recognise the central mass as our great and glorious sun, diminished by incessant contraction, though still vast and brilliantly hot. One of the lesser fragments which he cast off has consolidated into our earth, while other fragments, greater and smaller, have formed the rest of the host of planets. There are many features in the planets which seem to corroborate this view of their origin. They all revolve around the sun in the same direction; they all rotate on their own axes in the same direction, that direction being also coincident with the sun's rotation on its axis. Most astronomers are agreed that the history of the solar system has been something of the kind that I have ventured to describe. Astronomers were thus the first evolutionists; they had sketched out a majestic scheme of evolution for the whole solar system, and now they are rejoiced to find that the great doctrine of Evolution has received an extension to the whole domain of organic life by the splendid genius of Darwin.

At its first separation from the shrinking central nebula, our earth was probably a mass of glowing gas, of far greater volume than it is at present. Gradually the earth parted with its heat by radiation, and commenced to shrink also. The temperature was so high, that iron and other still more refractory substances were actually in a state of vapour, but, as the temperature fell, these substances could not remain in the gaseous form; they condensed first into liquids, these liquids coalesced into a vast central mass, and still that mass went on cooling until its surface, passing through the various stages of incandescence, sank at length to a temperature comparatively cool. Still the earth was swathed with a deep and dense mantle of air, charged with an enormous load of watery vapour; but, as the temperature of the surface gradually decreased, at length the watery vapours were condensed and descended to form the oceans with which our earth is so largely covered. At this point the functions of the astronomer are at an end: he has traced in outline the manufacture of the earth from the primeval nebula; he has accounted for its revolution round the sun, for its rotation on its axis; he has accounted for the shape of the earth and for its internal heat. His work being done, he now hands over the continuance of the history to the biologist.

The lifeless earth is the canvas on which has been drawn the noblest picture that modern science has produced. It is Darwin who has drawn this picture. He has shown that the evolution of the lifeless earth from the nebula is but the prelude to an organic evolution of still greater interest and complexity. He has taken up the history of the earth at the point where the astronomer left it, and he has made discoveries which have influenced thought and opinion more than any other discoveries that have been made for centuries. We here encounter a very celebrated difficulty. The theory of Darwin requires life to begin with, but how did that life originate? I need hardly remind you of the celebrated controversy which has taken place on this subject. It has been contended that life can never be produced except from life; but just as stoutly has the opposite view been maintained. Can it be possible that the wondrous and complex phenomena known as life are purely material? Can a particle of matter which consists only of a definite number of atoms of definite chemical composition manifest any of those characters which characterize life? Take as an extreme instance the brain of an ant, which is not larger than a quarter of a good-sized pin's head. It would require a volume to describe what we know of the powers of ants. Huber showed this long ago, and Lord Avebury has lately reminded us of it, while adding further discoveries of his own.

I here quote Darwin's vivid description; but it is only right to add that many different species of ants are referred to, though included under the common designation: "Ants certainly communicate information to each other, and several unite for the same work, or for games of play. They recognise their fellow-ants after months of absence, and feel sympathy for each other. They build great edifices, keep them clean, close the door in the evening, and post sentries. They make roads as well as tunnels under rivers, and temporary bridges over them by clinging together. They collect food for the community, and when an object too large for entrance is brought to the nest, they enlarge the door, and afterwards build it up again. They store up seeds of which they prevent the germination, and which if damp are brought to the surface to dry. They keep aphides and other insects as milch cows. They go out to battle in regular bands, and freely sacrifice their lives for the common weal. They emigrate according to a peculiar plan. They capture slaves. They move the eggs of their aphides, as well as their own eggs and cocoons, into warm parts of the nest, in order that they may be quickly hatched." *

Well may Darwin speak of the brain of an ant as one of the most wondrous particles of matter in the world. We are apt to think that it is impossible for so minute a piece of matter to possess the necessary complexity required for the discharge of such elaborate functions. The microscope will no doubt show some details in the ant's brain, but these fall hopelessly short of revealing the refinement which the ant's brain must really have. The microscope is not adequate to show us the texture of matter. It has been one of the greatest discoveries of modern times to enable us to form some numerical estimate of the exquisite delicacy of the fabric which we know as inert matter. Water, or air, or iron may be divided and subdivided, but the process cannot be carried on indefinitely. There is a well-defined limit. We are even able to make some approximation to the number of molecules in a given mass of matter. It has been estimated that the number of atoms in a cubic inch of air may be approximately expressed by the number 3, followed by no fewer than twenty ciphers. The brain of the ant doubtless contains more atoms than an equal volume of air; but even if we suppose them to be the same, and if we take the size of an ant's brain to be a little globe one-thousandth of an inch in diameter, we are able to form some estimate of the number of atoms it must contain. The number is to be expressed by writing down 6, and following it by eleven ciphers. We can imagine these atoms grouped in so many various ways that even the complexity of the ant's brain

* Darwin, "Descent of Man," p. 147.

may be intelligible when we have so many units to deal with.

An illustration will perhaps make the argument clearer. Take a million and a half of little black marks, put them in a certain order, and we have a wondrous result—Darwin's "Descent of Man." This book merely consists of about a million and a half letters, placed one after the other in a certain order. Whatever be the complexity of the ant's brain, it is still hard to believe that it could not be fully described in 400,000 volumes, each as large as Darwin's work. Yet the number of molecules in the ant's brain is at least 400,000 times as great as the number of letters in the memorable volume in question.

It would seem that by merely studying the behaviour of an infusion of hay or a tincture of turnips in a test tube, we do not rise to the full magnificence of the problem as to whether life can have originated on the globe from the particles of inorganic matter.

Unusual, indeed, must be the circumstances which will have brought about such a combination of atoms as to form the first organic being. But great events are always unusual. Because we cannot repeatedly make an organized being from inert matter in our test tubes, are we to say that such an event can never once have occurred with the infinite opportunities of nature? We have in nature the most varied conditions of temperature, of pressure, and of chemical composition. Every corner of the earth and of the ocean has been the laboratory in which these experiments have been carried on. It is not necessary to suppose that such an event as the formation of an organized being shall have occurred often. If in the whole course of millions of years past it has once happened, either on the land or in the depths of the ocean, that a group of atoms, few or many, have been so segregated as to have the power of assimilating outside material, and the power of producing other groups more or less similar to themselves, then we have but little more to demand from the "Theory of Spontaneous Generation."

The more we study the actual nature of matter the less improbable will it seem that organic beings should have so originated. One of the most obvious contrasts between organic and inorganic bodies seems to be the power of motion often inherent in the organized body, which is not possessed by the inorganic body; but this is really a superficial view of the question. Take any mass of inorganic matter, a drop of water or a grain of sand. Each of these bodies is composed of a certain number of ultimate atoms. We have no hope that we shall ever have a microscope sufficiently powerful to detect these atoms; but we nevertheless know that they exist, and we know several of their properties. We know, for instance, that even in solid bodies these particles are not at rest, that they are in rapid and ceaseless motion, even though the body may be as rigid as a diamond. In ultimate analysis we see that the atoms of inorganic matter seem to have that mobility which is frequently noticed as a characteristic of vital action. A mere arrangement of the movements of the atoms of a grain of sand could confer on the little object some of the attributes of an organized body.

The method Darwin adopts is of the most captivating simplicity. When the history of Science in the last century comes to be written, the interest will culminate in the supreme discovery of Natural Selection.

There are so many modifying circumstances to be taken into account that it is not often easy to trace the actual course of natural selection; but the leading idea is so simple that, once it is properly stated, I do not see how any reasonable person can refuse his assent. There is a well-known proverb, "As like as two peas," and at a superficial glance two peas are no doubt very like each other. They are like in their size, shape, and colour; they are like in their internal structure; but, when we look closely into the subject, no two peas are exactly alike. Take any two peas from a sack, and after a brief examination we can detect innumerable points of difference. Weighed in a careful balance, they have not the same actual weight; gauged with a pair of callipers, they have not the same size; and these differences extend to every minute part of the structure. One pea will have more nourishment stored up for the benefit of the future plant. Another will be better able to resist hurtful influences. That two peas should be so absolutely identical in every feature as to be indistinguishable is an impossibility, or, as a mathematician would say, the chances are infinitely against such an occurrence. If we find that two peas are never really alike, we shall also find that no two organisms of any kind are really alike when attention is directed to minute points of distinction. A shepherd will laugh to scorn the idea that any two of his flock are so alike that they could be mistaken. Even his dog knows better than that. A poultry fancier will see in his pets conspicuous marks of difference which are barely apparent to the unskilled eye.

I need not multiply illustrations; the innumerable variety of roses and of geraniums, of apples, and of other fruits, will show how universal is the law of variety among all the productions of the organic world.

The great doctrine of Natural Selection is founded upon this susceptibility to variation. Suppose that you wished to improve the peas in your garden, it is quite possible to do so in a few years in the following manner: Take 100 peas, sow them and preserve the seed. You will have some thousands of seeds, but no two peas will be exactly alike; pick out the hundred heaviest seeds and sow them again next season. You will have a crop of thousands, from which you are again to pick out the heaviest hundred. As this process is repeated year by year you will find that within certain limits the peas are gradually increased in size from one generation to another, and thus it is that improved varieties can be artificially established. The success of this process depends merely upon taking judicious advantage of the variability inherent in the organic world. This we may call an artificial selection as opposed to the natural selection.

What we have here described as being produced artificially in the pea is going on everywhere on the grandest scale in nature. Take an illustration this time from animal life; and I choose, as one of the most widely known instances, some incidents in the history of the common herring, which exists in such countless myriads in our oceans. Those who frequent the sea are well acquainted with certain features in the life of the herring. The herring is a fish deservedly prized for food, but it is not only mankind that are fond of devouring it;

a similar taste is widely spread among the fowls of the air and the fishes of the sea. The herring has no defence from innumerable enemies but its agility and its caution. Around the shoal swarm troops of porpoises, while pollack and various other predatory fish devour the herrings in myriads. The female herring lays a stupendous quantity of eggs. It is perfectly certain that only a very minute fraction of these eggs ever reach maturity. If only one per cent. of the eggs grew to full size and reproduced more herrings, the herring population of the sea would multiply enormously every year. This cannot always, or indeed often, be the case, and we are thus compelled to believe that out of every million herring eggs only a small fraction usually come to maturity. To those who have ever observed the herring this appalling mortality will not seem strange.

To begin with, when the eggs are laid the flat fishes congregate and feast thereon to such an extent that fishermen repair to these spots and catch the flat fish in scores with their stomachs filled with the eggs of the herring. No doubt there are many other enemies at this stage, so that vast multitudes of the herring eggs never become hatched at all; even those that are hatched have indeed a bad time of it. Around our coasts we see in the autumn shoals of the tiny herrings pursued and devoured by hosts of young codfish and mackerel. Sometimes the fish surround the shoal completely, and the miserable prey cluster together near the top of the water in a vain hope of safety; but, alas! here the enemies from the air attack them. Sea-gulls crowd to the spot and swallow the young herrings in mouthfuls, and once a shoal has been thus imprisoned between air and water, the slaughter is truly prodigious.

The voracity of enemies is not the only danger to which young herrings are exposed; often they are left on the beach by the falling tide, and may be seen lying in hundreds along the sea margin. I purposely leave out of account all mere human enemies. The efforts of man in catching herrings are quite insignificant in comparison with their more numerous and incessantly voracious destroyers. Indeed Professor Huxley states that the codfish caught in our seas each season would, if they had not been caught, have eaten as many herrings during the next season as those which have actually fallen to the nets of the fisherman. The survivors of this fearful massacre are naturally objects of interest. How is it that they have been spared when so many myriads of their brothers and sisters have been annihilated? No doubt their safety is partly due to the chapter of accidents. They happened to be out of the way when the mackerel made a fatal rush. The sea-gull had eaten so many that when it came to their turn he positively could not eat any more. They got into the middle of the shoal afterwards and escaped the fish that preyed on its margin. But, making every allowance for the benefit of the accidents, I think we must credit the surviving herrings themselves with some share in their success. The few that have survived were on the whole certainly not the most stupid. They must have had quick sight, they must have had nimble fins, they must have had vigilance and activity. They must have been skilful in procuring food as well as alert in avoiding danger. They had no maternal solicitude to watch over them.

Every little herring had to forage for himself, and to hide from or elude his enemies as well as he could; he had no kind warning that the tide was falling and that he would be left high and dry if he did not keep away from the edge. I think we must admit that the few herrings that survive out of a million eggs are above the average in whatever qualities best adapt the herring for fighting his battle of life. I will not say that they must be actually the very best of the million, but I think we must admit that they were among the best.

What we have here attempted to illustrate takes place in the whole realm of organized life. The organic beings, animal and vegetable, tend to increase faster than the limit to the supply of food or the presence of enemies will permit. Many must therefore perish. No two of these organisms are exactly identical. There will be trifling differences (sometimes, indeed, the differences are by no means trifling). It thus happens that in the struggle for life one individual will have a slight advantage over another. It therefore may be anticipated that the more favoured individuals will be those which survive; their peculiarities will be more or less inherited by their descendants. Thus the variations which are useful to the animal will in successive generations be gradually added to, and in course of time the widest changes in organization can thus arise.

It may at first seem hard to realise that so trifling a change as that between one generation and the next can ever by repetition amount up to so great a change as that between one species of animal and another; still less can we imagine at first how animals so widely distinct as, for instance, a bird and a fish can have originated by natural selection from some common ancestor. The whole question is, no doubt, complicated; but it is easy to show how minute differences between one generation and the next, all tending in one direction, speedily reach to an appreciable aggregate.

Let me give an illustration. I know some tender mothers who like to have their darlings photographed every year in order to preserve a permanent record of their development. No doubt the mother would have no difficulty in distinguishing between the photographs of her child at two years old or at three, or even between those of her boy at thirteen and at fourteen. But suppose that, instead of having the child photographed only once a year, he were to be photographed every week from birth until he was full grown. This is not at all an impracticable suggestion; there would be little more than a thousand photographs altogether. An album could easily be made which would hold them all. Of course the prudent mother would mark the dates on the back; but suppose this was not done, and the whole thousand photographs got into confusion, would it be possible to arrange them all in order again? Certainly no outsider could do it; he could sort them in a general way, so as to have the babies at one end, and the young men at the other, and the boys in the middle. But could he put the whole thousand in regular order from one end to the other? He could not. I doubt very much whether even the mother herself could do it without numerous mistakes.

Now if this be granted, the difficulty sometimes felt in

believing natural selection to be the cause of species may be lessened. Great as is the difference between a newborn infant and a man of twenty, the one passes into the other by such imperceptible gradations that the boy of this Monday is hardly distinguishable from the boy of last Monday or of next Monday. We thus see that if we divide the growth of an individual man into one thousand stages the passage from one stage to the next is almost imperceptible. In the same way, if we subdivide the growth of a species into a thousand parts or a million parts, we shall have gradations quite comparable with those we meet with in the ordinary variation from one generation to the next.

Nor is it hard to see how the process of natural selection has gradually produced diverging branches from the parent stem. The variations which occur may be of use to the organism in various ways. Among the progeny of a single pair there may be two individuals, A and B, which are specially favoured; but they may be favoured in different ways. A may have some increased facility in catching his prey; B, by his peculiar colour, or greater activity, may have superior success in eluding his enemies. The descendants of A will gradually from one generation to the next strengthen and reinforce the special feature which characterized A. The descendants of B will grow more and more adapted for eluding their enemies. The influence of natural selection is in both cases promoting the survival of the fittest, but each generation will see the cousins more and more widely separated. In no case, indeed, would the process be so simple as that here described —a multitude of circumstances will occur to complicate it;

but enough has been said to show that in the great principle of natural selection we have a means of producing animals and plants which in the course of time will differ widely from other organisms from the same progenitors.

No one has ever seen a new species developed by natural selection; but this is because no one has ever lived long enough for that purpose. The circumstantial evidence in favour of natural selection is indeed so strong that no unprejudiced person can refuse to accept it. That evidence has of late years been poured out with a profusion which could hardly have been anticipated at the time when the "Origin of Species" was published. Entombed within solid rocks we find fossil remains of the former inhabitants of our earth. There lies in these rocks a record of vast extent and of the utmost interest; but that record is to a great extent screened from our view. Here and there fossils have been brought to light; but the greater part of the earth has never been examined, and we have as yet only the veriest fragments of the geological record before us. But these fragments of the record are of great importance; they show us several of the links which connect one class of animals with another in the way the Darwinian theory suggests; and they encourage us to hope that, when the geological record shall have been fully explored, we shall have glimpses of a majestic panorama of the salient points in the history of life on our globe.

Mathematicians are long accustomed to the use of what is known as the infinitesimal calculus. It is indeed chiefly the infinitesimal calculus which has raised the science of mathematics to its present position, and which has given to that science a potent grasp over some of the inmost recesses of nature. Suppose, for instance, to take one of the most profound problems, we proceed to investigate on mathematical principles the movement of one of the planets. The sun, in the first place, attracts the planet, and in virtue of that attraction the planet would move in a certain path which could be determined with comparative ease. But the actual problem is by no means so simple. The planet is acted on by other planets; its orbit is thus deflected slightly from the simple form it would otherwise have; and while the orbit preserves a general resemblance to the ellipse, it is in reality a path of no little complexity. But still the mathematician can follow the planet with his figures he can point out with accuracy where the planet was at any ancient date; he can show where it will be at any future date. It is the infinitesimal calculus, the invention of Newton and Leibnitz, which enables this to be done. By this subtle and exquisite contrivance we attack the problem in detail. It is comparatively easy to find out the direction in which the planet is moving at any instant, as well as its velocity. This will enable us to ascertain where it will be in the next moment of time. We then repeat the operation and carry on this process as long as we like, and thus discover where the planet will be at any future date. The success of the process consists in attacking the question in detail. Is there not in this a striking analogy to the great principle of Darwin? In each case great effects are produced by the constant addition of innumerable small tendencies, all in the same direction. As the infinitesimal calculus of Newton has led us to a knowledge of the physical laws which regulate the universe, so the infinitesimal calculus of Darwin has afforded the solution of the profound problem presented by organic life.

It must have been with prophetic insight that Cuvier exclaimed, "Shall not natural history some day have its Newton?" At the time these words were uttered the Newton of natural history had been born, and his immortal work has revolutionized knowledge.

INDEX.

INDEX.

A

Air, great wave caused by Krakatoa explosion, 326-330
Andromeda, nebula in, 124
  photograph of, 315-317
Andromedes, 245, 246
Ant, brain of, 351-353
Astrology, survivals of, 196
  the number seven, 197
  days of the week, 198-200
Atmosphere, of moon, 87; of planets, 86

B

Beagle, voyage of the, 343, 344

C

Carbon, formation of, in trees, 42-44
Chart of the heavens, 311
Climatic changes, 4
Coal, prehistoric sunbeams, 44
Colours of stars, Doppler's theory, 280
  affected by motion, 278-281
Constellations, changes in forms of, 264, 267
Cuvier quoted, 364

D

Day, length of, increasing, 64, 66
  ancient five-hours' day, 66
  future 1,400-hours' day, 72, 73
Days of week, names of, 198-200
Darwinism and astronomy, 343-364
  "The Origin of Species," 344
  natural selection, 345, 355, 356, 361, 362
  the past of the sun, 346-348
  history of solar system, 348
  genesis of earth, 349
  organic evolution, 350
  spontaneous generation, 354
  accumulations of variations, 359-361
Denning, Mr. W. F., observation of a shooting star, 211-214
Distances of stars, 259, 260
Doppler, theory of star colours, 280

E

Earth, attraction by the sun, 2, 5
  elements common to it and sun, 19
  tides and the moon, 63, 74
  tides and the sun, 75
  antiquity of, 65, 66
  genesis of, 349
  length of day increasing, 64, 66
  ancient five-hours' day, 66
  future 1,400-hours' day and month, 72, 73
  speed of rotation and the moon, 67
  moon receding from, 67
  ancient propinquity of moon, 68
  will present a fixed face, 74
  as seen from moon, 82, 95
  accumulation of meteoric débris on, 230

Extent of starry heavens, 255, 304
range of telescope, 256-258
distances, 260

F

FALLING stars, fire-balls (see Meteors)

G

GALILEO, view of Venus, 141
Georgium Sidus, 201
Great spiral nebula, 140
Green, N. E., drawings of Mars, 159, 161, 162
Gulliver's Travels, 41, 179

H

HALL, Prof. Asaph, discovery of moons of Mars, 168-172
Heavens, chart of, 311, 312
Herring, 357, 358
Herschel, Sir W., as an observer, 54
and Saturn's rings, 121
Huggins, Sir William, discoveries in nebula of Orion. 134, 136
work in spectrum analysis, 262

I

INFINITESIMAL calculus, 362, 363

J

JANSSEN's photographs of the sun, 295
Jupiter, orbit, 180, 181
rotation, 182
belts, 184
phases, 185
solidity of, doubtful, 185, 187
great red spot in, 186, 187
bulk of, 188
mass, 188, 189
internal heat, 189
clouds, 190, 191, 194
solar heat on, 191-192
photograph of, 298

K

KNOBEL, observation of Mars, 164
Krakatoa, the eruption, 319-342
investigation by the Royal Society, 320
description of locality, 321
previous eruptions, 321
warnings, 322
the catastrophe, 323, 324
compared with other eruptions, 325
the great air wave, 326-329
its rate of motion, 330
area of the sound, 331-334
great sea-waves, 334
sky phenomena, 335
dust clouds, 336-338
after-glow, 339-341

L

LEONIDS, 238, 242
Lick Observatory, 103-106
the great refractor, 105
Light and colour rays, 277
of 18,000 years ago, 260

M

MAGNETIC needle and sunbeams 1
Mars, discovery of satellites of, 75, 76, 151, 168-172
and Venus, 141
rotation of, 144, 153, 154
revolution and orbit, 151, 157, 158
position in solar system, 150
and the earth, 152, 156
atmosphere of, 162
through the telescope, 153, 164
clouds on, 163
in opposition, 154-156
colours of surface, 163
south pole, pictures of, 159
white polar regions, 162
Mr. N. E. Green's drawings, 159, 161, 162
mapping of, 160
zero of longitudes, 161
Knobel's observations, 164
Schiaparelli's "canals," 165-167
Swift's guesses, 179

Material unity of the Universe, 263
Mercury, rotation and revolution, 145
Schiaparelli, 145-146
constant face to the sun, 146
tidal action on, 148
early discovery of, 197
Meteoric dust, 208-209
débris on the globe, 230
Meteors, influx of into the sun, 21-23
shooting-star, autobiography 203-209
constitution of, 203
flight, 203, 215
wanderings in space, 204
combustion, 207
height of, 209, 210, 213
Mr. W. F. Denning's observations, 211-214
fireballs of 1877-8, 217
1879, at York, 218, 219
1876, in America, 220
brilliancy of, 218
detonation, 221
energy of, compared with powder, 223, 224
energy of, compared with steam, 224
luminous trails of, 225-227
star showers, 228
periodicity of, 235, 237
early records of showers, 236
telescopic shooting stars, 229, 230
November showers of 1866, 231-234
November showers of 1698, 237
Leonids, 238, 242
the Great Shoal, 238-245
its width, 239
its intersection of earth's orbit, 242, 245
Perseids and Andromedes, 245
Milky Way, 121
Months, future, of 1,400 hours, 73
Moon, smallest of visible orbs, 49
dimensions, 50
unchanging face, 52
dark side of, 53-55
Moon (*continued*)—
rotation on axis, 55-57
the rotation paradox, 56
revolution, 57
lunar history, 57
ancient heated condition, 58
cooling of, 61
active lunar volcanoes, 58
lunar tides, 58-62
their effect, 63
absence of water on the, 59
of life, 84
of ice, 85
of air, 86, 88
what became of lunar water, 85
and terrestrial tides, 63, 74
and earth's speed of rotation, 67
recession of, from the earth, 67
ancient propinquity to earth, 68
mountains on, 90
craters, 90
the crater Ptolemy, 75
why does the moon not fall? 78, 79
non-luminous, 80
earth seen from, 82, 95
old, in new moon's arms, 82
whether inhabited, 82
through the telescope, 83, 84
indications of gaseous material on, 87
weights on, 94
origin of, 69-71
future career, 71-73

N

NATURAL Selection, 345, 355-356
Nebula in Andromeda, 124, 315-317
Great Spiral, 140
Orion, 127, 128, 133, 265, 317
Huggins' discoveries, 134, 136
Nebulæ, 124, 125, 132
and spectrum analysis, 137
Newton's discoveries, 77, 79-80
Niagara, debt of, to the sun, 46
November star showers (*see* Meteors)

O

Observatory, women's work in the, 97, 169
prosaic labours in, 98-99
conditions of observation, 100
impediments to work, 101
the Lick, 103-106
the Lick refractor, 105
meridian circle, 107-110
equatorial, 110
Orion, Great Nebula in, 127, 133-134, 265, 317
composition of, 131
presence of hydrogen in, 136-138
unknown spectrum lines in, 137
magnitude of, 138
Orionis Theta, 129, 130

P

Perseus, 121, 122
distance of cluster, 123
Perseids, 245
Photographing the stars, 292, 318
atmospheric difficulties, 294
Janssen's sun-pictures, 295
photographs of moon, 296
photographs of planets, 297
of Jupiter, 298
of Saturn, 299
of extra-telescopic, 300, 301
Mr. Roberts's work, 303, 315
instruments for photography, 305-310
charting the heavens, 311, 312
work at the Draper Memorial, 318
Planets, rotation of, 54
atmosphere of, 86
how to weigh, 115, 172-176
Mars, Venus, Jupiter, 142
compared with stars, 149-150
and their satellites, 151, 168
relative size of, and sun, 183
heated stage of, 193
names of, 195, 200, 201
Pleiades, 266, 316

R

Refraction, 102, 103
Roberts, Dr. Isaac, and celestial photography, 303
charting the heavens, 313
photograph of the Andromeda Nebula, 315, 317
photograph of the Pleiades, 316

S

Sandwich Islands and lunar landscape, 91, 92
Saturn, period of revolution, 113, 114
bands, 115
weight, 116
rings, 116-118, 121
photograph of, 299
Schiaparelli, observation of Mercury and Venus, 145-147
his "canals" on Mars, 165-167
Sea-waves, great, caused by Krakatoa, 334
Senses, two, useless on the moon 92, 93
Shooting stars (*see* Meteors)
Sound, eruption of Krakatoa, 331-334
detonation of fireballs, 221
Spectroscope and star-movements, 262
motion in line of sight, 268-272
explanation of, 272-289
musical illustration of, 287-289
light and colour rays, 277
colour affected by motion, 278, 279, 281
value of the dark lines, 283
Spectrum analysis, 19, 135-137, 262
elements common to earth and sun, 19
material unity of the universe, 263
Spontaneous generation, 354
Stars, growth and decay of, 35, 37
dark, 37, 38
double, 129
colour of, 278-281

Stars (*continued*)—
  triple, 130
  number of, 248, 254
  suns, 251-253
  extent of starry space, 255, 304
  light of 18,000 years ago, 260
  no "fixed," 264
  change of groupings, 264
  movements in space, 267
  motion and spectroscope, 268-272
  photography of, 292-318
    invisible, 300, 301
Star-worship, 200
Sun, attraction of, and the earth, 2, 5
  heat-supply constant, 3, 5, 6
    expenditure of heat, 7-9, 11, 16
  elements common to it and earth, 19
  the "fuel" problem, 6, 7, 24, 25
  not explained by chemical action, 17-20
  nor by mechanical, 21
  true explanation, 24-34
  dimensions of, compared with earth's, 12
  density of, compared with earth's, 25
  prominence of, corona, 14
  rotation of, 53
  influx of meteors, 21-23
  temperature and radiation, 30-32
  future of, ultimate dark and cold, 35, 36
  nebular origin, 39, 46, 346-8
  pre-nebular stage, 47, 48
  what we owe to the, 40
  tidal action, 75
  heat of, on Jupiter, 191-193
  Janssen's photographs of, 295
Sunbeams and magnetic needle,
  out of cucumbers, 41, 42
  pre-historic in coal, 44
  all artificial light due to, 45
  and water power, 46
Swift, Dean, his guesses, 41, 179

T

Telescope and the moon, 83, 84
  range of vision, 256-258
Tidal action on earth, 63, 74-75
  on moon, 58, 62, 63
  on Venus and Mercury, 147-148
Transit of Venus, 158
Tycho Brahe, 98

U

Unity, material, of universe, 263

V

Vega, light-distance of, 259
Venus and Mars, 141
  Galileo's view of, 141
  heat, light, atmosphere, 143
  rotation, length of day, 144. 145
  Schiaparelli's observations, 147
  one face to the sun, 147
  tidal action on, 148
  transit of, 158

W

Water in the moon, 85
Weights on the moon, 94
Weighing planets, 115, 172-179
Women and astronomical work, 97. 169

Z

Zero of longitudes on Mars, 161